OPERATIONS RESEARCH SOCIETY OF AMERICA

Publications in Operations Research

Number 1

PUBLICATIONS IN OPERATIONS RESEARCH

Operations Research Society of America

Editor for Publications in Operations Research
DAVID B. HERTZ

No. 1.   QUEUES, INVENTORIES AND MAINTENANCE
Philip M. Morse

No. 2.   FINITE QUEUING TABLES
L. G. Peck and R. N. Hazelwood

No. 3.   EFFICIENCY IN GOVERNMENT THROUGH SYSTEMS ANALYSIS
Roland N. McKean

No. 4.   A COMPREHENSIVE BIBLIOGRAPHY ON OPERATIONS RESEARCH
Operations Research Group, Case Institute

No. 5.   PROGRESS IN OPERATIONS RESEARCH, VOLUME I
Edited by Russell L. Ackoff

No. 6.   STATISTICAL MANAGEMENT OF INVENTORY SYSTEMS
Harvey M. Wagner

No. 7.   PRICE, OUTPUT, AND INVENTORY POLICY
Edwin S. Mills

No. 8.   A COMPREHENSIVE BIBLIOGRAPHY ON OPERATIONS RESEARCH, 1957–1958
Operations Research Group, Case Institute

No. 9.   PROGRESS IN OPERATIONS RESEARCH, VOLUME II
David B. Hertz and Roger T. Eddison

No. 10.   DECISION AND VALUE THEORY
Peter C. Fishburn

QUEUES, INVENTORIES AND MAINTENANCE

The Analysis of Operational Systems with Variable Demand and Supply

By PHILIP M. MORSE

MASSACHUSETTS INSTITUTE OF TECHNOLOGY

JOHN WILEY & SONS, INC.
New York · London · Sydney

SIXTH PRINTING, APRIL, 1967

PREFACE

SEVERAL YEARS AGO, in connection with the development of a program of training in operations research at the Massachusetts Institute of Technology, it was decided to start a long-term, cooperative study of some of the basic theories likely to be of general use in operations research. One of those chosen as likely to provide opportunities for thesis research and for practical application in many military and industrial operations was queuing or waiting-line theory. The subject has indeed proved of interest; several doctoral and master's theses have been written on various aspects, and the calculation of extensive tables is being carried out, using the high-speed digital computer Whirlwind at the Institute. The Army Office of Ordnance Research has supported some of this research and computation, through its Contract Number DA-19-020-ORD-2684.

As the tables were being produced, it became apparent that publication of tables alone would not be enough. What was needed, in addition to tables, was a general description of the subject, with definitions of terms and an outline of the various fields of application of the theory. The writer started this as a short preface to the tables, but it soon became apparent that what appeared to be needed could not be compressed into a short preface. As it now turns out, the present monograph is the first of two or perhaps three monographs on queuing theory. This one is the expanded introduction, defining terms, indicating applications and outlining some of the analytic aspects of the theory. The second one will have a discussion of some of the computational methods and machine techniques used in getting numerical answers to queuing problems, and will provide tables of some of the more useful solutions for systems of the sort discussed in Chapters 7 and 8 of this book. A possible third volume will discuss in detail solutions applicable to maintenance problems of the sort sketched in Chapter 11 of this book, again providing tables of values corresponding to the more frequently encountered maintenance operations.

The present volume, therefore, does not pretend to be an exhaustive treatise on queuing theory. Its purpose is primarily expository, to present enough of the concepts, to define some of the terms and to illustrate a few of the analytic techniques, so that the newcomer to the field can begin to find his way around, can start to solve his own problems.

Acknowledgments for help in getting it written are due to many. Discussions of various aspects of the theory with colleagues, such as H. P. GALLIHER, and with students, such as H. N. GARBER and R. M. OLIVER, have often clarified a point. Friends active in operations research, such as M. L. ERNST, G. E. KIMBALL and A. VASZONYI, have helped provide some realism to the practical examples given. MRS. CLAIRE SHOULDERS has typed the manuscript, and M. M. A. SIMOND, P. L. DUREN and R. M. OLIVER have helped read proof. They and many others should be credited for much of the book's usefulness, should not be blamed for its errors.

PHILIP M. MORSE

Cambridge, Massachusetts
December, 1957

CONTENTS

vii

Appendixes

INTRODUCTION

IN MOST OPERATIONAL PROBLEMS involving flow, the first step is to ensure that mean flow capacities can handle average flow, so that persistent bottlenecks do not occur. In the study of the flow of aircraft in and out of airports, of ships in and out of harbor, of orders and sales through a store, of items into and out of a warehouse, of machines into and out of a maintenance repair shop, of bills through an accounting department, or in many other examples of operational dynamics, if we do not design the system so that its mean capacity is at least as large as the average flow, a "traffic jam" will build up until flow is reduced or capacity is increased.

But even if mean capacities can handle average flows, transient and, in certain cases, permanent "traffic jams" can occur because the actual flow or the actual capacity to handle the flow fluctuates, being sometimes larger and sometimes smaller than its mean value. It is the purpose of this treatise to describe how the effects of such fluctuations can be analyzed, and in many cases of practical importance, how one can obtain quantitative predictions of the effects. This is not intended to be a highly theoretical treatise on the subject, giving all possible methods of computation; instead, the discussion will concentrate on a single fairly simple technique of analysis, by means of which answers can be calculated for many problems of practical interest. Those who wish to use more "high-powered" mathematical techniques or to solve very difficult problems should turn to the extensive literature in this field, some of which is listed in the bibliography.

Nor is this a collection of "recipes" to be applied blindly to any and all situations involving queues. Rather, we seek to display the funda-

1

mental properties of operations involving variable arrivals and delays, and to demonstrate some of the theoretical techniques which can be used to analyze and predict their behavior. The operational situations encountered in practice differ enough in character, and the criteria imposed by management differ enough in nature, that it is not possible to provide ready-made formulas to fit all or even most situations. The goal of this monograph is to provide understanding and familiarity with techniques, so that the reader may be able to set up his own mathematical model to fit his particular operation, and compute his own formulas to fit his particular management criterion for optimization. More and better queuing models should be our aim!

Theoretical research into the properties of queues began in connection with problems of telephone operation. In the design of automatic telephone exchanges, one had to know the effect of fluctuations of service demands, as varying numbers of customers began dialing numbers, on the utilization of the automatic equipment in the telephone exchange. Erlang, an engineer with the Copenhagen telephone exchange, analyzed the situation very much as we will do at first. His work was begun in 1905, and until about ten years ago most of the work on the theory of queues was done in connection with telephone problems. Only recently, since the development of the more general outlook on operational problems, symbolized by the adoption of the term "operations research," has it been realized that the theory begun specifically for telephone problems has many other applications in connection with a wide variety of operations. In adopting the earlier work and extending it, the more general point of view had to be disentangled from the specific terminology and approach suitable for telephone traffic problems. Thus, though a portion of the theory expounded in the succeeding pages is displayed or is inherent in papers and books on telephone traffic, it has been found necessary to modify the symbolism and the vocabulary to some extent in order to make it less difficult to extend the theory to operational problems of wider interest.

Chapter 1

REPRESENTATION IN TERMS
OF
PROBABILITIES

MOST OF THE OPERATIONAL FLOW PROBLEMS mentioned in the Introduction can be broken down into elements, each of which has the following basic behavior: A sequence of *units* arrive at some *facility* which *services* each unit and eventually *discharges* it. For the port, the units are cargo ships, the facilities are the docks, the service is the loading-unloading operation. For store sales, the unit is any one of a given item which is for sale, or rather its absence from the store shelves caused by the arrival of a customer who buys one (or more) of the item and removes it from the store. The facility is the shelf or drawer which is emptied by the sale, and the service is the process of refilling the vacant place by another unit, by ordering from the wholesaler or factory and getting it delivered. For machine maintenance, the units are the individual machines, which "arrive" by getting out of order; the service facility is the repair crew, and the service operation consists in getting the machine in working order again.

It often happens that the service facility has several "channels" in parallel, each of which can service the arriving unit. In a parking lot, the arriving units are the automobiles, the service channels are the available parking spaces and the "service process" is the leaving of the car until it is taken out again. A similar correspondence can be made with a library reading room. Telephone conversations also correspond to the same pattern; the arrivals are the customers picking up their phones to make calls, the "service" is the telephone conversation and the channels are the lines into and out of the exchange.

In some cases units must pass through a sequence of servicing operations which must be carried out one after the other. Various kinds of production lines are of this type. The flow of automobile traffic along a road having a sequence of traffic lights is an example.

In all of these situations, if there are variations in the regularity of arrivals or in the length of time required to service a unit, or both, then all aspects of the operation will exhibit fluctuations. Sometimes more units will arrive than the service facility can immediately accommodate, and a queue of varying length will form; sometimes service channels will be idle; different units will wait different times, and the discharge of units from the facility will not be regular. Every part of the operation will vary in a more or less random way and every measurable quantity associated with the operation will be a *stochastic* variable, fluctuating with time above and below some average value or rate.

State Probabilities

It is not advisable or appropriate to try to calculate the exact behavior of these stochastic variables with time. Usually a probabilistic picture will give sufficient insight for one to be able to calculate the important planning factors and predict the system's overall behavior. The system can be in a number of possible *states*, specified by the number of units in the queue, waiting for service, the number of units in service, the particular phase of each in its service channel, etc. Instead of trying to predict in detail how the state changes with time, we can compute the *probabilities* that the system is in each of the possible states. From these probabilities we can calculate average values of the various quantities of interest (average length of queue, mean number of idle channels, average time spent by a unit in the system, etc.) and derived probabilities (such as the probability that the queue is longer than a certain amount or that a unit has to spend longer than a certain time in the system).

If the mean rate of arrival and the mean rate of service per channel are constant (that is, if the fluctuations in both are short-time fluctuations around constant mean values), the state probabilities and the derived averages will be independent of time. If, however, there are also long-term variations in the mean arrivals or service rates, which can be expressed by saying that the average values change relatively slowly with time, the state probabilities will also change with time.

The average or expected values we may wish to compute vary with the problem we are analyzing. For ships in port, we may wish to calculate the mean time spent by a ship in port, including waiting for dock space and unloading and loading time, and we may wish to balance the cost of these delays against the cost of building more dock space (increasing mean service rate). In the case of the store sales, we may wish to balance the sales lost when the store is out of stock against various systems of reordering (reorder an item after every sale or reorder a lot when the store has run out, or some intermediate arrangement), or against the average number of items kept in stock. For the maintenance operation we may wish to balance the average loss caused by idle machines waiting repair against the cost of the maintenance crew. For traffic lights or highway toll booths, we may wish to compute the probability that the queue of waiting cars will become longer than a certain operational limit.

Our program, in analyzing the operational situation, is first to learn how to express the short-time fluctuations of arrivals and services, in terms of probabilities. From these and from the structure of the system, we must then learn how to compute the state probabilities and, finally, how to calculate the expected average values of the various quantities of practical interest in the problem under study.

Chapter 2

PROBABILISTIC DESCRIPTION
OF
ARRIVALS AND SERVICE TIMES

IN MANY OPERATIONAL SITUATIONS it is impossible to predict ahead of time just how long the service operation will take before completion. Various reasons for delay may arise, in a more or less random fashion, which could not have been foreseen. A ship being unloaded may have its cargo placed in the wrong order; an airplane wishing to land may be delayed by ground fog or by momentary blocking of the landing strip; the telephone operator seldom knows how long the customer is going to take to finish his telephone conversation; and the store, when reordering items from the factory, has no control over fluctuations in mail service, for example.

In other cases, it may be possible to predict, at least approximately, how long the service operation will take, but it is *not worth making the prediction*. It may be easier for a gas station to use the same service procedure for a driver who wants two gallons of gasoline as for one who wishes twenty gallons, a quart of oil and his tires checked. It may be better to use the same unloading facilities and the same stevedore crew for any of a variety of ships and cargoes. It may be simpler to use the same maintenance crew to repair any of a wide variety of machine breakdowns. In other words, it may be operationally appropriate to consider a variety of arriving units to be *indistinguishable* as far as the service operation is concerned. If the various units of this general class arrive in a random order, there will again be a random fluctuation in the length of the service operation. In each of these situations the service operation will best be described in terms of probabilities. Our first task is to see how this can be done.

Service Time Distribution

Suppose that we measure the time taken for the service operation to be completed on a series of a hundred or so units, which we have decided to treat as the same in regard to service. We could time the unloading of various ships using the same docks, or note the various lengths of time

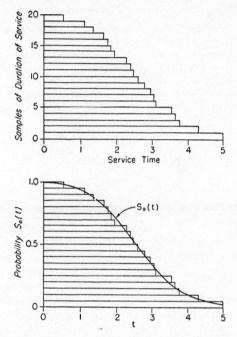

Fig. 2.1. Block diagram of a sample of measured service times, each measurement a block laid horizontally and arranged vertically in the order of length. The second graph is the same, but with its vertical scale divided by the total number in the sample. The solid curve is a smoothed-out estimate of service-time distribution $S_0(t)$ corresponding to the sample.

taken between the ordering of an out-of-stock item and its delivery at the store, or we could record the durations of a sequence of telephone calls. By arranging this sequence of recorded times in order of decreasing length, we can plot the number of service operations that *take longer* than a given time (see Fig. 2.1), and then by dividing by the total number of cases in the sample, we can obtain a curve for the *probability* $S_0(t)$ that the service operation on this class of unit *will take longer* than a certain time. Presumably, if the situation remains the same, another sample of measured times will yield another experimentally determined curve of probability which will be roughly equal to the first; also, presumably, the more samples we take, the smoother the curve will become.

The probability function $S_0(t)$ (sometimes called the *service-time distribution*) is all we need for our probabilistic analysis, as long as we make sure that there is no regular pattern in the occurrence of long and short service times, as long as the distribution of the sequence of service durations is random in time. All curves of $S_0(t)$ will start at unity at $t=0$,

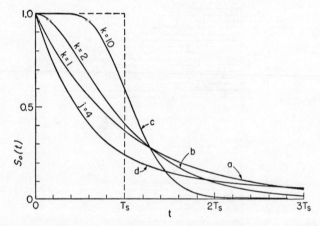

Fig. 2.2. Service-time distribution function $S_0(t)$, the probability that the service operation takes longer than time t. Curve a ($k=1$) is for exponential service, see Eq. 2.6. Dashed curve is for constant service time. Time $t = T_s = (1/\mu)$ is the average service time. See also Figs. 5.1 and 5.6.

for it is certain (that is, the probability is unity) that a service operation takes longer than zero time. All of them will tend monotonically toward zero as t increases (that is, there will be no peaks or valleys in the curve). For most cases of practical interest, $S_0(t)$ goes to zero exponentially as t goes to infinity. As indicated in Fig. 2.2, the smaller the variation between service times the nearer the curve will approach a "step function" (the dashed curve) which is the form of $S_0(x)$ when all service operations take the same time. In this latter case (*constant service-time* case), when the service operation on every arriving unit of the class takes exactly time T_s for completion, it is certain ($S_0=1$) that *every* service time takes longer than t if t is less than T_s, and it is certain that *no* service time ($S_0=0$) is longer than t if t is greater than T_s. Very few actual situations correspond to this limiting example, however; most of them produce a curve for $S_0(t)$ more like curves a or b of Fig. 2.2.

The *area under curve* $S_0(t)$ turns out to equal the *average length of time* T_s of the service operation for the class of units under study. This can be shown most easily by first computing the probability that the service operation is completed a time between t and $t+dt$ after service started. This quantity is equal to the difference between $S_0(t)$ (the probability that service takes longer than t) and $S_0(t+dt)$ (the probability that service takes longer than $t+dt$). By Taylor's theorem,

$$S_0(t) - S_0(t+dt) = S_0(t) - S_0(t) - \frac{dS_0}{dt}\, dt = s(t)\, dt$$

$$(2.1)$$

where $\qquad s(t) = -(dS_0/dt) \quad \text{or} \quad S_0(t) = \int_t^\infty s(t)\, dt$

The quantity $s(t)$ is the *probability density* that a service operation is completed at time t. It is a *rate*, since its dimensions are probability divided by time. If we imagine a whole set of service operations all started at the same instant and, of course, ending at different times, then $s(t)$ would measure the mean rate at which these operations would be ending at time t.

The *average duration* of the service operation then is

$$T_s = \int_0^\infty t\, s(t)\, dt = -\left[t\, S_0(t) \right]_0^\infty + \int_0^\infty S_0(t)\, dt = \int_0^\infty S_0(t)\, dt \qquad (2.2)$$

if we integrate by parts and use Eq. 2.1. The quantity in square brackets is zero at $t=0$ because S_0 is not infinite, is zero at $t \to \infty$ because S_0 goes to zero faster than (A/t) at that limit (otherwise there would be no average service time). The units of T_s (minutes, hours, days) are, of course, the same as the units of t in the curve of $S_0(t)$. We have thus proved the statement made earlier that the area under S_0 equals T_s.

To compute the mean deviation of the service time above and below this average value T_s (the "spread" of the variation of service times), we first calculate the mean square of the duration. Again using integration by parts and discarding the term in brackets,

$$(t^2)_{\text{av}} = \int_0^\infty t^2\, s(t)\, dt = -\left[t^2 S_0 \right]_0^\infty + 2\int_0^\infty t\, S_0(t)\, dt = 2\int_0^\infty t\, S_0(t)\, dt \qquad (2.3)$$

The *mean square deviation* from T_s is then

$$\int_0^\infty (t - T_s)^2\, s(t)\, dt = (t^2)_{\text{av}} - T_s{}^2 = \int_0^\infty (2t - T_s)\, S_0(t)\, dt = (\Delta t_s)^2 \qquad (2.4)$$

and the square root of this *variance*, Δt_s, is called the *standard deviation* of the variable service time. It is zero for the constant service time case (S_0 a step function) and increases as curve S_0 departs more and more from the step-function shape.

There are times when we may not wish to start our observations of service duration at the beginning of service. We may wish to approach the service operation at some random time and, if it is engaged in service, time the completion of service from this arbitrarily chosen starting point. For example, if another unit arrives before the facility is through with the previous arrival, we may wish to know how long it must wait before the facility is free. If one starts observing at time x after the beginning of service (having found that the service is still busy at time x), the probability that the service will be completed in a time between y and $y+dy$ after the beginning of observation is $s(x+y)\,dy/S_0(x)$, according to Eq. 2.1 and the definition of S_0. But the probability of starting to observe the service channel between x and $x+dx$ after start of service, and finding it still busy then, is proportional to $S_0(x)\,dx$, where the proportionality factor must be adjusted so that the integral of this, over all possible values of x, equals unity. Reference to Eq. 2.2 shows that the probability required is $(1/T_s)\,S_0(x)\,dx$. The product of the two is the probability that the service observation is started between x and $x+dx$ and the service is finished between time y and $y+dy$ later.

Suppose arrivals were sufficiently frequent that whenever the service channel finished with one unit it could start immediately on another. The probabilities just described may be used to compute the chance that *no service termination* occurs during an arbitrarily chosen interval of time t. The chance of starting the time interval between x and $x+dx$ from the beginning of service and having the service finish between y and $y+dy$ later is $[S_0(x)\,dx/T_s][s(x+y)\,dy/S_0(x)] = (1/T_s)s(x+y)\,dx\,dy$, and the chance that y is larger than t, averaged over all possible starting times x, is

$$V_0(t) = (1/T_s)\int_0^\infty dx \int_t^\infty s(x+y)\,dy = \int_t^\infty S_0(x)\,(dx/T_s) \qquad (2.5)$$

This is the probability that an observer coming up to a service channel at some random instant and finding the channel busy then, would find it *still occupied by the same unit* a time t later. The related curves of s, S_0 and V_0 for different service characteristics are shown in Figs. 2.2 and 2.3.

Curves c correspond to a situation where nearly all service operations take the same time; the limiting case, when S_0 is a completely sharp step function, the density s is a delta function and V_0 is a segment of a straight line (the dashed curves), is called the *constant service-time* case. Curves a correspond to the other limit, where probabilities S_0 and

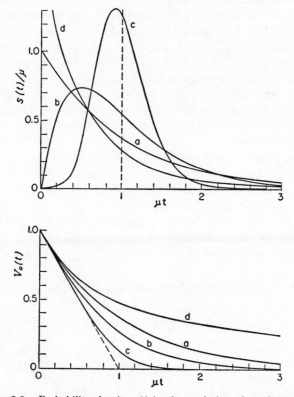

Fig. 2.3. Probability density $s(t)/\mu$ of completion of service at time t and probability $V_0(t)$ that no service completion occurs in an interval of length t chosen at random, for service characteristics corresponding to those shown in Fig. 2.2. Dashed curve is limiting case of constant service time.

V_0 are equal, that is, when the probability of prolongation of service is independent of how long ago the service started. From Eq. 2.5 we see that when $S_0 = V_0$,

$$(dS_0/dt) = -\mu S_0; \quad \mu = (1/T_s)$$

so that
$$S_0(t) = V_0(t) = e^{-\mu t}; \quad s(t) = \mu\, e^{-\mu t}$$

$$\Delta t_s = T_s = (1/\mu) \tag{2.6}$$

This case, analogous to radioactive decay (where the chance of survival of an individual nucleus is independent of the length of time it has already survived), is called the *exponential service* case.

A surprisingly large number of service operations exhibit distribution functions S_0 which are equal to the exponential curve a, within the limits of accuracy of the measurements. Telephone conversations, many repair operations and various other service functions are statistically close enough to this case so that calculated averages assuming an exponential service distribution correspond quite closely to the measured averages. There are a few cases where the distribution is "hyper-exponential," as shown in curves d; here very short and very long intervals predominate.

Arrival Distribution

Irregular arrivals may be described in terms of probabilities in a manner quite analogous to service times. One measures the times between successive arrivals, and from these constructs a curve of probability $A_0(t)$ that the next arrival comes later than time t *after the previous arrival* (that is, that no arrival occurs in time t after the previous one). Also one has the probability density $a(t)$, such that the chance that the next arrival comes between t and $t+dt$ after the previous one is $a(t)\,dt$. As before

$$a(t) = -[dA_0(t)/dt] \quad \text{or} \quad A_0(t) = \int_t^\infty a(t)\,dt \qquad (2.7)$$

Also we have the probability that no arrivals occur in an interval of time t chosen at random if

$$U_0(t) = \lambda \int_t^\infty A_0(t)\,dt = \lambda \int_0^\infty dx \int_t^\infty a(x+y)\,dy \qquad (2.8)$$

where λ, the "mean rate of arrival," is defined as the reciprocal of

$$T_a = (1/\lambda) = \int_0^\infty A_0(t)\,dt = \int_0^\infty t\,a(t)\,dt \qquad (2.9)$$

the mean time between arrivals. Note that λ and μ are reciprocals of mean times, not mean values of reciprocals.

The case of perfectly *regularly spaced* arrivals corresponds to the case where $A_0(t)$ is a step function:

$$A_0(t) = \begin{cases} 1 & (t<T_a) \\ 0 & (t>T_a) \end{cases}; \quad U_0(t) = \begin{cases} 1-(t/T_a) & (t<T_a) \\ 0 & (t>T_a) \end{cases} \qquad (2.10)$$

$$\Delta t_a = 0$$

The other limit, where the chance of occurrence of the next arrival is independent of the time since the last arrival, corresponds to

$$A_0(t) = U_0(t) = e^{-\lambda t}; \quad a(t) = \lambda\, e^{-\lambda t}$$

$$\Delta t_a = T_a = (1/\lambda) \tag{2.11}$$

This is the distribution of arrivals called the *Poisson distribution*, though to be consistent in our descriptions we might better call it the *exponential arrival* case. Texts on probability theory demonstrate that this distribution corresponds to completely random arrivals.

In the case of arrivals, we sometimes wish to know the *probability that n arrivals occur* within an interval of time of duration t. If this interval commences just after an arrival, the probability will be called $A_n(t)$; if the interval is placed at random in time, it will be called $U_n(t)$. We have already shown how to compute U_0 and A_0 from the probability density $a(t)$. It is not too difficult to show that these other probabilities are related by the equations

$$A_n(t) = \int_0^t a(x)\, A_{n-1}(t-x)\, dx$$

$$U_n(t) = \lambda \int_0^\infty dx \int_0^t a(x+y)\, A_{n-1}(t-y)\, dy \tag{2.12}$$

$$= \lambda \int_0^t A_0(x)\, A_{n-1}(t-x)\, dx$$

For exponential (Poisson) arrivals we have

$$U_n(t) = A_n(t) = [(\lambda t)^n / n!]\, e^{-\lambda t} \tag{2.13}$$

Curves for a, A_0 and U_0 are similar to those for s, S_0 and V_0 shown in Figs. 2.2 and 2.3.

Having become familiar with the statistical representation of arrivals and service operations, we must now see how, from the functions a and s (or A_0 and S_0) we can compute the average delays, lengths of queue, idle times and so on, which are likely to be needed in evaluating the various operations these functions represent. To do this we first investigate how we can compute state probabilities from the arrival and service probabilities.

Chapter 3

SINGLE EXPONENTIAL CHANNEL

$\mathbf{A}$T THIS POINT generalities will be less understandable than specific examples. Suppose that we consider for a while a single facility serving one kind of unit, with a service-time distribution $S_0(t)$ and "mean service rate" $\mu = (1/T_s)$. The arriving units obey the arrival distribution $A_0(t)$, with "mean arrival rate" $\lambda = (1/T_a)$. No arriving unit enters the service channel unless and until the channel has finished with the previous unit. If service is busy, the arriving unit waits in a queue, in order of arrival, until service has finished with all previous arrivals, at which time it immediately enters the channel, is serviced, and then departs. (This set of rules is often called "strict queue discipline; first come, first served.")

The various states of this system can be characterized by the total number of units in the system, the one in service and the number in the queue, if there are any. If the arrival and service probabilities A and S do not change with time (that is, if the experimental distributions are the same no matter when the sample measurements were taken), we can expect that the system will settle down to a statistical steady state, such that the probability that the system is in a particular state (with n units in the system, for example) is independent of time. But to find these average probabilities we shall nearly always have to compute probabilities which do depend on times, specifically on the time since the last arrival and the time since the service facility started work on a new unit. This complication occurs because we must compute the relative magnitudes of the state probabilities by computing the rates at which the system can change from one state to another by arrivals or by completion of service, and it usually happens that these transition rates vary with time after arrival or after service starts.

14

In fact, only when transitions from one state to another involve exponential processes can we eliminate this complication. As was noted in the previous section, only for a facility with exponential service-time distribution is the chance of service completion at any given instant, $s(t)\,dt$, equal to a constant times the probability $S_0(t)$ that the service lasted as long as t. In all other cases the ratio between $s(t)$ and $S_0(t)$ depends on t, the time since service started. Also for arrivals, only for Poisson (that is, exponential) arrivals is the ratio between $a(t)$ and $A_0(t)$ independent of t, the time since the previous arrival. For these exponential transitions the rate of transition is simply proportional to the state probability for the initial state, and the problem of balancing transitions is enormously simplified.

Equations of Detailed Balance

To see how this goes, suppose our simple one-channel system has exponential service-time and arrival-time distributions. The change in the probability P_n that there are n units in the system (which change will be set equal to zero to obtain the steady-state case) will be caused by new arrivals and by completions of service. For example, the chance that state n will go into state $n+1$ in the next instant of time dt, because of an arrival, will in this case, as we have just seen, be equal to P_n times the chance (see Eq. 2.13) that one arrival will occur in dt, $A_1(dt) = (\lambda\,dt)\,e^{-\lambda\,dt}$, which equals $P_n\lambda\,dt$ when we neglect higher powers of dt. The chance that two arrivals will occur in the next dt will be $A_2(dt)$, which is proportional to dt^2 and can be neglected, as can be all larger numbers of arrivals. On the other hand, the probability that P_n will be increased, through change from state $n-1$ to n because of an arrival, is equal to $P_{n-1}A_1(dt) \rightarrow P_{n-1}\lambda\,dt$, and the chance of transition into state n from states $n-2$, $n-3$, etc., is negligible compared to dt when dt is made small enough.

Likewise the transitions involving state n caused by completion of service, which are of first order in dt, are only those from state n to $n-1$, equal to $\mu\,dt\,P_n$, and from $n+1$ to n, equal to $\mu\,dt\,P_{n+1}$.

To put it another way, we can say that the value of the P_n's at $t+dt$ are related to their values at t in a fairly simple way *if* the processes causing the transitions from state n to state m do have the absence of specific dependence on t, which we have pointed out is true for exponential processes. In that case the probability $P_n(t+dt)$ of being in state n at time $t+dt$ is equal to the sum of the probabilities $P_m(t)$ of being in state m at time t, each times the transition probability $T_{mn}(dt)$ that the system will change from state m to state n in time dt:

$$P_n(t+dt) = \sum_m T_{mn}(dt)\, P_m(t)$$

The probability of *staying* in state n during dt is the probability that no units arrive or are serviced in dt,

$$T_{nn} = A_0(dt)\, S_0(dt) = e^{-(\mu+\lambda)\,dt} \simeq 1 - (\mu+\lambda)\, dt$$

to the first order in dt. The chance of changing from state m to state n (if $m < n$) is the probability that $m-n$ units have arrived or that $l-n+m$ have arrived and l have been serviced in time dt (similarly for $m > n$). The only such quantities of first order in dt are

$$T_{n+1,n} \simeq A_0(dt)\, S_1(dt) \simeq \mu\, dt$$

and $\qquad\qquad T_{n-1,n} \simeq A_1(dt) S_0(dt) \simeq \lambda\, dt \qquad\qquad$ (for $n>0$)

Inserting these into the general equation and expanding $P_n(t+dt)$ into $P_n(t)+dP_n$ gives us

$$dP_n = [\lambda P_{n-1} + \mu P_{n+1} - (\lambda+\mu)P_n]\, dt \qquad\qquad (3.1)$$

If this is equal to zero, then P_n will be independent of time. We should repeat that these expressions, equating the transitions into and out of the various states, *only* have this simple form with constant coefficients when *all* transitions are exponential processes (in the sense of Chapter 2) and when the mean arrival rate λ and mean service rate μ, defined in Eqs. 2.6 and 2.9, are independent of time. For the present we assume that this condition holds; time-dependent effects will be discussed in a later chapter.

Setting expression 3.1 for dP_n for different n's, equal to zero, gives rise to a series of simultaneous algebraic equations for the steady-state probabilities P_n. The equation for P_0 has a special form, for there is no P_{-1} from which to transfer to P_0 by arrival of a unit and there is no possibility of moving out of state $n=0$ by completion of a service operation; the service operation is idle when no unit is in the system. Consequently the equations relating the state probabilities are

$$\mu P_1 - \lambda P_0 = 0$$
$$\mu P_{n+1} + \lambda P_{n-1} - (\lambda+\mu)P_n = 0 \qquad (n>0)$$

(3.2)

These equations represent the detailed balancing of transitions between states for a statistically steady state. The term with negative sign represents transitions *out* of state n per unit time; those with positive sign represent transitions *into* state n.

This set of simultaneous algebraic equations is easy to solve. If we express all P's in terms of P_0 we have

$$P_n = \rho^n P_0; \quad \rho = (\lambda/\mu) = (T_s/T_a) \tag{3.3}$$

where ρ, the ratio between mean arrival rate and mean service rate, the mean fraction of the time the service channel could be used, is appropriately called the *utilization factor*. Using this simple system as an example, let us now show how various quantities of practical interest can be found and used to provide criteria for operational decisions.

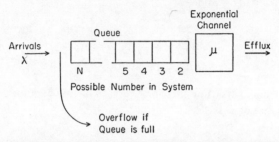

Fig. 3.1. Schematic representation of a single exponential service channel with a queue of maximum allowed length $N-1$, with Poisson arrivals.

We first take an example with an upper limit to the queue. An exemplification of this simple system would be a gasoline filling station with a single pump and space for no more than N cars in all ($N-1$ cars waiting, 1 car getting gasoline). Cars wishing gasoline, arriving when the queue has less than $N-1$ cars, will wait; those arriving when the queue is $N-1$ cars long will go elsewhere for gasoline. (One can picture other sales operations corresponding more or less closely to this.) Here there is only a finite number of states, for values of n from 0 to N. Equations 3.2 hold for n from zero to $N-1$. The equation for $n=N$ is

$$\lambda P_{n-1} - \mu P_n = 0$$

and solution 3.3 holds for $0 \le n \le N$.

To derive mean values for measures of effectiveness of the system, we need the relations

$$[1+x+x^2+\cdots+x^N](1-x) = 1-x^{N+1}$$

$$[1+2x+3x^2+\cdots+Nx^{N-1}](1-x)^2 = 1-(N+1)x^N+Nx^{N+1} \tag{3.4}$$

$$[1+4x+9x^2+\cdots+N^2x^{N-1}](1-x)^3$$
$$= (1+x)[1-(N+1)^2x^N-N^2x^{N+1}]+4N(N+1)x^{N+1}$$

The value of P_0 is obtained from the requirement that the sum of all the P's is unity:

$$1 = \sum_{n=0}^{N} P_n = P_0(1+\rho+\cdots+\rho^N); \quad P_0 = \left[\frac{1-\rho}{1-\rho^{N+1}}\right]; \quad P_n = \left[\frac{1-\rho}{1-\rho^{N+1}}\right]\rho^n$$

(3.5)

The mean number in the system (in queue and in service) is

$$L = \sum_{n=0}^{N} n P_n = \rho\frac{1-(N+1)\rho^N+N\rho^{N+1}}{(1-\rho)(1-\rho^{N+1})}$$

$$\rightarrow \begin{cases} \rho+\rho^2 & (\rho\ll1) \\ \frac{1}{2}N+\frac{1}{12}N(N+2)(\rho-1) & (\rho\rightarrow1) \quad (3.6) \\ N-(1/\rho) & (\rho\gg1) \end{cases}$$

where ρ is the utilization factor (λ/μ). The mean-square fluctuation from this value of L is

$$(\Delta L)^2 = \sum_{n=0}^{N} n^2 P_n - L^2$$

$$= \frac{\rho-(N+1)^2\rho^{N+1}(1-\rho)^2-2\rho^{N+2}+\rho^{2N+3}}{(1-\rho)^2(1-\rho^{N+1})^2} \rightarrow \begin{cases} \rho+2\rho^2 & (\rho\ll1) \\ \frac{1}{12}N(N+2) & (\rho\rightarrow1) \\ (1/\rho)+(2/\rho^2) & (\rho\gg1) \end{cases}$$

The mean number in queue is

$$L_q = \sum_{n=1}^{N} (n-1) P_n = \rho^2\frac{1-N\rho^{N-1}+(N-1)\rho^N}{(1-\rho)(1-\rho^N)}$$

$$\rightarrow \begin{cases} \rho^2+\rho^3 & (\rho\ll1) \\ \frac{1}{2}(N-1)+\frac{1}{12}(N-1)(N+7)(\rho-1) & (\rho\rightarrow1) \quad (3.7) \\ N-1-(1/\rho) & (\rho\gg1) \end{cases}$$

We note that the mean number in the system is small when ρ is small, but the mean fluctuation about this length, $\Delta L \simeq \sqrt{\rho}$, is large compared to L itself when ρ is small. This, of course, is not an efficient way to run a service facility, since the fraction of time the facility is idle, P_0, is nearly unity when ρ is small. There is one countervailing advantage when ρ is small, however—nearly all prospective customers are served. P_N is the fraction of the time that the queue has maximum length and, according to our assumption, is therefore equal to the fraction of customers who go elsewhere. This is quite small when ρ is small.

Balance between Service Cost and Customers Lost

On the other hand, if we reduce the rate of service μ so that the utilization factor ρ becomes large, the fraction of customers lost P_N increases rapidly, becoming approximately $1 - (1/\rho)$ when ρ is much larger than unity. In other words, the facility is being used to within $(1/\rho^N)$ of its full capacity ($P_0 \simeq 1/\rho^N$ is the fraction of time service is idle), but only $(1/\rho)$ of the prospective customers are served. Obviously some sort of balance should be made. This can be done if we know the cost of increasing the service rate and if we can measure the rate of arrival of prospective customers (this is not equal to the rate of arrival of actual customers, for during the fraction of time P_N when the queue has its maximum length, prospective customers don't stop).

Incidentally, we can estimate the rate λ by measuring L_q or some of the P_n's, since we know the value of μ, for we presumably have checked the service-time distribution to see whether it is reasonably close to exponential in type (otherwise we should not be trying to apply this particular example!). In fact, we can check the validity of our assumptions as to customer actions by measuring the P_n's and seeing whether they are a constant times some fraction to the nth power. (Plotting P_n against n on semilog paper, the curve should be a straight line if customers stay or not, depending on queue length; the slope will then give the value of ρ, and knowing μ, one obtains λ, the arrival rate of prospective customers.)

Suppose it costs $E\mu$ dollars per unit of time to provide service having a mean rate of μ services per unit of time (μ measured as indicated in Chapter 2). In other words, suppose the cost of service is strictly proportional to the speed of the service; two men will service a car twice as fast as one man, and so on, E being the mean cost per unit serviced. And suppose the average sales corresponding to a single service operation yield a gross profit of G dollars. If all prospective customers were served, this would produce a gross profit λG per unit of time; but only $(1 - P_N)$ of the prospective customers are actually served, so our actual gross profit per unit of time is

$$\lambda G(1 - P_N) = \mu G(1 - P_0) = \frac{\lambda G(1 - \rho^N)}{(1 - \rho^{N+1})}$$

Our net profit per unit time is, of course, this minus the cost of service:

$$\lambda G\left[\frac{1 - \rho^N}{1 - \rho^{N+1}} - \frac{E}{\rho G}\right] = \lambda\mu G\frac{\mu^N - \lambda^N}{\mu^{N+1} - \lambda^{N+1}} - E\mu \tag{3.8}$$

If we regard λ, G and E as fixed, we can vary μ to obtain a maximum net profit per unit time. Differentiating the quantity with respect to μ and setting the differential equal to zero gives us the equation for this maximum,

$$\rho^{N+1} \frac{N-(N+1)\rho+\rho^{N+1}}{(1-\rho^{N+1})^2} = \frac{E}{G} \tag{3.9}$$

The left-hand side of this equation is plotted in Fig. 3.2, for several values of N. This term is very small when ρ is small, is equal to $N/2(N+1)$ when $\rho=1$, and approaches unity as ρ approaches infinity.

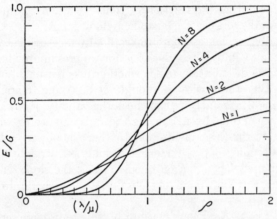

Fig. 3.2. Values of utilization factor $\rho = (\lambda/\mu)$ for optimum profit, for different values of ratio of average cost E of service per unit to mean profit G per service, for different values of N, maximum allowed number of units in queue plus service. From Eq. 3.9.

If E is larger than G (that is, if the cost of service per unit serviced is greater than the gross profit per unit serviced), there is no solution and the facility had better go out of business. If E is less than G, however, there is a solution; and the nearer (E/G) is to unity, the larger ρ should be. If E is about $\frac{1}{2}G$, we should adjust service so that service rate is about equal to arrival rate and all but $1/(N+1)$ of the prospective customers are served. If E is larger than $\frac{1}{2}G$, ρ should be larger than unity (in other words, as the margin of profit diminishes, we should reduce our rate of service to less than λ, so as to cut idle time to a minimum). If E is less than $\frac{1}{2}G$, we should reduce ρ (that is, speed up service) so as to get as large a fraction of prospective customers as possible even at the cost of additional idle time (since this is cheap). Incidentally, we also can see that increasing the size of N, the maximum queue length, pays off. Holding everything else constant, increasing N increases the number of customers served and, therefore, the profits also.

Thus, our mathematical model provides us with decision criteria for the operation. The rules devised, however, apply only when the system obeys (at least approximately) the assumptions made in the model, that arrivals and service are exponential and that arriving units stay in the queue if the queue is less than $N-1$ long, go elsewhere if its length is $N-1$. The actual operation need not correspond exactly to the model; if it corresponds approximately, our answers should hold with at least an equal degree of approximation.

Infinite Queues

We note that when the maximum queue length is very large the steady-state solution which we have just studied differs radically in character, depending on whether ρ is a little less than 1 or a little greater than 1. In the first case, the probability P_N that a maximum-length queue occurs is extremely small; in the second case, it is the largest of all the P's. When ρ is a little less than 1, the mean length is effectively independent of N if N is very large; when ρ is a little greater than 1, the mean length is large and roughly proportional to N.

There are a few operational situations which can give rise to very long lines (a ticket window for a popular play, for example, and the toll booth on a toll bridge). In these cases, arriving units are willing to (or have to) join the queue no matter how long it is. If service rate μ is greater than arrival rate $\lambda(\rho<1)$, steady state corresponds to a mean queue length much smaller than N, and the system's properties are independent of the value of N as long as it is large enough. On the other hand, when λ is larger than μ, the larger N is, the less likely we are to find the system in a steady-state situation. As soon as λ is made larger than μ, the queue tends to increase in length, but it will take so long to reach the new large value of L that a steady state is not likely to be reached before the operational situation changes again.

We will revert to the non-steady-state solutions later in our discussion. Here we will note that the steady-state solutions given in Eqs. 3.5 to 3.8 will not apply, in practice, for N very large whenever ρ is larger than unity. When operations with large N occur in practice, every effort is made to keep the mean service rate μ larger than arrival rate λ, so with the solutions for large N, only those for $\rho<1$ are of practical utility. Since in these cases the results depend very little on the exact value of N, as long as it is large, we can use the solutions for $N\to\infty$, which are simple in form. The steady-state solutions for infinite possible queue *are valid only* for $\rho < 1$; there are no steady-state solutions for $\rho > 1$. But, as we have seen, the possibility of a steady-state situation for large N and $\rho > 1$ is not likely in practice, so this limitation to the range $0 < \rho < 1$ is not serious. Transient solutions, more appropriate for the $\rho > 1$ situation, will be discussed later.

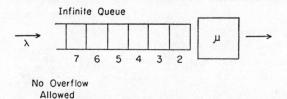

Infinite Queue

λ 7 6 5 4 3 2 μ

No Overflow
Allowed

Fig. 3.3. Representation of a single exponential service channel with infinite queue (no overflow allowed), with Poisson arrivals. Open end of queue channel and absence of overflow arrow indicate that the queue is infinite in possible length.

The steady-state solutions for $N \to \infty$ (where *every* arriving unit joins the queue)

$$P_n = (1-\rho)\rho^n; \quad L = \rho/(1-\rho) = \lambda/(\mu-\lambda); \quad \rho = (\lambda/\mu)$$
$$L_q = \rho^2/(1-\rho) = \lambda^2/\mu(\mu-\lambda); \quad \Delta L = \sqrt{\lambda\mu}/(\mu-\lambda)$$

(3.10)

are valid only for $\mu > \lambda$. There are no steady-state solutions, in this case, for $\rho > 1$. The fraction of time the service facility is busy is $1 - P_0$, as before; here it equals ρ, the utilization factor (as long as $\rho < 1$). The mean wait W of an average arriving unit, from the time it joins the queue until it is discharged from the service facility, can be obtained from the consideration that if the mean arrival rate is λ, on the average the wait W times the arrival rate λ must equal the mean number of units waiting (in this connection, see the paragraph preceding Eq. 7.18), that is, $W = (L/\lambda) = 1/(\mu-\lambda)$. Likewise, the mean wait in queue before the unit is serviced, for this case where every unit joins the queue, is $W_q = (L_q/\lambda) = \lambda/\mu(\mu-\lambda)$ (as long as $\mu > \lambda$). Thus, queue length and waiting times are strongly dependent on ρ when ρ approaches unity. If we try to cut down on idle time $(1-\rho)$, we automatically increase the mean delay of the units, which have to wait in line.

Balance between Mean Wait and Service Cost

This suggests a possible practical problem. Suppose that the system is a harbor for unloading ships, the arrival distribution of the ships is Poisson with mean rate λ ships per week, and the service-time distribution is exponential, with a maximum mean rate of μ unloadings per week. If the ships are routed to this harbor, they have no choice but to wait at anchor till the dock is free. (We assume here that the rule of "first come, first served" is obeyed; other possible arrangements (priorities) will be discussed later.) If the harbor is to accommodate the ships routed to it, it must be able to handle them at least as fast as they arrive, that is, ρ must be less than unity. But it may be worthwhile to find out *how much* less than unity ρ should be made. For example, if the harbor facilities are owned by the shipping company, it would be worthwhile trying to balance the cost occasioned by the delay of shipping with the cost of running the dock.

Suppose again that the cost per unloading operation of running the service facility (the unloading dock in this instance; we are treating here the case where there is only one dock in the harbor that can unload the ships under study) is $D\mu$, proportional to the speed of service. And suppose that the average cost of having one ship idle in the port (the cost of crew, overhead, etc.) is proportional to the mean wait in port, CW. Then we would wish to adjust μ (or ρ, since we assume that λ is fixed) so that total cost per ship unloaded, $D\mu + CW = D\mu + C/(\mu - \lambda)$, is minimum. Setting the derivative of this with respect to μ equal to zero yields the required optimal value of

$$\mu \text{ (for least cost)} = \lambda + \sqrt{C/D} \qquad (3.11)$$

Therefore, if cost C of ship delay per week (C for crew cost) is small compared to the cost D per operation per service rate of operating the dock (D for dock cost), the optimum service rate need not be much larger than arrival rate; we should keep dock utilization high (ρ near unity) at the expense of ship delays. But if crew cost C is large compared to dock cost factor D, the optimum value of μ would be considerably larger than λ; we could afford to have our efficient dock idle much of the time in order to reduce costly ship delays. In practice, the values of λ and μ can be obtained by studying the arrival-time and service-time distributions, and the cost of delay per ship per week (or per whatever other unit of time is convenient, as long as λ and μ are given in the same units) can be figured from usual cost data. The value of D can be obtained by computing the cost $E(\mu)$ per unloading operation for the current value of μ and estimating the cost per operation $E(\mu + a)$ if the unloading rate were to be increased to $\mu + a$ (increased by a operations per week). Part of the cost E will be fixed charges, independent of μ; the rest, proportional to μ, the part we want, is obtained by subtracting and dividing by a: $D = (1/a)[E(\mu + a) - E(\mu)]$.

Now let us return to the general problem of units arriving at a single exponential service facility and investigate other possible behavior patterns for the arriving units.

We may find, of course, that the arriving units do not make their decisions to wait for service simply on whether the queue is less than $N-1$ long. They may estimate the length of time they will have to wait in line, and may stay or not depending on this estimate. The mean wait in queue of a unit in an exponential service system is proportional to the length of the queue when the unit joins it.

On the average, each unit ahead of the new unit takes a time $T_s = (1/\mu)$ to be serviced; therefore, if the queue has length n when the new unit joins, the expected wait before the unit enters service will be (n/μ).

Effect of Customer Impatience

Now suppose these units (prospective customers, for example) having had experience with the service facility, tend to stay only when they expect the wait will be short, and tend not to join the queue if they estimate the wait will be long. A mathematical model that will correspond to this tendency is to assume that the fraction of prospective customers which joins the queue is $e^{-\alpha t}$, where t is the customer's estimate of his waiting time and α is a measure of the average impatience of customers. In other words, the fraction of prospective customers which joins the queue when its length is n is $e^{-\alpha n/\mu}$, a quantity which diminishes as n increases (and also as μ decreases).

In this case our equations for detailed balance of transitions for the steady-state case are (compare with Eq. 3.2)

$$\mu P_1 - \lambda P_0 = 0; \quad \gamma = e^{-\alpha/2\mu}$$
$$\mu P_{n+1} + \lambda\gamma^{2n-2}P_{n-1} - (\mu + \lambda\gamma^{2n})P_n = 0 \quad (n > 0)$$

(3.12)

where we have adjusted our arrival rates to correspond to the fraction of prospective customers which elects to stay. The solutions of this set of equations are

$$P_n = P_0\rho^n\gamma^{n^2-n} = P_0\rho^n\, e^{-n(n-1)\alpha/2\mu}$$

These probabilities fall off very rapidly with increasing n, so it is hardly necessary to terminate the series even though there may be a practical restriction on length of queue. To put it another way, if the fact that the queue cannot be longer than some maximum length has an important effect on the results, then the effect of customer avoidance of long waits, which we are investigating here, will not be important, and we can probably use the results of the earlier analysis given in Eqs. 3.6, 3.8 and 3.9. On the other hand, if the effect we are now studying is more important, it means that a queue of maximum length seldom occurs, and we will not change the results appreciably if we assume that all values of n are allowed (since the occurrence of large n's is extremely

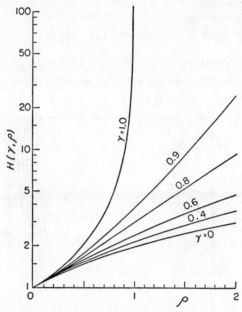

Fig. 3.4. Plots of function $H(\gamma,\rho)$, defined in Eq. 3.13, as a function for different values of γ.

unlikely). Therefore, we will here make no restriction on the magnitude of n. Since queues never tend to infinity even for $\rho > 1$ in this case, we need not impose the restriction $\rho < 1$ here, as we had to do for Eqs. 3.10.

To discuss measures of effectiveness we need to define a function

$$H(\gamma,\rho) = \sum_{n=0}^{\infty} \rho^n \gamma^{n(n-1)} \rightarrow \begin{cases} 1+\rho & (\gamma \rightarrow 0) \\ 1/(1-\rho) & (\gamma \rightarrow 1) \end{cases} \quad (3.13)$$

Curves of this function for different values of ρ and γ are given in Fig. 3.4. Curves for the logarithmic derivative times ρ

$$\rho[H_\rho(\gamma,\rho)/H(\gamma,\rho)] = \rho \frac{\partial}{\partial \rho} \ln [H(\gamma,\rho)]; \quad H_\rho = \frac{\partial}{\partial \rho} H = \sum_{n=1}^{\infty} n\rho^{n-1}\gamma^{n(n-1)}$$

are shown in Fig. 3.5. In terms of these functions, the constants for the system are

$$P_n = [\rho^n \gamma^{n(n-1)} / H(\gamma, \rho)]; \quad L = \rho[H_\rho(\gamma, \rho) / H(\gamma, \rho)]$$

$$L_q = L - 1 + P_0 = \frac{\rho H_\rho(\gamma, \rho) + 1 - H(\gamma, \rho)}{H(\gamma, \rho)} \tag{3.14}$$

The mean-square deviation, if needed, can be obtained in terms of the derivative of H with respect to γ. Figure 3.5 shows that as customer impatience increases (γ decreases), the length of queue diminishes markedly.

Measurement of the P_n's will show whether this situation obtains in an actual system. Plotting the P_n's against n on semilog paper will not give a straight line as it did in the previous model. The plot will curve

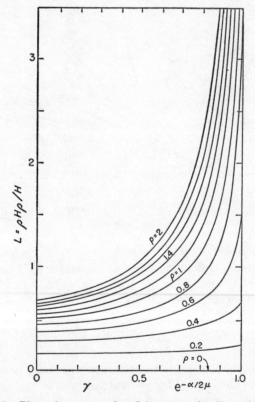

Fig. 3.5. Plots of mean number L in system for "impatient customers," according to Eq. 3.14. Parameter γ is "impatience factor"; probability of new arrival joining the queue is γ^{2n} if the queue, on arrival, is length n. Parameter ρ is utilization factor (λ/μ).

downward, and from the curvature one will be able to compute an approximate value of γ. If $\gamma = 0.9$, and if $\gamma^2 = e^{-\alpha/\mu} = 0.81$ (then $\alpha/\mu = 0.211$), it means that about a fifth of the prospective customers will not wait if the queue is one unit long, about a third will not wait if the queue length is 2, about a half will turn away if queue length is 3, and so on. If $\gamma = 0.8$ ($\alpha/\mu = 0.446$), it means that about a third will not join the queue even if its length is only 1, three-fifths will not join if it is 2, and about three-quarters of them will go elsewhere if 3 are in the queue when they arrive, and so on.

In this case also we can adjust μ for optimum profit, once costs and the average behavior of the customer are known. We should know, of course, mean gross profits G per actual customer and mean cost E per customer (we assume these costs are independent of rate μ, so that service cost per unit of time is μE). We now assume that as service rate is changed, the prospective customers learn by trial and error that μ is being changed and adjust their habits so that the fraction that stays in line is still $e^{-\alpha\tau}$, where τ is the newly estimated delay time. In other words, as μ is changed, the factor $\gamma = e^{-\alpha/2\mu}$ in Eqs. 3.12 and 3.13 changes accordingly, increasing if μ increases and decreasing if μ is decreased. (There are a number of measurements of the alteration of traffic flow as street traffic conductivities are changed, and of the change in customer buying habits as product accessibilities are modified, which indicate that people actually do adjust their average behavior in response to changing delays, in a manner rather like this.) Consequently, in our equation for net profit per unit time, we can assume λ, α, E and G are fixed, and adjust μ for maximum.

The number of service operations per unit time is the channel capacity μ times the fraction of the time the channel is busy $(1-P_0)$. Therefore the net profit per unit time is

$$\{\mu G[H(\gamma,\rho)-1]/H(\gamma,\rho)\} - \mu E = \left(\frac{\lambda G}{\rho}\right)\left[1 - \frac{1}{H(e^{-\beta\rho/2},\rho)} - \frac{E}{G}\right]$$

where $\beta = (\alpha/\lambda)$ is a constant property of prospective customers and we have absorbed the μ into the variable $\rho = (\lambda/\mu)$. Therefore, we can differentiate this with respect to ρ and set the result zero to obtain an optimum value of ρ and thus of μ. The resulting equation, if we write out the series, is

$$1 - \frac{1}{\Sigma \rho^n\, e^{-n(n-1)\beta\rho/2}}$$

$$-\frac{\Sigma n\rho^n\, e^{-n(n-1)\beta\rho/2} - (\rho\beta/2)\Sigma n(n-1)\rho^n\, e^{-n(n-1)\rho\beta/2}}{[\Sigma \rho^n\, e^{-n(n-1)\rho\beta/2}]^2} = \frac{E}{G} \qquad (3.15)$$

which is the analogue of Eq. 3.9 in the present case. The quantity on the left side, when $\beta > (\frac{1}{2})$, starts from zero as $(3\beta + \frac{1}{2}\beta^2)\rho^4$ when ρ is small compared to unity, and approaches $\rho^2/(1+\rho)^2$ when ρ is much larger than $(1/\beta) = (\lambda/\alpha)$ (that is, when $\alpha \gg \mu$). We see once again that if $E > G$, there is no solution (this is not surprising, for our "net profit" would be negative even if the facility had no idle time). For small values of (E/G) (cost per service small compared to gross profit per service) we should make ρ small (service rate μ large compared to arrival rate λ) so that as many prospective customers are served as possible, even though idle time P_0 is large; whereas if (E/G) is larger than $\frac{1}{2}$ (but less than 1), ρ should be increased and, in some cases, made larger than unity (in this case we reduce service rate to reduce idle time, even though it means loss of prospective customers). We also note that as β is made larger (γ smaller), corresponding to greater "impatience" on the part of the customers and less willingness to wait in line, the change in ρ required as (E/G) changes becomes more and more. For very impatient customers it is necessary to increase service rate very much before it will attract many more prospective customers. As we have indicated, β, E and G can be measured, so that the optimum value of ρ can be computed for any specific case.

In all of the simple cases discussed heretofore, as in the more complicated systems to be treated later, one consequence of the fluctuations in arrivals and service times shows up in our solutions every time: If we wish to accommodate a large proportion of arriving units, we *must provide a surplus of service* to take care of fluctuations; we must expect the service facility to be idle part of the time in order to be able to handle the surges in arrivals that occur from time to time. Every reduction in idle time either loses customers or increases delays, the more rapidly the smaller the fraction of time idle. The present examples allow for this provision, for they have been calculated for the "random" situation, the exponential case. If actual arrival or service distributions are appreciably nearer regularity than this, some relaxation of planned idle time can be allowed, but unless we are sure of this, any reduction of excess service capacity is likely to result in loss of prospective customers or increase in waiting time, or both. Vice versa, if the fluctuations are "more random" than the exponential, our provisions will not be adequate. The effects of arrival or service distributions on the dynamics of the system, the quantitative restatement of this paragraph, will be given in Chapter 5.

Chapter 4

MULTIPLE
EXPONENTIAL CHANNELS

T HE NEXT EXAMPLE in increasing degree of complication is that of a service facility with M equal exponential channels, each of mean service rate μ, arranged "in parallel." Units are again supposed to have a Poisson arrival distribution, with "mean arrival rate" λ. If they join the queue, they stay in order of arrival, in a single queue, until they come to the front of the line, when they enter the first unoccupied channel. Examples of this sort of system are restaurants with counter seats and automobile parking facilities. We assume here that service times are exponentially distributed; if measurements indicate that the actual distributions differ appreciably from this, one of the examples discussed later may be a more appropriate model. For "short order" restaurants and for parking lots near a shopping center, it is likely that short stays may be prevalent enough to make the exponential distribution a good approximation.

Service Channels in Parallel

Again we can characterize the state of the system by n, the number of units present. When n is less than M, there is no queue; all units present are being serviced. When n is larger than M, there is a queue $(n-M)$ long (if the operational situation allows queues). When $n(<M)$ channels are occupied, the rate of transition from state n to state $n-1$ by completion of service is $n\mu P_n\, dt$, since any one of the n-filled channels may complete its service in the next instant dt. The chance of two or more channels completing service in the same instant dt is proportional to a higher power of dt, and may be neglected as before. The equations

of detailed balance for steady-state operation are therefore

$$\mu P_1 - \lambda P_0 = 0$$

$$(n+1)\mu P_{n+1} + \lambda P_{n-1} - (n\mu + \lambda)P_n = 0 \quad (0 < n < M) \quad (4.1)$$

$$M\mu P_{n+1} + \lambda P_{n-1} - (M\mu + \lambda)P_n = 0 \quad (M \leq n)$$

As before, the negative terms represent transitions out of the state considered, the positive terms transitions into the same state, either by

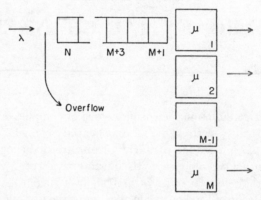

Fig. 4.1. Representation of multiple exponential-channel service facility. Arrivals are Poisson, number of equivalent parallel channels is M, and maximum length of queue is $N - M$.

arrival or completion of service. If there is a maximum length of queue $N - M$ such that arrivals will not join if $n = N$ but will join if $n < N$, then the equation for $n = N$ is

$$\lambda P_{N-1} - M\mu P_N = 0 \quad (N \geq M)$$

Successive solution of these equations, starting at $n = 0$, gives

$$P_n = \frac{(M\rho)^n}{n!} P_0 \quad (0 \leq n \leq M)$$

$$(4.2)$$

$$P_n = \frac{M^M}{M!}\rho^n P_0 \quad (M \leq n \leq N)$$

where $\rho = (\lambda/M\mu)$, the utilization factor for the whole system, is the ratio between mean rate of arrivals and the maximum possible rate of service of all M channels. (Incidentally, this model corresponds to a restaurant operation only if the restaurant is really staffed for all M places, if the service rate per customer is independent of the number of customers seated. If "saturation effects" show up before $n = M$, another model should be used.)

To express the measures of effectiveness compactly, we define a set of functions $E_m(x)$ and $D_m(x)$, such that

$$e^x E_m(x) = \sum_{n=0}^{m} (x^n/n!)$$

$$E_m(x) \rightarrow \begin{cases} (x^m/m!) \, e^{-x} & (m \ll x) \\ 1 - [x^{m+1}/(m+1)!] \, e^{-x} & (m \gg x) \end{cases} \quad (4.3)$$

$$D_m(x) = E_{m+1}(x) - [x/(m+1)]E_m(x)$$

Properties of these functions are listed in Appendix 2. Values of E_m and D_m are given in Table V.

We first study the no-queue case, where arrivals do not wait if no space is available $(N = M)$. This is usually the case with parking lots, and often the case with restaurants. Here

$$P_n = [e_n(\rho M)/E_M(\rho M)] \qquad (0 \leq n \leq M)$$

$$e_n(x) = (x^n e^{-x}/n!)$$

$$L = \sum_{n=0}^{M} nP_n = M\rho \frac{E_{M-1}(\rho M)}{E_M(\rho M)} \rightarrow \begin{cases} M - (1/\rho) & (\rho \gg 1) \\ \rho M & (\rho \ll 1) \end{cases} \quad (4.4)$$

$$(\Delta L)^2 = \rho M \frac{E_M(\rho M)E_{M-1}(\rho M) - M e_M(\rho M)D_{M-1}(\rho M)}{[E_M(\rho M)]^2}$$

$$\rightarrow \begin{cases} (1/\rho) & (\rho \gg 1) \\ \rho M & (\rho \ll 1) \end{cases}$$

Curves of L for some values of M and ρ are shown in Fig. 4.2. The quantity $P_0 = e^{-\rho M}/E_M(M\rho)$ is the fraction of times the facility is completely idle, P_M the fraction of times it is full and L is the mean number of filled channels. The value of ΔL shows that there is considerable fluctuation about this mean utilization. The average rate of service of units is μL, which is λ when ρ is small and is μM when ρ is large.

As before, probably the best way to see whether the actual operation corresponds to this model is to measure the various P_n's, to clock the fraction of the time the system has n units being served, for different

n's. A listing of the times of all arrivals and departures for a day or so will provide sufficient data for this to be done. If a plot of $n!P_n$ against n on semilog paper yields a straight line (or one nearly straight for the larger values of n), the model is appropriate, and from the slope of the line one can obtain a value of $\rho M = (\lambda/\mu)$. A measurement of the service-

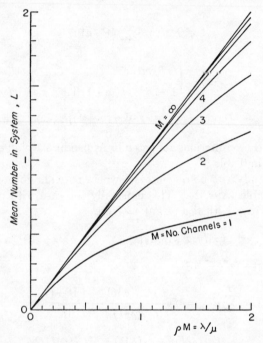

Fig. 4.2. Mean number of units in system for Poisson arrivals, at rate λ, to a system of M parallel exponential service channels, each of rate μ, with no queue allowed ($N = M$), as function of $M\rho = (\lambda/\mu)$ for different values of M. See Fig. 11.7.

time distribution (which should also be made, to see whether it is exponential, before the present model is used) will yield a value of μ and thus λ can be evaluated.

Optimizing the Number of Channels

In this case one might expect that the cost of service will be proportional to the number of channels M and not proportional to μ, since in both restaurants and parking spaces the mean length of "service" (of stay) is not changed much by improving the "service" (increasing the service staff). The average gross profit per customer served, not counting the cost of service, may be called G, and the gross profit per unit time is μLG. The net profit per unit time is thus

$$\mu LG - ME = \lambda G[E_{M-1}(\lambda/\mu)/E_M(\lambda/\mu)] - ME$$

where E is the cost, per channel per unit time, of the service facility. From this expression one can find the optimum value of M (number of parking spaces or number of utilizable seats in the restaurant) to yield maximum net profit for given values of λ, μ, G and E. We first divide by μG and then examine the changes of value of the resulting expression as M is increased successively by unit increments. The increase in the second term is constant $(E/\mu G)$, the increase in the first term is

$$\left(\frac{\lambda}{\mu}\right)\left[\frac{E_M(\lambda/\mu)}{E_{M+1}(\lambda/\mu)} - \frac{E_{M-1}(\lambda/\mu)}{E_M(\lambda/\mu)}\right]$$

$$\rightarrow \begin{cases} 1 & (\mu M \ll \lambda) \\ (\lambda^{M+1} e^{-\lambda/\mu}/\mu^{M+1} M!) & (\mu M \gg \lambda) \end{cases} \quad (4.5)$$

Plots of this against (λ/μ) for a few values of M are given in Fig. 4.3.

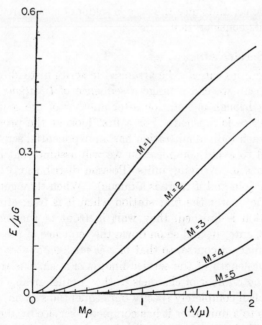

Fig. 4.3. Determination of optimum number of service channels. Existing values of ratio (λ/μ) and of ratio $(E/\mu G)$ of service cost to mean gross profit, per busy channel per unit time, determine a point on the chart. The M for the curve nearest this point is the number of channels which will produce greatest net profit. See Eq. 4.5; also, Eq. 10.4 and Fig. 10.2.

When this quantity is larger than $(E/\mu G)$, further increase of M will increase net profit; when it is less than $(E/\mu G)$, further increase will decrease net profit. The value of M which makes it most nearly equal to $(E/\mu G)$ is the number of channels that yields the largest net profit per unit time.

The ratio $(E/\mu G)$ is the ratio of service-cost rate per channel to gross-profits rate per busy channel. If it is greater than unity, there is a net loss per unit operation and there is no optimum solution. If it is less than unity but not much less (not much margin of profit), M should be unity unless $\rho \gg 1$, and we should turn away many prospective customers in order to cut down idle time. If $(E/\mu G)$ is considerably less than $\frac{1}{3}$, M can be larger than unity; we should have several channels, even though some of them will usually be idle, so that we can accommodate as many prospective customers as possible.

The modifications to these solutions to allow for a possible queue, limited either by space considerations or by customer impatience, can be added without much difficulty, combining the methods used in Chapter 3 with the state probabilities of Eq. 4.2. The formulas are not simple in appearance, and since the case is seldom encountered in practice, we will omit its consideration.

Sequential Service Lines

Service facilities can also be arranged in series instead of in parallel. By this we mean we can arrange a sequence of l *stations* such that a unit must go through one station after another of the sequence before the whole service is finished. For a first look at the process, we will assume that each individual station has an exponential service-time distribution, and to avoid complication we will assume that each has the same mean rate μ. Arriving units (Poisson distribution) first join the queue (if they join and if there is a queue). When they get to the head of the line, they enter the first station when it is free; after service at this first station is finished, they wait in front of the second station until it is free, enter it, and so on down the sequence of l stations. This pattern is similar, of course, to that of a *production* or *service line*. The integer l is the length of the service line; it is analogous to the integer M, which is the number of channels in the parallel arrangement.

Before we can completely specify our sequential system, we must say what happens to a unit after it has completed service by the nth station in the line. If the $(n+1)$'st station has already finished its previous unit, it is free and can take the next unit as it emerges from the nth station. But if the $(n+1)$'st station is not free, the emerging unit could

(1) emerge from the nth station and wait in a queue till the $(n+1)$'st is free; or (2) stay in the nth station, *blocking* it from taking on another unit, even though it is idle and another unit may be waiting in the $(n-1)$'st station, until the $(n+1)$'st becomes free to take the waiting unit, thus unblocking the nth station; or (3) all units in service have to stay in their respective stations until *all* stations complete service on the units in them, when all units move at once, each into the next station, the one in the lth station leaving the line and one from the queue moving into the first station (if there is no unit in the queue, all units wait until another unit arrives, when they all move).

In service lines of type 1, if the queues before each station are unbounded in length, then each station acts independently of every other and there is no blocking. If the queues are finite in length before the 2nd, 3rd $\cdots$ to lth station, blocking of the preceding station occurs whenever a queue reaches its maximum length; the preceding station must stay idle, even though its own queue exists, until the following queue drops below its maximum length. Type 2 lines are really type 1 lines with finite queues of zero length. Type 3 lines, where all units must move together, are sometimes called "unpaced belt production lines." Lines in cafeterias are either type 1 with finite queues or type 2 lines.

As a simple example of how the behavior of these systems can be worked out, we take a two-station service line of type 2 (no queues ahead of station 1 or between the stations), as shown in the upper diagram of Fig. 4.4. The particular state of the system is specified by specifying the states of the two stations. The second station can either be empty (0) or full (1), whereas the first station can be empty (0) or full and working (1) or blocked (b) because it has finished its service but the second station is still occupied. The probability functions can be labeled with two subscripts, the first for the state of the first station, the second for that of the second. State 11 can go to state $b1$ or 10 by completion of service of either first or second station; state $b1$ can go to state 01 by completion of service of station 2 (as soon as the unit in station 2 is ejected, the unit blocking station 1 enters station 2, and since there is no queue allowed ahead of station 1 in this example, station 1 remains empty until a new arrival comes along), and so on. The detailed balance equations for steady state are

$$\mu P_{01} - \lambda P_{00} = 0; \quad \mu P_{10} + \mu P_{b1} - (\mu + \lambda) P_{01} = 0;$$

$$\lambda P_{00} + \mu P_{11} - \mu P_{10} = 0; \quad \mu P_{11} - \mu P_{b1} = 0; \quad \lambda P_{01} - 2\mu P_{11} = 0 \tag{4.6}$$

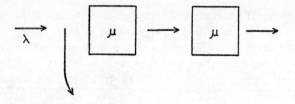

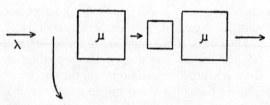

Fig. 4.4. Representation of two-station service lines corresponding to Eqs. 4.7 and 4.8.

For example, the only way to get out of state (00) is to have an arrival $(-\lambda P_{00}$ in the first equation), and the only way to get into this state is to have service completed on a unit in station 2 (μP_{01}). For steady state, these rates of transition must balance.

The solution is

$$P_{00} = (2/S); \quad P_{01} = (2\rho/S);$$

$$P_{10} = (\rho^2 + 2\rho)/S; \quad P_{b1} = P_{11} = \rho^2/S \tag{4.7}$$

where $\rho = (\lambda/\mu)$ and the quantity $S = 3\rho^2 + 4\rho + 2$ is the constant factor, which is adjusted so that the sum of all the P's is unity.

We note that the mean number of units in the system is

$$L = P_{01} + P_{10} + 2(P_{11} + P_{b1}) = (5\rho^2 + 4\rho)/S \rightarrow \begin{cases} 2\rho - \frac{3}{2}\rho^2 & (\rho \ll 1) \\ 1 & (\rho = 1) \\ \dfrac{5}{3} - \dfrac{32}{45\rho} & (\rho \gg 1) \end{cases}$$

but the mean number of busy service stations is

$$B = P_{01} + P_{10} + P_{b1} + 2P_{11} = (4\rho^2 + 4\rho)/S \rightarrow \begin{cases} 2\rho - 2\rho^2 & (\rho \ll 1) \\ \frac{8}{9} & (\rho = 1) \\ \frac{4}{3} - \frac{4}{9\rho} & (\rho \gg 1) \end{cases}$$

and the fraction of prospective customers turned away is

$$F = P_{10} + P_{b1} + P_{11} = (3\rho^2 + 2\rho)/S \rightarrow \begin{cases} \rho - \frac{1}{2}\rho^2 & (\rho \ll 1) \\ \frac{5}{9} & (\rho = 1) \\ 1 - \frac{2}{3\rho} & (\rho \gg 1) \end{cases}$$

Because of the "blocking effect," occurring when station 1 is finished but cannot take on another unit since station 2 is not ready to accept the readied unit, this sequential facility cannot be as efficient as a single-station line. Even when $\rho \rightarrow \infty$ and the facility can pick up an arriving unit nearly any time it can take one, each unit is busy only two thirds of the time ($B \rightarrow \frac{4}{3} = 2 \cdot \frac{2}{3}$). Because of blocking, the maximum utilization possible is $\frac{2}{3}$.

The decrease in useful time caused by blocking can be reduced by allowing a queue in front of the second station. For example, if we allow a queue of length 1 before the second station, but none before the first, our allowed states are (00, 01, 02, 10, 11, 12, b2), where the 2 in the second place indicates that station 2 is busy and its queue is also full (blocking can occur only when the queue for station 2 is filled). The equations of detailed balance yield the following solution:

$$P_{00} = (\rho + 4)/S; \quad P_{01} = (\rho^2 + 4\rho)/S; \quad P_{02} = (2\rho^2/S)$$

$$P_{10} = (\rho^3 + 3\rho^2 + 4\rho)/S; \quad P_{11} = (\rho^3 + 2\rho^2)/S; \quad P_{12} = P_{b2} = (\rho^3/S)$$

(4.8)

where $\rho = (\lambda/\mu)$ and $S = 4\rho^3 + 8\rho^2 + 9\rho + 4$.

In this case the mean number of units in the system, L, the mean number of stations busy, B, the fraction of times the first station is filled, preventing an arrival from entering, F, and the fraction of time, T_2, station 2 is busy $(T_2 = T_1)$ are

$$L = (9\rho^3 + 12\rho^2 + 8\rho)/S \rightarrow \begin{cases} 2\rho & (\rho \ll 1) \\ \frac{2}{2}\frac{9}{5} & (\rho = 1) \\ \frac{9}{4} & (\rho \gg 1) \end{cases}$$

$$B = (6\rho^3 + 10\rho^2 + 8\rho)/S \rightarrow \begin{cases} 2\rho \\ \frac{2}{2}\frac{4}{5} \\ \frac{3}{2} \end{cases} \qquad (4.9)$$

$$F = (4\rho^3 + 5\rho^2 + 4\rho)/S \rightarrow \begin{cases} \rho - \rho^2 & (\rho \ll 1) \\ \frac{1}{2}\frac{3}{5} & (\rho = 1) \\ 1 - \dfrac{3}{4\rho} & (\rho \gg 1) \end{cases}$$

$$T_1 = T_2 = \tfrac{1}{2}B$$

In this case the maximum utilization of the stations is $\frac{3}{4}$. The fraction of prospective customers turned away is somewhat smaller than for the example with no queue between stations, being 0.52 compared to 0.56 at $\rho = 1$, but this improvement in customer acceptance (for the same value of ρ) is hardly noticeable.

In these cases, where blocking can occur, we see that the fluctuations in arrival and service times actually prevent the full utilization of the service facility. No matter what value of μ we choose, the fraction of time busy cannot be increased above the maximum value (in these examples $\frac{2}{3}$ or $\frac{3}{4}$) fixed by the setup.

Many other sorts of service facilities, with exponential units, can be simulated and solved by the methods we have been outlining here. Some of them will be taken up later. We shall now see whether we can extend our mathematical model to situations with service-time and arrival-time distributions appreciably different from the exponential type.

Chapter 5

SIMULATION OF
NON-EXPONENTIAL DISTRIBUTIONS

W E MENTIONED EARLIER that only exponential facilities (and Poisson arrivals) give rise to simple linear equations for detailed balance of transitions between states, independent of time. For other types of distributions we normally have to solve much more complicated sets of equations. Yet many operational situations correspond to service-time distributions which are appreciably different from exponential. Our next task is to show that a fair number of these *can be simulated* by a suitably chosen set of exponential facilities, with appropriate rules for transition. This is not to say that the service facility in question necessarily has the actual structure corresponding to the model which simulates its statistical behavior; all that is necessary for our analysis is that the model *does* simulate this behavior. If the model can be built up from exponential elements, the equations to be solved will be considerably simplified.

Simulation by Series Arrangement

To show how we can proceed, we shall consider the statistical properties of a facility consisting of two exponential parts, called *phases*, with the following rules for transfer: (1) only one unit is allowed, at a time, in the facility; (2) the entering unit must first go through the first phase, which has exponential time distribution with mean rate of completion 2μ; (3) when it has finished phase 1, it immediately goes on to phase 2, which also is exponential with rate 2μ; (4) when phase 2 is finished, the unit is discharged from the facility, and only then can a new unit be introduced to phase 1. Although we know this facility is compound, it can be considered as a single service facility, since it only allows one unit in it at a time (it is thus *not* a service line, with two stations). Let us see what service-time distribution it has, viewed as a single facility.

The chance that the first phase finishes between x and $x+dx$ after the unit enters the facility is $2\mu\,e^{-2\mu x}\,dx$, according to Eq. 2.6, and the chance that the second phase, starting at x, completes at a time between $t-x$ and $t-x+dt$ later is $2\mu\,e^{-2\mu(t-x)}\,dt$. Consequently, the probability that the facility completes both phases and discharges the unit a time between t and $t+dt$ after service was started is

$$s(t)\,dt = 4\mu^2\,dt\int_0^t e^{-2\mu(t-x+x)}\,dx = 2\mu(2\mu t)\,e^{-2\mu t}\,dt$$

and the basic service-time distribution, the probability that the whole two-phase service is not yet completed is

$$S_0(t) = \int_t^\infty s(t)\,dt = \int_{2\mu t}^\infty y\,e^{-y}\,dy = (1+2\mu t)\,e^{-2\mu t}$$

which corresponds to curve b of Fig. 2.2. We note that it differs appreciably from a, the exponential distribution.

Therefore this facility, *viewed as a single facility*, has a service-time distribution which is not exponential, though each of its phases is exponential. Vice versa, if we find a facility which has service-time distribution curves similar to curves b of Fig. 2.2 or 2.3, we can use the combination of two exponential phases just described as the *statistical equivalent* of the actual facility in our mathematical model of the process. Then, by considering the different phases separately, we can reduce the equations for the state probabilities to simple linear equations of the general form we have been treating. The actual service operation may not be physically separable into distinct phases, but if its distribution function has the form given in this demonstration, introducing "virtual phases" into the model enables us to simplify the analysis considerably.

The mean time of completion of the service is, by definition,

$$T_s = \int_0^\infty (1+2\mu t)\,e^{-2\mu t}\,dt = (1/\mu)$$

so that μ is the mean rate of completion of the service, as required (this is, of course, why we chose the rate 2μ for each of the phases, so that the mean time to complete *both* phases would be twice $\frac{1}{2}\mu$).

We can form a whole set of model service facilities by adding more and more phases. For example, a facility with k phases, each exponential and each with rate $k\mu$, arranged so that the unit must pass sequentially through all k phases before it is discharged and a new unit can enter, has probability functions

$$s(t) \, dt = (k\mu)^k \, dt \int_0^t e^{-k\mu(t-x_2)} \, dx_2 \int_0^{x_2} e^{-k\mu(x_2-x_3)} \, dx_3 \cdots$$

$$\cdot \int_0^{x_{k-1}} e^{-k\mu(x_{k-1}-x_k+x_k)} \, dx_k \qquad (5.1)$$

$$= (k\mu t)^{k-1}[e^{-k\mu t}/(k-1)!]k\mu \, dt; \quad T_s = (1/\mu)$$

$$S_0(t) = e^{-k\mu t} \sum_{n=0}^{k-1} (k\mu t)^n/n!; \quad \Delta t_s = (1/\mu\sqrt{k})$$

We note that, in this case, distribution function $S_0 = E_{k-1}(k\mu t)$ of Eq. 4.3 and Table V. The expression for the standard deviation Δt_s (see Eq. 2.4) shows that the variability of service times diminishes as k increases. Curves b and c in Figs. 2.2 and 2.3 are for $k=2$ and $k=10$ respectively. Curves a are for $k=1$, which is the exponential case. The case of constant service time, with S_0 a true step function, is the case $k \rightarrow \infty$.

These distributions, called *Erlang distributions*, provide a family of service-time distributions which range all the way from the "pure random" exponential type to the completely regular, constant service-time situation. They will not fit all possible service-time distributions, but they will fit many (and perhaps most) of the ones encountered in practice. And, as we have indicated, they allow an interpretation of states in terms of exponential phases, which allows us to use the simple linear equations of detailed balance between states, thus considerably simplifying their solution.

The same procedure can be followed for arrivals. Suppose that we have an infinitely large supply depot of units, and suppose that these units, in order to "arrive" at the service facility, have to pass through an "arrival timing channel," which receives a unit from the supply depot, holds it for a variable time and then releases it to go on to the service facility, taking in a new unit from the depot as soon as it releases the previous one. If the timing channel has an exponential holding-time distribution with mean rate λ, then the output of this channel, the arrivals at the service facility, will have a Poisson distribution with mean arrival rate λ. If the arrival timing channel has two equal exponential phases in series, each of rate 2λ, such that a new unit enters phase 1 only after the previous unit leaves phase 2, then the arrival distribution (see Eqs. 2.7 and 2.8), the output of this channel, is the second Erlang type:

$$a(t) = 2\lambda(2\lambda t)\, e^{-2\lambda t}$$

$$A_0(t) = (1 + 2\lambda t)\, e^{-2\lambda t}; \quad U_0(t) = (1 + \lambda t)\, e^{-2\lambda t}$$

which is "less random" than the Poisson distribution; there are fewer very short or very long intervals between arrivals.

Going on as before, if the arrival timing channel, which regulates the exit from the supply depot of units sent on to arrive at the service facility, has l phases, each exponential with rate $l\lambda$, the resulting arrival distributions will be

$$a(t) = l\lambda(l\lambda t)^{l-1}[e^{-l\lambda t}/(l-1)!]; \quad T_a = (1/\lambda)$$

$$A_0(t) = e^{-l\lambda t} \sum_{n=0}^{l-1} [(l\lambda t)^n/n!] = E_{l-1}(l\lambda t)$$

$$U_0(t) = e^{-l\lambda t} \sum_{n=0}^{l-1} \left(1 - \frac{n}{l}\right)\frac{(l\lambda t)^n}{n!} = D_{l-1}(l\lambda t) \tag{5.2}$$

$$A_n(t) = e^{-l\lambda t} \sum_{s=0}^{l-1} [(l\lambda t)^{s+nl}/(s+nl)!]; \quad \Delta t_a = (1/\lambda\sqrt{l})$$

$$U_n(t) = e^{-l\lambda t} \sum_{s=0}^{l-1}\left[\left(1 - \frac{s}{l}\right)\frac{(l\lambda t)^{nl-s}}{(nl-s)!} + \left(1 - \frac{s+1}{l}\right)\frac{(l\lambda t)^{nl+s+1}}{(nl+s+1)!}\right]$$

Note the connection between these functions and the function $E_n(x)$ of Eq. 4.3 and Appendix 2.

Figure 5.1 gives curves for S_0 or A_0 and V_0 or U_0 as functions of λt or μt. We note that as k or l increases, the variability Δt of the interval decreases inversely as the square root of k or l, and the curve for S_0 or A_0 approaches closer to the step-function shape. The most convenient way of deciding whether a given operational situation may be simulated by a system having l or k-stage arrival or service channels is to plot up a curve for S_0 or A_0 from operational data, as indicated in Fig. 2.1. The vertical scale is fixed, since the curve starts at unity for $t=0$; the horizontal scale is fixed by determining the mean time $(1/\mu)$ or $(1/\lambda)$ between arrivals or for service completions, and measuring t in units of this mean time. We can then see whether the resulting curve corresponds to one of those shown in the upper half of Fig. 5.1 within the accuracy of the data. If it does not, it may fit one of the set of curves given in the upper half of Fig. 5.6.

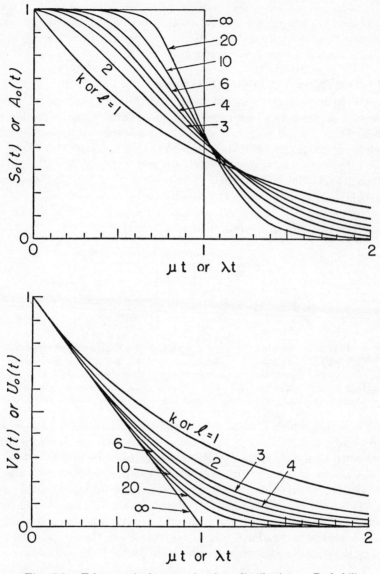

Fig. 5.1. Erlang arrival or service-time distributions. Probability that the next arrival or the next service completion will occur *after* time interval t. For S_0 or A_0, the interval starts just after the last arrival or service completion. For V_0 or U_0, time in the interval t is started at random. These distributions may be simulated by the systems represented in Figs. 5.2 and 5.3. Case k or $l = 1$ is the simple exponential case. See also Fig. 5.6 and Table V.

If the data represent a probability that an interval started at random does not contain an arrival or a service completion, then the curves for V_0 or U_0 are to be used for comparison.

Effects of Service-Time Distributions

To illustrate the way we use these models, let us examine the simple case of a single service facility with no queue (arriving units finding the channel busy do not wait). We considered this case for Poisson arrivals and exponential service earlier (Eqs. 3.5 to 3.8 for $N=1$), where we found that the probability that the service facility is busy is $P_1 = \rho/(1+\rho)$, which is also the fraction of arriving units which do not stop, and $P_0 = 1/(1+\rho)$ is the fraction of time the facility is idle.

Now suppose that arrivals are still Poisson $(l=1)$ but the service facility is the Erlang k type. This means that it behaves as though it

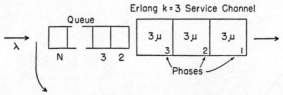

Fig. 5.2. Sequence of service phases having the Erlang service-time distribution corresponding to the curves for $k=3$ in Fig. 5.1. Each phase of service is exponential; a unit enters phase 3 first, then goes to 2, to 1 and then out; no other unit can enter phase 3 until the previous unit leaves phase 1. Eq. 5.3 gives results for the case of no queue, $N=1$.

had k phases, which the unit must traverse in turn before a new unit can be admitted. The possible states of the system are therefore either zero when no unit is in the facility or 1 to k, when there is a unit in one of the phases of service. We will label these phases in reverse order of occupation, so that the arriving unit will first go through phase k, then $(k-1)$, and so on, till it comes to phase 1, after which it is discharged and the state is zero until the next unit arrives, when it goes back to state k, and so on (we have assumed no queue can form). The detailed balancing equations interrelating the state probabilities are thus

$$k\mu P_1 - \lambda P_0 = 0; \quad k\mu P_{n+1} - k\mu P_n = 0 \quad (0 < n < k)$$
$$\lambda P_0 - k\mu P_k = 0 \tag{5.3}$$

(We remember that the mean rate of service of a single phase is $k\mu$ in order that the rate for the whole unit may be μ.) This solution of this set of equations is quite simple:

$$P_0 = 1/(1+\rho); \quad P_1 = P_2 = \cdots = P_k = \rho/k(1+\rho)$$

$$P_{\text{full}} = \sum_{n=1}^{k} P_n = \rho/(1+\rho) \tag{5.4}$$

In this simple case of no queue (Poisson arrivals), we are equally likely to find the unit in any of the k phases. We note that the values of the probabilities that the facility may be empty or full are exactly equal to those for exponential service ($k=1$). The behavior of the system is *independent of the shape of the service-time distribution.* (To be more accurate, it is the same for any Erlang distribution; to say it is the same for *any* distribution is a dangerous extrapolation to make in general, though one can show it is actually true in this case!)

A similar analysis can be made for the multiple-channel case, for M channels in parallel, each of k-Erlang type and of overall service rate μ, with Poisson arrivals and no queue allowed. Each channel can be unoccupied (state 0) or can have a unit in the nth phase, where n goes from 1 to k (k being the first phase entered and 1 being the last, as before). Since all channels are equivalent, we need only count the number of channels in phase 1, the number in phase 2, etc., to determine the state of the system; we need not bother to specify *which* channels are in state 1, etc. The state probabilities can then be written $p(n;s_1,s_2,\cdots,s_k)$, where s_1 is the number of channels in phase 1, s_2 the number in phase 2, etc., and $n = \Sigma s_i$ is the number of units in the system, which can be as small as zero or as large as M, the number of channels. A representation is given in Fig. 5.3.

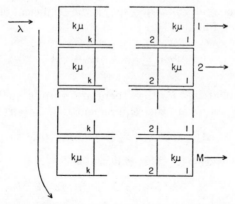

Fig. 5.3. Representation of a service facility with M channels in parallel, each of k-Erlang type, fed with Poisson arrivals. The system represented has no queue. See Eqs. 5.5.

Looking at the possible transitions, we see that a shift of phase inside one channel (say from phase i to phase $i-1$) would reduce s_i by unity and increase s_{i-1} by unity. This would occur at a rate $k\mu$ per channel, and if s_i+1 channels were in phase i to begin with, the factor multiplying p for this term would be $(s_i+1)k\mu$. Arrivals (rate λ) would change a channel from state 0 to state k unless all channels are full, in which case nothing would occur—the arrival would go elsewhere. The general equations for steady-state balance all have the same general form:

$$
\begin{aligned}
(1-\delta_{0s_k})\lambda p(n-1;s_1,\cdots,s_k-1) & \\
+(1-\delta_{Mn})k\mu(s_1+1)p(n+1;s_1+1,s_2,\cdots,s_k) & \\
+k\mu(s_2+1)p(n;s_1-1,s_2+1,s_3,\cdots,s_k)+\cdots & \quad (5.5)\\
+k\mu(s_k+1)p(n;s_1,\cdots,s_{k-2},s_{k-1}-1,s_k+1) & \\
-[nk\mu+(1-\delta_{Mn})\lambda]p(n;s_1,s_2,\cdots,s_{k-1},s_k)=0 &
\end{aligned}
$$

where $\Sigma s_i = n$ and where δ_{nm}, the Kronecker delta, is zero unless $n=m$, when it is unity.

The solution to this set of equations is

$$
p(n;s_1,\cdots,s_k) = A(\lambda/k\mu)^n/(s_1!s_2!\cdots s_k!)
$$

(where A is a constant, determined later), a fairly obvious generalization of Eq. 4.2. If now we remember that the coefficient of $x_1^{s_1}x_2^{s_2}\cdots x_k^{s_k}$ in the expansion of $(x_1+x_2+\cdots+x_k)^n$ is just $[n!/(s_1!s_2!\cdots s_k!)]$, we see that the state probability $p(n;s_1,\cdots,s_k)$ is the coefficient of $x_1^{s_1}x_2^{s_2}\cdots x_k^{s_k}$ in the "generating function"

$$
F_M(x_1,x_2,\cdots,x_k) = A\sum_{n=0}^{M}[(\lambda/k\mu)(x_1+x_2+\cdots+x_k)]^n/n! \quad (5.6)
$$

and that the probability P_n that there are n units in the system (all values of the s's, subject to the requirement that $\Sigma s = n$) is the value of

$$
A(\lambda/k\mu)^n(x_1+x_2+\cdots+x_k)^n/n!
$$

when $x_1 = x_2 = \cdots = x_k = 1$. This is just

$$
P_n = A(\rho^n M^n/n!) \quad (\rho=\lambda/M\mu;\ A=P_0)
$$

which corresponds exactly to Eqs. 4.2 for M exponential channels. Therefore, for the multiple-channel facility, as well as for the single-channel case, when no queue is allowed and when arrivals are Poisson, the probabilities of various numbers of units being in the system are independent of the type of Erlang service distribution exhibited by the channels, as long as the mean service rate μ and number of channels M are unchanged. The probability that the facility is full and other arrivals turn away is P_M, and the probability that it is empty is P_0, both given in Eqs. 4.4.

Effects of Arrival-Time Distributions

One might be tempted to say that the answers we get can be obtained without all the machinery we have used, and that it is obvious that the dependence of P_0 and P_{full} are independent of the form of the service-time distribution and depend only on the value of ρ, the ratio between arrival and service rate. For in the single-channel case the mean ratio between the amount of time the unit is busy and the amount of time it is empty should just equal ρ (it takes, on the average, a time $1/\mu$ to complete service and then the unit will have to wait, on the average, a time $1/\lambda$ for another unit to come along; thus $P_{\text{full}}/P_0 = \rho$; since $P_0 + P_{\text{full}} = 1$, we get Eqs. 5.4). That this is a somewhat slippery sort of reasoning is indicated by the fact that it might persuade us that Eqs. 5.4 for P_0 and P_{full} should hold even if the *arrival time* distribution differs from Poisson. We will now demonstrate that this last statement is *not* correct.

To keep the problem as simple as possible to begin with, we take an l-Erlang arrival distribution impinging on a single exponential channel. The model corresponding to this is an arrival-timing channel of l phases, each of rate $l\lambda$. The state of this system can be represented by two integers, the first (1 up to l) labeling the phase the next unit is in as it passes along the arrival channel, and the second (0 or 1) indicating whether the exponential service channel is empty or full (if it is full, the next arrival will pass on, for we are still considering the no-queue case). We label the phases of the arrival-timing channel also in reverse order, the lth being the first phase the unit comes to as it enters from the unit storage depot and the 1st being the last phase it goes through before it arrives at the service facility. Since the supply depot of units is never empty, the arrival-timing channel is never empty and the first subscript on the state probability must be an integer between 1 and l. Phase $s+1$ "decays" into phase s, with a mean rate $l\lambda$, and phase 1 goes back to l, to begin a cycle again. At this last transition the "arriving" unit enters service if service is unoccupied, or else leaves uncared for.

Thus state $(s,0)$ (nothing in the service channel, next unit in the sth phase in the arrival-timing channel) can change into state $(s-1,0)$ with rate $l\lambda$ (unless $s=1$), and state $(s,0)$ can arise by transition from state $(s,1)$ by the service channel completing service (rate μ) or from state $(s+1,0)$ by the next unit completing the $(s+1)$'st phase in the arrival channel (rate $l\lambda$) *unless s is l*. Therefore, we have $l-2$ of the $2l$ equations of balance

$$l\lambda P_{s+1,0}+\mu P_{s,1}-l\lambda P_{s,0}=0 \qquad (1\leq s<l) \quad (5.7)$$

State $(l,0)$ can go to state $(l-1,0)$ with rate $l\lambda$, and state $(l,1)$ can go into state $(l,0)$ with rate μ, but there is no state $(l+1,0)$. State $(1,0)$

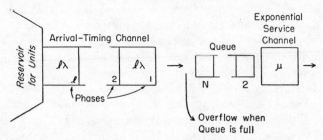

Fig. 5.4. Representation of an l-Erlang arrival distribution, feeding a single exponential channel, with queue of maximum length $N-1$. Eqs. 5.10 give results for zero-length queue, $N=1$.

does not go to state $(l,0)$ but to state $(l,1)$, for when the unit leaves phase 1 it arrives at an empty service channel and enters it. Therefore, the equation of balance for state $(l,0)$ is simply

$$\mu P_{l,1}-l\lambda P_{l,0}=0$$

This completes the set for empty service channel.

State $(s,1)$ can go *into* state $(s,0)$ at rate μ, *or* into state $(s-1,1)$ (when $s>1$) at rate $l\lambda$, whereas only state $(s+1,1)$ goes *to* state $(s,1)$. Therefore the next $(l-1)$ equations are

$$l\lambda P_{s+1,1}-(\mu+l\lambda)P_{s,1}=0 \qquad (1\leq s<l) \quad (5.8)$$

where, for $s=1$, state $(1,1)$ goes into either state $(1,0)$ or state $(l,1)$ (in the latter case the arriving unit being lost to the service channel). Finally, state $(l,1)$ can go into either state $(l,0)$ or state $(l-1,1)$, and it can arise by transition either from state $(1,0)$ (when the unit coming out of the arrival channel enters the service channel) or from state $(1,1)$ (when the unit coming out finds the service channel busy and loses interest in staying around any longer, so the final equation is

$$l\lambda P_{1,0}+l\lambda P_{1,1}-(\mu+l\lambda)P_{l,1}=0 \qquad (5.9)$$

The state probabilities for full service channel can be obtained in terms of $P_{1,1}$ by sequential substitution, giving $P_{s,1} = \left(1 + \dfrac{\mu}{l\lambda}\right)^{s-1} P_{1,1}$.

The equations for empty service channel are a bit more messy, but a little algebraic manipulation will yield the solutions

$$P_{s,0} = \left[\left(1 + \frac{\mu}{l\lambda}\right)^{l} - \left(1 + \frac{\mu}{l\lambda}\right)^{s-1}\right] P_{1,1}$$

The value of $P_{1,1}$ is then determined by requiring that the sum of all the $2l$ probabilities adds up to unity. We have

$$P_{\text{full}} = \sum_{s=1}^{l} P_{s,1} = \sum_{n=0}^{l-1} q^{n} P_{1,1} = \frac{q^{l}-1}{q-1} P_{1,1}$$

$$= \left(\frac{l\lambda}{\mu}\right)\left[\left(1 + \frac{\mu}{l\lambda}\right)^{l} - 1\right] P_{1,1} \tag{5.10}$$

$$P_{\text{empty}} = \sum_{s=1}^{l} P_{s,0} = \left[\left(l - \frac{l\lambda}{\mu}\right)\left(1 + \frac{\mu}{l\lambda}\right)^{l} + \left(\frac{l\lambda}{\mu}\right)\right] P_{1,1}$$

and
$$P_{\text{full}} + P_{\text{empty}} = l\left(1 + \frac{\mu}{l\lambda}\right)^{l} P_{1,1} = 1$$

where $q = 1 + (\mu/l\lambda)$ and the quantities P_{full} and P_{empty} are the probabilities that the service channel is busy or is empty, respectively. The ratio $(P_{\text{full}}/P_{\text{empty}})$ is certainly not equal to $\rho = (\lambda/\mu)$ as it was in the previous two cases (compare with Eq. 5.4). A non-Poisson arrival distribution thus produces a different ratio between P_{full} and P_{empty}; it also makes other differences.

The probability P_{full} that the service channel is busy

$$P_{\text{full}} = \rho\left[1 - \left(1 + \frac{1}{l\rho}\right)^{-l}\right] \rightarrow \begin{cases} \rho - \rho(l\rho)^{l} & (l\rho \ll 1) \\ 1 - [(l+1)/2l\rho] & (l\rho \gg 1) \end{cases} \tag{5.11}$$

is, in this case, *not* equal to the fraction of arriving units which find a full service channel and leave without being serviced (which we might call the fraction of customers lost, P_{lost}). For now we can no longer say that times of arrivals are completely independent of times of completion of service, and therefore the *average probability* of finding the service channel busy is not necessarily equal to the probability *the arriving unit* will find the service channel busy. To find the value of P_{lost} we must look at the state transitions involved when a unit leaves the arrival-timing channel and compare the mean rate at which units arrive when the service facility is busy, with the rate of arrival when the facility is empty.

The transitions involved here are from state $(1,0)$ to state $(l,1)$ and from state $(1,1)$ to state $(l,1)$, which are the ones involved in Eq. 5.9. We see that the rate of transition from state $(1,0)$ to $(l,1)$ is $l\lambda P_{1,0}$ (which is the transition involved when the arriving unit finds the service channel empty and enters it), whereas the transition rate from $(1,1)$ to $(l,1)$ is $l\lambda P_{1,1}$ (which is the change corresponding to the case where the arriving unit finds the service facility busy and does not stop). Therefore, the ratio between the probability P_{served} that the arriving unit enters the service channel and the probability P_{lost} that the arriving unit finds the service channel busy and passes by is equal to the ratio between $P_{1,0}$ and $P_{1,1}$, which equals $[1+(\mu/l\lambda)]^l - 1$. From the value this ratio and from the fact that the sum $P_{\text{served}} + P_{\text{lost}}$ must equal unity, we finally obtain

$$P_{\text{served}} = 1 - \left(1 + \frac{\mu}{l\lambda}\right)^{-l}; \quad P_{\text{lost}} = \left(1 + \frac{\mu}{l\lambda}\right)^{-l} \qquad (5.12)$$

which does not correspond to Eq. 5.11 for P_{full} and for $P_{\text{empty}}(=1-P_{\text{full}})$.

We can perhaps see how these complications come about as we alter the arrival statistics, by going to the limiting case for perfectly regular arrivals (A_0 a true step function) and exponential service. This is the case for $l \to \infty$, and formulas 5.11 and 5.12 can be modified to give the answers for this limiting case by using the formula

$$\underset{l \to \infty}{\text{Lim}} \; [1 + (x/l)]^l = e^x \qquad (5.13)$$

which is one of the definitions of the exponential function. But it may help our understanding of the whole process if we work out this limiting case from the beginning, by another method.

For when arrivals are perfectly regular, each coming a time $(1/\lambda)$ after the previous one, we can follow each cycle in detail. At each arrival, the arriving unit either finds the service channel empty (in which case it enters) or it finds it full (in which case it passes on). In either case, just after each arrival the service facility is *always full* (this corresponds to Eq. 5.9 in the previous analysis, which said that both state $1,0$ and state $1,1$ went on to state $l,1$).

In the special case of the exponential service channel, we do not have to distinguish between those services that were started at the arrival in question and those started earlier; all we need to know is that the service channel is certainly filled just after each arrival, and that for an exponential service the probability that the channel is still busy a time t after an arrival is simply $e^{-\mu t}$. For any other service-time distribution we would have to distinguish between those services started at that arrival and those started at earlier arrivals; but for exponential service we can be sure that the probability $p_f(t)$ that *it is still full* a time t after each arrival (and before the next arrival) is $e^{-\mu t}$, and the related probability $p_e(t)$ that the channel is empty at time t is $1 - e^{-\mu t}$. Therefore, p_f starts at unity after each arrival, drops exponentially in the intervals between arrivals, and rises discontinuously to unity at the next arrival; p_e starts at zero and rises, dropping again to zero at the next arrival.

The probability $p_f(t) = e^{-\mu t}$ cannot be equal to the quantity P_{full} of Eq. 5.11, for $p_f(t)$ depends on the time after last arrival, whereas P_{full} is independent of time. As a matter of fact, P_{full} is the *average value* of $p_f(t)$, averaged over a whole cycle:

$$P_{\text{full}} = \lambda \int_0^{1/\lambda} e^{-\mu t}\, dt = (\lambda/\mu)(1 - e^{-\mu/\lambda}) \qquad (5.14)$$

which corresponds to Eq. 5.11 if we use the limiting value given by Eq. 5.13. As we have seen, P_{lost} is not equal to the *average* value P_{full} of $p_f(t)$, but is equal to the probability that the *arriving unit* finds the service channel full, which is $p_f(1/\lambda) = e^{-\mu/\lambda}$, as Eq. 5.12, in its limiting form, shows. Whenever arrivals are not completely random (Poisson, $l = 1$) then times of completion of service are not independent of arrival times, probabilities of finding the service channel full are not independent of time after last arrival, and therefore P_{full} is not equal to P_{lost}.

Nevertheless, the probabilities P_{full} and P_{empty} obtained from linear Eqs. 5.5 to 5.9 are correct if we consider them as average values over time, and thus as not appropriate to use in computing P_{lost}.

The more general case, of Erlang l arrivals and Erlang k service, can be worked out by the methods we used in solving Eqs. 5.5 to 5.9. For the no-queue case the possible states can be labeled again by a pair of numbers (n,s), where n, as before, runs from l to 1 but where s now runs from k to 0. We start by solving for the set $P_{n,k}$ in terms of $P_{1,k}$, then go on to the set $P_{n,k-1}$ and so on. The algebra is tedious and we learn nothing new, so the calculations will not be set forth.

Simulation by Parallel Arrangement

We can also devise systems to simulate service operations or arrivals which are "more random" than the Poisson distribution. We noted in Eq. 2.11 that the root-mean-square deviation Δt_a of arrival intervals in the Poisson distribution is T_a itself; the mean spread is equal to the mean spacing; roughly speaking, there are about equal numbers of very short, average, and very long intervals. A distribution which might claim to be called "more random" than Poisson would have to have a value of Δt_a *larger* than T_a. On the other hand, a better definition of "random" might be that given preceding Eq. 2.11, in which case the "hyper-Poisson" case treated here would just be a distribution with $(\Delta t_a/T_a)$ larger than Poisson.

Since running exponential channels in series produces a variability in service or arrival times Δt *less* than the value $(1/\mu)$ or $(1/\lambda)$ for the exponential case, we might expect that an arrangement of channels in parallel would produce a variability greater than the exponential. This turns out to be true. Suppose our service channel is made up of two independent *branches*, one of rate $2\sigma\mu$, the other of rate $2(1-\sigma)\mu$ (where σ can be restricted to the range $0<\sigma\leq\frac{1}{2}$ without loss of generality).

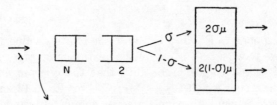

Fig. 5.5. Simulation of a system having a service-time distribution with more variability than the exponential channel; see Eq. 5.15. Incoming units are sent at random to one or another branch, with relative frequency σ and $1-\sigma$. The two branches are each exponential, with differing service times, as shown. Only one unit at a time is allowed in the double-branched channel.

When a unit enters service, it is assigned to one or the other branch at random, the choice going to the $2\sigma\mu$ branch, on the average, a fraction σ of the time, and going to the $2(1-\sigma)\mu$ branch $(1-\sigma)$ of the times, on the average. When it enters one or the other branch, the whole service facility is then busy, and no other unit can enter either branch until the occupied branch completes its task and discharges its unit. Then, if a queue is present, the next unit is assigned to one or the other branch, again in a random manner, and the channel is busy again.

It is not difficult to see that the mean chance that a unit will complete its service, in such a channel, in a time between t and $t+dt$ is $s(t)\,dt$, where

$$s(t) = 2\sigma^2\mu\,e^{-2\sigma\mu t} + 2(1-\sigma)^2\mu\,e^{-2(1-\sigma)\mu t} \qquad (0<\sigma\leq\tfrac{1}{2}) \qquad (5.15)$$

This is to be compared with the $a(t)$ for the Erlang case, given in Eq. 5.2. The mean time to complete service here has been adjusted to be $(1/\mu)$, so the mean service rate for the channel made up of the two parallel branches, operated as described, is just μ. The root-mean-square deviation of the service time is the square root of

$$(\Delta t_s)^2 = \int_0^\infty s(t)t^2\,dt - T_s{}^2 = \frac{1}{\mu^2}\left[1 + \frac{(1-2\sigma)^2}{2\sigma(1-\sigma)}\right] = \frac{j}{\mu^2}$$

where j equals the expression in the brackets, which is never smaller than unity when $0 < \sigma \leq \tfrac{1}{2}$. Variance Δt_s is equal to $(1/\mu)$ when $\sigma = \tfrac{1}{2}$ (here both channels are identical and the behavior is the same as a single exponential channel), and is larger than $(1/\mu)$ when $\sigma < \tfrac{1}{2}$, going to infinity as $\sigma \to 0$. Thus this mechanism can simulate a service channel which is hyper-exponential. (Quantity j plays the same role here that integer k plays with the Erlang distribution; it measures departure from "pure random.")

It is not difficult to see why this is so. A hyper-exponential channel has "bunches" of short service times even more often than the exponential case, and has very long service times somewhat more often. When σ is small, the $2\sigma\mu$ branch has a mean time $(1/2\sigma\mu)$, longer than the average $(1/\mu)$, and the $2(1-\sigma)\mu$ has a shorter time. This latter branch is chosen more often, also; so the time distribution consists, in part, of service times less than the mean, but once in a while the slow branch is assigned, and a very long service time is likely to result. This increased appearance of very short and very long intervals is the hyper-exponential characteristic, and just what is needed to make Δt_s larger than $(1/\mu)$.

The service-distribution function and the related functions are (see Eqs. 2.6 and 2.12)

$$S_0(t) = \sigma\,e^{-2\sigma\mu t} + (1-\sigma)\,e^{-2(1-\sigma)\mu t}$$

$$V_0(t) = \tfrac{1}{2}\,e^{-2\sigma\mu t} + \tfrac{1}{2}\,e^{-2(1-\sigma)\mu t}$$

$$S_1(t) = \mu t[2\sigma^3\,e^{-2\mu\sigma t} + 2(1-\sigma)^3\,e^{-2\mu(1-\sigma)t}]$$

$$\qquad\qquad + \frac{\sigma(1-\sigma)}{1-2\sigma}[e^{-2\mu\sigma t} - e^{-2\mu(1-\sigma)t}] \quad (5.16)$$

$$V_1(t) = \mu t[\sigma^2\,e^{-2\mu\sigma t} + (1-\sigma)^2\,e^{-2\mu(1-\sigma)t}]$$

$$\qquad\qquad + \frac{\sigma(1-\sigma)}{1-2\sigma}[e^{-2\mu\sigma t} - e^{-2\mu(1-\sigma)t}], \quad \text{etc.}$$

which are to be compared with the corresponding functions S_n and V_n

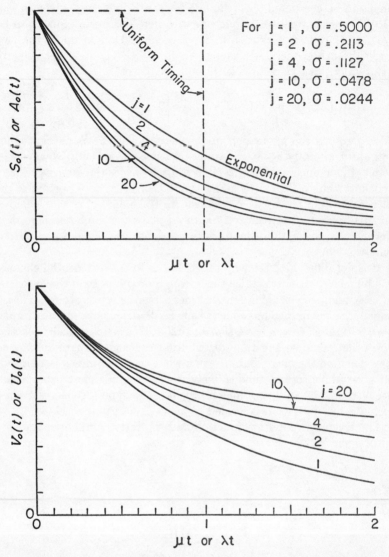

Fig. 5.6. Family of arrival or service-time distributions, corresponding to the system represented by Fig. 5.5. Values of σ are chosen so that the variability Δt is equal to $\sqrt{j}/\mu$ or $\sqrt{j}/\lambda$, and thus ranges from $(1/\mu)(\sigma = \frac{1}{2})$, the exponential or Poisson case, to infinity $(\sigma = 0)$. These are to be compared to the set of Erlang distributions shown in Fig. 5.1, which have variabilities less than $(1/\mu)$. Between the two sets, most operational situations can be simulated. See also Table VI.

(or A_n and U_n, which are the same functions for arrivals) for the Erlang distributions, given in Eqs. 5.2. Figure 5.6 shows curves for S_0 and for V_0 for various values of j, for which $\Delta t_s = \sqrt{j}/\mu$, larger than the variance $(1/\mu)$ that the exponential channel has. The curves for (s/μ) and S_0 show that more short intervals occur than for the exponential case. Extension of the curves beyond $\mu t = 2$ would show more very long intervals also, since the area under each of the S_0 curves must equal unity.

One could also use this two-branch channel for an arrival-timing channel, to produce "hyper-Poisson" arrivals. The distribution functions a, A_n and U_n would have the form of the s, S_n and V_n of Eqs. 5.15 and 5.16, except that λ would be substituted for μ.

Examples with Hyper-Exponential Distributions

To illustrate how we can use this model to analyze the operation when either arrival or service is hyper-exponential, we shall consider here only two simple cases: the first, a hyper-exponential service channel with Poisson arrivals and no queue; the second, an exponential channel with hyper-Poisson arrivals and no queue. Other systems involving wide-variance service or arrivals will be discussed in later sections.

With no queue allowed, a two-branch service facility has only three states: one with no unit present (0), one with the $2\sigma\mu$ branch busy (1), and one with the $2(1-\sigma)\mu$ branch busy (2). The equations for steady state are

$$2\sigma\mu P_1 + 2(1-\sigma)\mu P_2 - \lambda P_0 = 0$$

$$\lambda\sigma P_0 - 2\sigma\mu P_1 = 0; \quad \lambda(1-\sigma)P_0 - 2(1-\sigma)\mu P_2 = 0$$

$$P_0 = \frac{1}{1+\rho}; \quad P_1 = P_2 = \frac{\frac{1}{2}\rho}{1+\rho}; \quad \rho = (\lambda/\mu) \tag{5.17}$$

$$P_{\text{full}} = P_1 + P_2 = \rho/(1+\rho)$$

The values of P_0 and P_{full} are the same as those given in Eqs. 5.4 for other service-time distributions, as could be expected.

In the case of the hyper-Poisson arrivals and a single exponential channel, no queue, there are two states for the arrival-timing channel (first subscript on P), the next unit coming in branch 1, $(2\sigma\lambda)$, or in branch 2, $(2\lambda - 2\sigma\lambda)$, and two states for the service channel (second subscript) no unit present (0) or the channel busy (1). State 10 can go into either state 11 or state 21 by having the unit in branch 1 go into service and a new unit enter either branch 1 or 2; similarly, state 20 goes into either 11 or 21. State 11 goes into state 10 or into 11 or 21, according as the service channel or the arrival-timing channel finishes first, and so on. The equations are

$$\mu P_{11} - 2\sigma\lambda P_{10} = 0; \quad \mu P_{21} - 2(1-\sigma)\lambda P_{20} = 0$$

$$2\lambda\sigma^2 P_{11} + 2\sigma(1-\sigma)\lambda P_{21} + 2\sigma^2\lambda P_{10}$$
$$+ 2\sigma(1-\sigma)\lambda P_{20} - (\mu+2\sigma\lambda)P_{11} = 0$$

$$2\sigma(1-\sigma)\lambda P_{11} + 2(1-\sigma)^2\lambda P_{21} + 2\sigma(1-\sigma)\lambda P_{10}$$
$$+ 2(1-\sigma)^2\lambda P_{20} - [\mu+2(1-\sigma)\lambda]P_{21} = 0$$

$$P_{10} = \frac{\frac{1}{2}}{1+2\sigma\rho}; \quad P_{11} = 2\sigma\rho P_{10}$$

$$\tag{5.18}$$

$$P_{20} = \frac{\frac{1}{2}}{1+2(1-\sigma)\rho}; \quad P_{21} = 2(1-\sigma)\rho P_{20}$$

$$P_{\text{empty}} = \frac{1+\rho}{(1+2\sigma\rho)[1+2(1-\sigma)\rho]}$$
$$= \frac{1}{1+\rho} + \frac{\rho^2[1-4\sigma(1-\sigma)]}{(1+\rho)(1+2\sigma\rho)[1+2(1-\sigma)\rho]}$$

$$P_{\text{full}} = 1 - P_{\text{empty}}$$

The last pair of equations shows that the service channel for hyper-Poisson arrivals is *more* often empty than when arrivals are Poisson (when $P_{\text{empty}} = 1/(1+\rho)$, as indicated in Eq. 5.4). Comparison with Eq. 5.10 shows us for that case, for Erlang (which might be called sub-Poisson) arrivals

$$P_{\text{empty}} = \frac{1}{1+\rho} - \frac{\frac{1}{2}[(l-1)/l] + \frac{1}{6}[(l-1)(l-2)/\rho l^2] + \cdots}{(1+\rho)[1+(1/l\rho)]^l} \tag{5.19}$$

$$(l\text{-Erlang arrivals})$$

the service channel is *less* often empty than for Poisson arrivals. Thus, for a single exponential channel, for a given value of ρ, the chance that the channel is idle is least for completely regular arrivals ($l\to\infty$) (see Eq. 5.14).

$$P_{\text{empty}} = 1 - \rho + \rho\, e^{-1/\rho} \quad \text{(regular arrivals)}$$

As the variability of arrivals is increased ($l\to1$), the fraction of time the channel is idle increases, according to the formula

$$P_{\text{empty}} = 1 - \rho + \rho\left(1+\frac{1}{l\rho}\right)^{-l} \quad (l\text{-Erlang arrivals})$$

until for $l=1$,

$$P_{\text{empty}}=1/(1+\rho) \qquad \text{(Poisson arrivals)}$$

which is the same as the limiting hyper-Poisson case for $\sigma\to\frac{1}{2}$ $(j=1)$. For still greater variability of arrival we use Eqs. 5.18, which show that idle time increases still further, until in the limit of $\sigma\to0$ $(j\to\infty)$ the idle time has its maximum value $(1+\rho)/(1+2\rho)$. The greater the variability of arrivals, the more often is the service channel idle, even though mean arrival rate is kept the same.

The situation turns out to be quite similar when we consider the fraction of customers lost. This fraction (again for a single exponential service channel) is *least* for regular arrivals.

$$P_{\text{lost}}=e^{-1/\rho} \qquad \text{(regular arrivals)}$$

As variability of arrivals is increased (and keeping ρ unchanged), the fraction of lost customers increases according to Eq. 5.12

$$P_{\text{lost}}=\left(1+\frac{1}{l\rho}\right)^{-l} \qquad \text{(l-Erlang arrivals)}$$

until for $l=1$,

$$P_{\text{lost}}=\rho/(1+\rho)=1-P_{\text{empty}} \quad \text{(Poisson arrivals)}$$

To see whether P_{lost} increases still further for still more variability of arrival, we will have to compute it for the hyper-Poisson case of Eq. 5.18, which means that we must find the probability that an *arriving unit* finds the service channel busy. The third and fourth equations of 5.18 show that the contribution to P_{11} or P_{21} by P_{11} or P_{21} (corresponding to the case where the arriving unit finds the service channel busy) is via the combination $A\sigma P_{11}+A(1-\sigma)P_{21}$, and the contribution by P_{10} or P_{20} (corresponding to the arrival finding the service channel empty) is via the combination $A\sigma P_{10}+A(1-\sigma)P_{20}$. The value of A is determined from the requirement that the sum of these two must equal unity for the pair of them to be probabilities. We obtain $A=2$, so that

$$P_{\text{lost}}=2\sigma P_{11}+2(1-\sigma)P_{21}=\frac{2\rho-4\sigma(1-\sigma)\rho(1-\rho)}{(1+2\sigma\rho)[1+2(1-\sigma)\rho]}$$

$$=\frac{\rho}{1+\rho}+\frac{\rho}{1+\rho}\frac{1-4\sigma(1-\sigma)}{(1+2\sigma\rho)[1+2(1-\sigma)\rho]} \qquad (5.20)$$

$$\text{(hyper-Poisson arrivals)}$$

and
$$P_{\text{served}} = 1 - P_{\text{lost}} = 2\sigma P_{10} + 2(1-\sigma)P_{20}$$

$$= \frac{1+4\rho\sigma(1-\sigma)}{(1+2\sigma\rho)[1+2(1-\sigma)\rho]}$$

Therefore, as arrival variability increases still further, the fraction of customers turned away increases further, beyond the value for Poisson arrivals, until finally as $\sigma \to 0$ the fraction of customers lost reaches its limiting value $2\rho/(1+2\rho)$. As arrival variability is increased, idle time and fraction of potential customers that has to be turned away *both increase.* Increased variability means an increase in "bunching" of the arrivals; more and more arrivals come close together with long waits in between, a situation which increases the chance of an arrival finding the service channel busy and also increases the chance that the channel is idle, waiting for the next "bunch" to come along. The range of variation of P_{lost} is very small when $\rho \gg 1$; variation of P_{empty} is small when $\rho \ll 1$. Both show the greatest dependence on arrival variability when ρ is near unity.

Changing the variability of *service time* has no such effect (at least for the one-channel, no-queue case) as long as arrivals are kept Poisson. For Poisson arrivals, $P_{\text{full}} = P_{\text{lost}} = \rho/(1+\rho)$ for an Erlang service channel for all values of k, and also for a hyper-exponential channel for all values of σ between ½ and 0 (all values of j between 1 and ∞).

Chapter 6

GENERAL CONSIDERATIONS, TRANSIENT SOLUTIONS

W E HAVE NOW COVERED the sorts of arrival and service-time distributions which are likely to arise in practice, and we have indicated a method of solution, using a model built up of exponential phases to simulate the Erlang family and the "hyper-exponential" family of distributions, which has the advantage of reducing the equations for detailed balance to a set of linear algebraic equations. There are other more powerful techniques for solving these problems which work for more general sorts of distributions, but they involve more sophisticated mathematical analysis and are usually more difficult. We intend to concentrate on the exploitation of this simpler method, and most of the rest of this treatise will be concerned with its application to certain classes of operational situations. We will not attempt to survey other techniques or to delve more deeply into basic theory, which could lead us into the whole subject of Markov processes and, indeed, into many aspects of the whole subject of probability theory.

However, before we turn to specific examples of practical interest, we should review the general pattern of our method of analysis and indicate briefly how solutions can be obtained for the non-steady state or transient behavior of systems.

The General Equations of Detailed Balance

Having simulated the actual system (if we can) by a set of exponential units, we lay out a possible set of states of the system. Enumeration of these states and the rules of transition between them specifies the nature of the arrivals and service operations the model will simulate, as well as the rules of formation and procedure in the queue. Since the elements are all exponential, our equations of detailed balance for the steady-state solution will be a set of linear equations for the probabilities P_n $(0 \leq n \leq N)$, say, where n is an index enumerating the state. These equations may be written

$$\sum_{n=0}^{N} E_{mn} P_n = 0 \qquad (0 \leq m \leq N) \quad (6.1)$$

where the coefficient E_{mn} represents the rate of transition from state n to state m, and coefficient E_{mm} is minus the rate of transition from state m to all other states. This set of equations must be solved to find expressions for the P's in terms of one of them, say, P_0; then P_0 is found by using the requirement that the sum of all the P's must equal unity. Usually the solution is simplified because many of the E's are zero (any state can change to only a few other states).

If this set of equations is to have a solution, the determinant of the E's must be zero. It is not hard to see that this is *always* the case with our equations. For $-E_{mm}$ (the rate of transition *out* of state m) must equal the sum of the coefficients E_{mn} (the rates of transition from state m to states n) summed over all values of n different from m, so that the sum of each column in the determinant of the E's is zero, which ensures that the determinant is zero. In other words, the sum of all the Eqs. 6.1, summed over all m's, is exactly zero, which must be true for a set of equations representing a detailed balance of transitions. (A good method for checking the correctness of these equations for a complicated system is to see if the sum of all the equations *is* actually zero.) Once the values of all the P's are determined, the properties of the system can be computed, as we have seen previously.

The transient solutions can be obtained in terms of the E's also. Referring to Eq. 3.1, we see that if the state probabilities change with time, the equations for their rates of change are

$$(dp_m/dt) = \sum_{n=0}^{N} E_{mn} p_n \qquad (6.2)$$

where we use the lower-case letters for the time-dependent probabilities. Solutions are obtained by setting $p_m(t) = \sum_s B_{ms} e^{-\gamma_s t}$, where the rates γ_s are the various solutions of the secular equation

$$\begin{vmatrix} (E_{00} + \gamma_s) & E_{01} & E_{02} & \cdots & E_{0N} \\ E_{10} & (E_{11} + \gamma_s) & E_{12} & \cdots & E_{1N} \\ \vdots & & & & \vdots \\ & & & & \\ E_{N0} & E_{N1} & E_{N2} & \cdots & (E_{NN} + \gamma_s) \end{vmatrix} = 0 \qquad (6.3)$$

where the diagonal terms E_{nn} are all negative and the non-diagonal terms E_{mn} ($m \neq n$) are all positive (or zero). This is an equation of the $(N+1)$'st order in the rates γ; there will be $N+1$ roots. Since the determinant of the E's is zero, the coefficient of the zero'th power of γ in the secular equation is zero; consequently, one root of this equation will always be $\gamma = 0$. Call this zero root γ_0. The other N roots, labeled in order γ_1 to γ_N, are all positive, and represent the transient behavior of the system. The coefficients B_{ms} must be adjusted to fit the initial conditions, at $t = 0$. The resulting p's are averaged state probabilities, and thus are not concerned with times after last arrival or after last completion of service. A few examples will show what is meant.

An Example of Transient Behavior

Taking the simplest case first, the time-dependent equations for the single exponential channel with no queue and with Poisson arrivals are

$$(dp_0/dt) = \mu p_1 - \lambda p_0; \quad (dp_1/dt) = \lambda p_0 - \mu p_1 \tag{6.4}$$

Setting $p_n = B_{n0} + B_{n1} e^{-\gamma_1 t}$, we see that for the term independent of t to satisfy Eqs. 6.4 it must be the steady-state solution, $B_{00} = P_0$; $B_{10} = \rho P_0$ ($\rho = \lambda/\mu$). The time-dependent term is obtained by first solving the secular equation obtained from $\mu B_{11} + (\gamma_1 - \lambda)B_{01} = 0$; and $\lambda B_{01} + (\gamma_1 - \mu)B_{11} = 0$, which is $(\gamma_1 - \lambda)(\gamma_1 - \mu) = \lambda\mu$, or $\gamma_1^2 - (\lambda + \mu)\gamma_1 = 0$. One root is $\gamma = 0$, which corresponds to the steady-state part, already taken care of. The other root is $\gamma_1 = \lambda + \mu$, and for this $B_{11} = -B_{01}$. Therefore the transient solutions are

$$p_0(t) = [1/(1+\rho)] + B_{01} e^{-(\lambda+\mu)t}$$
$$p_1(t) = [\rho/(1+\rho)] - B_{01} e^{-(\lambda+\mu)t} \tag{6.5}$$

We note that the time-dependent parts, by themselves, add up to zero, and the steady-state parts add up to unity. This always occurs, since the sum of all the p's must always add up to unity, independent of t.

The one constant B_{01} is adjusted to fit the initial conditions at $t = 0$. For example, if the service channel is opened at $t = 0$, there having been no arrivals before then, the initial values of the p's are $p_0 = 1$, $p_1 = 0$ and

$$p_0(t) = [\mu + \lambda e^{-(\lambda+\mu)t}]/(\lambda+\mu)$$
$$p_1(t) = \lambda[1 - e^{-(\lambda+\mu)t}]/(\lambda+\mu) \tag{6.6}$$

After a time greater than about $2/(\lambda+\mu) = 2T_a T_s/(T_a + T_s)$ the transient part has become quite small and the system has settled down to its steady state. The time $1/(\lambda+\mu)$ for the transient to die down to $(1/e)$ of its initial value is called the *relaxation time* of the system.

We should ask what these time-dependent p's represent. They certainly are not analogous to the quantities $p_f(t)$ discussed in Eq. 5.14, for t there was the time after the last arrival and t here is the time after arrivals start. We can think of p_0 and p_1 of Eq. 6.5 as representing average starting behavior of the system, averaged over a number of similar starts. For example, we could make records of the first hour after opening a facility in the morning for ten or maybe a hundred mornings, and from these records we could obtain an average behavior that would correspond to the functions $p_n(t)$ (assuming, of course, that other conditions remained the same on all the mornings in the sample). We might find that the initial fraction of prospective customers turned away because the service facility is busy is less than its steady-state value, during the first few relaxation times. This is not a surprising result, of course, but the point is that the *amount* of increase of the fraction may be computed.

To show that the transient behavior may be different for different service-time distributions even though the steady-state averages are the same, we shall work through the case of a one-channel $k=2$ Erlang service, with Poisson arrivals and no queue. As we saw in Chapter 5, the steady-state solution is $P_0 = \mu/(\lambda+\mu)$, as it is for any value of k, and $P_1 = \lambda/2(\lambda+\mu) = P_2$, where 1 and 2 represent the two phases of the service operation. From Eq. 5.3 we can obtain the time-dependent equations

$$\dot{p}_0 = 2\mu p_1 - \lambda p_0; \quad \dot{p}_1 = 2\mu p_2 - 2\mu p_1; \quad \dot{p}_2 = \lambda p_0 - 2\mu p_2 \qquad (6.7)$$

where the dot over the p's indicates differentiation with respect to time. To solve, we set $p_n = B_n e^{-\gamma t}$ and arrive at the equations

$$2\mu B_1 = (\lambda - \gamma)B_0; \quad 2\mu B_2 = (2\mu - \gamma)B_1$$
$$\lambda B_0 = (2\mu - \gamma)B_2 \qquad (6.8)$$

which can be solved only if the secular equation

$$(\gamma - 2\mu)^2(\gamma - \lambda) + 4\lambda\mu^2 = 0$$

is satisfied. The solutions of this equation

$$\gamma = 0; \quad \gamma = 2\mu + \tfrac{1}{2}\lambda \pm i\sqrt{4\mu^2 - (2\mu - \tfrac{1}{2}\lambda)^2} \qquad (6.9)$$

are the allowed values of the relaxation rate γ. The first root is the usual one for the steady-state solution; the other two roots are complex, whenever $\lambda \leq 8\mu$; the transient solution has damped oscillations, thus already showing a different behavior from the $k=1$ Erlang case given in Eqs. 6.6.

For each allowed value of γ, Eqs. 6.8 must be solved for the relative values of the B's. For the value with the positive imaginary part we have

$$2\mu B_1 = -[2\mu - \tfrac{1}{2}\lambda + i\sqrt{2\mu\lambda - \tfrac{1}{4}\lambda^2}\,]B_0$$

$$2\mu B_2 = -[\tfrac{1}{2}\lambda - i\sqrt{2\mu\lambda - \tfrac{1}{4}\lambda^2}\,]B_0$$

Note that the sum $B_0 + B_1 + B_2$, for this time-varying part, equals zero. The solutions for the other root for γ are the complex conjugates of these. To fit initial conditions, we set $B_0 = C_0\, e^{i\alpha}$ and adjust C_0 and α so that the real parts of the expressions $B_0\, e^{-\gamma t}$ and $B_1\, e^{-\gamma t}$ have the desired values at $t=0$. The value of $B_2\, e^{-\gamma t}$ must then come out so that the sum of all three is zero. The total expression for the p's must also include the steady-state solution.

For example, if the initial values are $p_0(0) = 1$, $p_1(0) = p_2(0) = 0$, we set

$$B_0 = \frac{\lambda}{\lambda+\mu}\left[1 + i\frac{\mu - \tfrac{1}{2}\lambda}{\sqrt{2\lambda\mu - \tfrac{1}{4}\lambda^2}}\right]$$

and obtain

$$p_0(t) = \frac{\mu}{\lambda+\mu} + \frac{\lambda}{\lambda+\mu}\Bigg[\cos\left(t\sqrt{2\lambda\mu - \tfrac{1}{4}\lambda^2}\,\right)$$

$$+ \frac{\mu - \tfrac{1}{2}\lambda}{\sqrt{2\lambda\mu - \tfrac{1}{4}\lambda^2}}\sin\left(t\sqrt{2\lambda\mu - \tfrac{1}{4}\lambda^2}\,\right)\Bigg]e^{-(2\mu + \tfrac{1}{2}\lambda)t}$$

$$p_1(t) = \frac{\tfrac{1}{2}\lambda}{\lambda+\mu}\Bigg\{1 - \Bigg[\cos\left(t\sqrt{2\lambda\mu - \tfrac{1}{4}\lambda^2}\,\right) \tag{6.10}$$

$$+ \frac{2\mu + \tfrac{1}{2}\lambda}{\sqrt{2\lambda\mu - \tfrac{1}{4}\lambda^2}}\sin\left(t\sqrt{2\lambda\mu - \tfrac{1}{4}\lambda^2}\,\right)\Bigg]\Bigg\}e^{-(2\mu + \tfrac{1}{2}\lambda)t}$$

$$p_2(t) = \frac{\tfrac{1}{2}\lambda}{\lambda+\mu}\Bigg\{1 - \Bigg[\cos\left(t\sqrt{2\lambda\mu - \tfrac{1}{4}\lambda^2}\,\right)$$

$$- \frac{\tfrac{3}{2}\lambda}{\sqrt{2\lambda\mu - \tfrac{1}{4}\lambda^2}}\sin\left(t\sqrt{2\lambda\mu - \tfrac{1}{4}\lambda^2}\,\right)\Bigg]\Bigg\}e^{-(2\mu + \tfrac{1}{2}\lambda)t}$$

Curves for the solutions 6.6 and 6.10 are given in Fig. 6.1. In the latter case we plot $p_1 + p_2$, the probability that the service facility is busy, rather than the probabilities p_2 or p_1 that the individual phases are filled, since these phases are only parts of our formal representation of the service process and may not have much operational significance.

We note, however, that when t is near zero, p_2 (phase 2 is the first phase entered by the arriving unit) rises from zero linearly with time ($p_2 \to \lambda t$), whereas p_1 (it is only entered after phase 2 is finished) rises quadratically

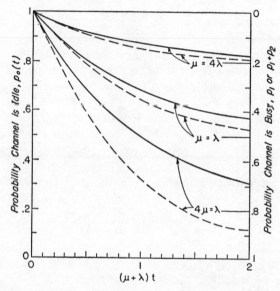

Fig. 6.1. Transient probabilities, that a single channel is empty or full, as functions of time, for the zero-queue case, for different ratios of λ to μ. Solid curves are for exponential service, dashed curves for $k=2$ Erlang service distribution. Asymptotic values for $t \to \infty$ are indicated by solid lines to the right of the indicated relations between λ and μ. Oscillatory character of the $k=2$ curves is indicated by the fact that the lower dashed curve falls below its asymptotic value at $(\lambda + \mu)t = 2$.

with time ($p_1 \to \lambda \mu t^2$). Of course, if λ becomes larger than 8μ, the roots γ become real and the trigonometric functions become hyperbolic ones, with no oscillation.

Transient Solution for Finite Queues

Some of the transient problems require more sophisticated techniques for their solution. For example, the single exponential channel, with N being the maximum number in the system (the steady-state solution is given in Eqs. 3.5 and 3.6), has time-dependent equations

$$\dot{p}_n = \mu p_{n+1} + \lambda p_{n-1} - (\lambda + \mu) p_n$$

$$\dot{p}_0 = \mu p_1 - \lambda p_0; \quad \dot{p}_N = \lambda p_{N-1} - \mu p_N$$

(6.11)

Setting $p_n = \rho^{\frac{1}{2}n} B_{n,s}\, e^{-\gamma_s t}$ and $\gamma_s = \mu x_s$, we obtain the algebraic equations

$$\sqrt{\rho}\, B_{1,s} + (x_s - \rho) B_{0,s} = 0$$

$$\sqrt{\rho}\, (B_{n+1,s} + B_{n-1,s}) + (x_s - 1 - \rho) B_{n,s} = 0 \qquad (6.12)$$

$$\sqrt{\rho}\, B_{N-1,s} + (x_s - 1) B_{N,s} = 0$$

By using the trigonometric identity

$$\sin(n+1)y + \sin(n-1)y = 2 \sin(ny)\, \cos(y)$$

we see that the second of the three Eqs. 6.12, when we try $B_{n,s} = \sin(ny)$, results in

$$2\sqrt{\rho}\, \cos(y)\, \sin(ny) = (\rho + 1 - x_s)\, \sin(ny)$$

which gives an equation relating x_s and y, independent of n, on dividing out by $\sin(ny)$. But $B_{n,s}$ cannot be proportional to $\sin(ny)$ alone, for such an assumption would not satisfy the "boundary conditions" of the first and last of Eqs. 6.12. However, we note that trying $B_{n,s} = \sin(n+1)y$ also reduces to the same equation for x_s, and that the combination $B_{n,s} = \sin(ny) - \sqrt{\rho}\, \sin(n+1)y$ satisfies also the first of Eqs. 6.12 as well as the second set. In addition, if we can make $\sin(N+1)y = 0$, we will reduce *all* of Eqs. 6.12 *to the single equation* $x_s = \rho + 1 - 2\sqrt{\rho}\, \cos y$. We can make $\sin(N+1)y = 0$ by setting $y = s\pi/(N+1)$, where s is one of the integers $1, 2, \cdots, N$; in fact, s is just the integer which is the second subscript of $B_{n,s}$ and also the subscript of $x_s = (\gamma_s/\mu)$, set there to distinguish between the N different solutions of the secular equation.

Therefore, the N solutions of Eqs. 6.11 are

$$p_n(t) = P_n + \rho^{\frac{1}{2}n} \sum_{s=1}^{N} C_s \left[\sin \frac{sn\pi}{N+1} - \sqrt{\rho}\, \sin \frac{s(n+1)\pi}{N+1} \right] e^{-\gamma_s t}$$

$$\text{(6.13)}$$

$$\gamma_s = \lambda + \mu - 2\sqrt{\lambda\mu}\, \cos \left(\frac{s\pi}{N+1} \right) = \mu x_s \qquad \begin{matrix} (s = 1,2,3,\cdots,N) \\ (n = 0,1,2,\cdots,N) \end{matrix}$$

where the coefficients C_s are chosen to fit the initial values of the p's at $t = 0$. Quantities P_n are the steady-state solutions given in Eq. 3.5. Determining the values of the C's can best be done in a manner analogous to that used in getting the coefficients of a Fourier series. For example, if $p_n(0)$ is zero except for $n = m$, and $p_m(0) = 1$ $(p_n = \delta_{nm})$, that is, if there are definitely m in the system at $t=0$, then the corresponding time-dependent solution is

$$p_n{}^m(t) = P_n + \frac{2\rho^{\frac{1}{2}(n-m)}}{N+1}\sum_{s=1}^{N}\left(\frac{1}{x_s}\right)\left[\sin\frac{sm\pi}{N+1} - \sqrt{\rho}\sin\frac{s(m+1)\pi}{N+1}\right].$$

$$\cdot\left[\sin\frac{sn\pi}{N+1} - \sqrt{\rho}\sin\frac{s(n+1)\pi}{N+1}\right]e^{-\gamma_s t}$$

(6.14)

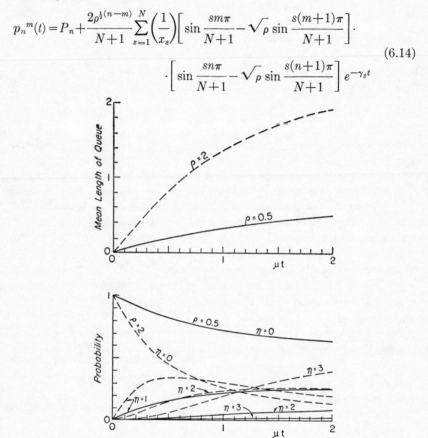

Fig. 6.2. Transient probabilities and mean queue lengths for a single exponential channel with maximum queue $N=3$, for $\rho=0.5$ (solid lines) and $\rho=2$ (dashed lines). Probabilities are $p_n{}^0$, the probability that n units are in the system at time t after start, as given in Eq. 6.14.

A few curves of $p_n{}^m(t)$ are given in Fig. 6.2, together with curves of mean queue length

$$L_q(t) = \sum_{n=1}^{N}(n-1)p_n{}^m(t)$$

These solutions start out $p_n{}^m(0) = \delta_{mn}$ and end up $p_n{}^m(\infty) = P_n$. The exponential factors γ_s are all positive, so all transient terms decay with time. The smallest value of γ_s is γ_1, which is close in value to $(\sqrt{\mu}-\sqrt{\lambda})^2$ when N is large. The largest value of γ_s is γ_N, which is close to $(\sqrt{\mu}+\sqrt{\lambda})^2$. Therefore, the transient solution has not become negligible compared to the steady-state solution until $(\gamma_1 t)$ is 3 or more. To put this statement in a more useful form, we can say that the *relaxation time* $(1/\gamma_1)$ of the one-channel exponential system is approximately $1/(\sqrt{\mu}-\sqrt{\lambda})^2 = (\sqrt{\mu}+\sqrt{\lambda})^2/(\mu-\lambda)^2$. It is a measure of the length of time required for the system to settle down to its steady-state condition. We note that as λ is increased, approaching the value of μ (or as service rate μ is reduced, approaching arrival rate λ), this relaxation time increases markedly. This is consistent with our general picture, for as λ approaches μ the amplitude of the fluctuations of queue size becomes quite large (see Eq. 3.7) and the system will take a long time to settle down to this nearly saturated condition.

In the special case of exact saturation ($\lambda=\mu$, $\rho=1$), the approximate expression for the relaxation time $(1/\gamma_1)$ breaks down and we must use a different form. When $\rho=1$, $\gamma_s=4\lambda \sin^2 [s\pi/2(N+1)]$, so that for N large, the relaxation time is approximately $(N+1)^2/\pi^2$, quite large if N is large.

Equation 6.14 is valid, of course, for λ larger than μ. In such cases, as we saw in Chapter 3, the steady-state situation corresponds to large queues and many "potential customers" are turned away. Whenever λ is considerably larger than μ, the exponential factors γ_s are again large and the system "settles down" fairly rapidly again. The formula $1/(\sqrt{\mu}-\sqrt{\lambda})^2$ for the relaxation time is again valid.

For any other set of initial conditions $p_n(t)=p_n{}^0$ (where $\Sigma p_n{}^0$ must equal unity to satisfy the usual rules for probability), the resulting solution can be built up from the unit solutions $p_n{}^m$ of Eq. 6.14,

$$p_n(t) = \sum_{m=0}^{N} p_m{}^0 p_n{}^m(t) \tag{6.15}$$

Transient solutions are not usually of much practical importance. Once in a while it is useful to make sure that the relaxation time is short compared with the duration of the operation. (If it is long, of course, only the transient solution will be valid.) And sometimes one wishes to find out what would happen if the arrival rate were suddenly increased to a value much greater than μ, to find out, for example, how soon the queue is likely to grow to unmanageable lengths. But in most cases the system has to be adjusted to respond fairly quickly (relaxation time short), and most of the time the steady-state situation will prevail.

Chapter 7

SINGLE CHANNEL, INFINITE QUEUES

As mentioned in Chapter 3, there are some operational situations in which every arriving unit must join the queue, no matter how long it happens to be. It was pointed out there that in such cases no steady-state solution exists for values of arrival rate λ larger than a certain maximum value, corresponding to the maximum rate at which units can be serviced. Since no arriving unit can escape passing through the service facility, when service cannot keep up with arrivals, the queue will keep on increasing in size until something is done about it.

For non-saturation cases, however, the steady-state solutions of infinite-queue systems are of definite practical interest. Their solution involves a few specialized techniques which will be worthwhile outlining. Primarily these techniques are required so that the state probabilities, which now are infinite in number, will add up to a convergent series. The requirement of convergence of the series of P_n's takes the place of the special equation of balance for the maximum value of n, which we have used in finite cases.

The General Equations

In all infinite-queue models the first few detailed-balancing equations, relating the states for which the service facility is not filled, are special equations, unduplicated later. But the equations for the states with filled service channels for different sizes of the queue form a sequence of related equations, repeating themselves indefinitely for larger and larger values of n. This last set, the *queue equations*, have the general form (see Eq. 6.1)

$$\sum_{s=1}^{l}(E_{k,s}{}^{0}P_{n-1,s}+E_{k,s}{}^{1}P_{n,s}+E_{k,s}{}^{2}P_{n+1,s})=0 \quad (k=1,2,\cdots,l) \quad (7.1)$$

where the E's are known constants related to the transition rates λ and μ, where n is the number of units in the system, and where the subscripts k and s correspond to various internal states of the service (or arrival) facility (assumed to be finite in number), which will be the same and have the same relationships no matter how many units are in the queue.

These queue equations can be solved by setting $P_{n,s} = B_s w^n$, whereupon they all reduce to a finite set of simultaneous equations

$$\sum_{s=1}^{l} (E_{k,s}{}^{0} B_s + E_{k,s}{}^{1} B_s w + E_{k,s}{}^{2} B_s w^2) = 0 \qquad (7.2)$$

for the unknowns B_s and w. In order that these homogeneous equations may have a solution, the determinant of their coefficients must be zero,

$$|E_{k,s}{}^{0} + E_{k,s}{}^{1} w + E_{k,s}{}^{2} w^2| = 0 \qquad (7.3)$$

which is the secular equation for w. There are $2l$ roots of this equation; they can be labeled w_i $(i = 1, 2, \cdots, 2l)$. Corresponding to each w_i is a set of related values of ratios between the B's, $B_s = \beta_{i,s} C_i$, so that the general solution of the queue equations 7.1 is a sum of $C_i \beta_{i,s} w_i{}^n$ over the i's. Some roots w_i have magnitude less than unity, some are larger. So that the series of the P's will converge, we must use the summation

$$P_{n,s} = \sum_i C_i \beta_{i,s} w_i{}^n$$

over *only* those values of i for which w_i has magnitude less than unity.

The coefficients C_i must now be determined. This is done by using the *initial equations*, representing those states in which the service facility is not completely filled and which have a form different from Eqs. 7.1. There turn out to be just enough of these equations to determine all the C's but one (if we have set up our model consistently!), and the last C is determined by the requirement that the sum of all the P's (clear out to $n \to \infty$) must be unity.

The Single Exponential Channel

We have already worked out one infinite-queue system (see Eq. 3.10), that for a single exponential channel and Poisson arrivals. Here $l = 1$, and the single queue equation is (see Eqs. 3.2)

$$\lambda P_{n-1} - (\lambda + \mu) P_n + \mu P_{n+1} = 0$$

Setting $P_n = B w^n$, we obtain the secular equation

$$w^2 - (1+\rho) w + \rho = 0 \qquad (\rho = \lambda/\mu)$$

which has roots $w = 1$, $w = \rho$. The first root is not less than unity, so it must be omitted and we have $P_n = B\rho^n$, which satisfies the initial equation $\mu P_1 - \lambda P_0 = 0$. The value of B is obtained by requiring that

$$1 = \sum_n P_n = B \sum_n \rho^n = B/(1-\rho); \quad B = 1 - \rho$$

The probabilities, the mean numbers in the system and in the queue, were written out in Eq. 3.10. The mean time spent in queue and the mean total time are, as noted previously, $W_q = (L_q/\lambda)$, $W = (L/\lambda)$. The probability that there are N or more units in the system (queue plus service) is Q_N, where

$$Q_N = \sum_{n=N}^{\infty} P_n = \rho^N \tag{7.4}$$

With a system in which every unit must join the queue, there is a chance, however small, that the queue will be longer than any given length, however large. All we can do is to make this chance small enough so it will not happen often.

Finally, it may be important that each unit should not wait too long before its service is completed. The average wait is, of course, W, but some units will arrive when the queue happens to be longer than L_q and will wait longer than this, so it would be useful to compute the probability that a unit will have to wait longer than time T. If no unit is present when the unit arrives, the probability that its service will take longer than T is (from Eq. 2.6) $V_0(T) = e^{-\mu T}$. If one unit is ahead of it, then the total wait will be for the completion of two services, that of the preceding unit and its own. The chance that the preceding unit's service will not be completed in time T is $V_0(T)$, and the chance that the first service is finished in time T, but not the unit's own service, is $V_1(T)$, which is obtained from V_0 by means analogous to those given in Eq. 2.12, and for exponential service is $(\mu T) e^{-\mu T}$. Likewise, if n units are ahead of the arriving unit, the chance that the unit will still be in the system after time T is

$$\sum_m V_m(T) = \sum_m [(\mu T)^m/m!] e^{-\mu T}$$

where the sum over m is from $m = 0$ to $m = n$ (the mth term representing the chance that just m services are completed). Multiplying this probability by the chance that the arriving unit will find n units ahead of it, and summing over n, gives us the average probability that the unit will be in the system a time longer than T,

$$G(T) = \sum_{n=0}^{\infty} P_n \sum_{m=0}^{n} V_m(T) = (1-\rho) \sum_{n=0}^{\infty} \rho^n \sum_{m=0}^{n} \frac{(\mu T)^m}{m!} e^{-\mu T} = e^{(\lambda - \mu) T}$$

There is also a probability $G_q(T) = \sum\limits_{n=1}^{\infty} P_n \sum\limits_{m=0}^{n-1} V_n(T)$ that the wait in queue will be longer than T.

For completeness, we collect here the expressions of operational interest for this simple system, the single exponential channel with Poisson arrivals, infinite queue and simple queue discipline:

$$P_n = (1-\rho)\rho^n; \quad Q_n = \rho^n$$

$$L = \rho/(1-\rho) = \lambda W; \quad L_q = \rho^2/(1-\rho) = \lambda W_q$$

$$G(T) = e^{-(1-\rho)\mu T}; \quad G_q(T) = \rho\, e^{-(1-\rho)\mu T} \tag{7.5}$$

$$\Delta L = \sqrt{\rho}/(1-\rho) \qquad\qquad [0 \le \rho = (\lambda/\mu) < 1]$$

A useful tool in our analysis of infinite-queue systems, which will be increasingly powerful as these systems become more complicated, is the *generating function*. We define the generating function in the present case to be

$$F(z) = \sum_{n=0}^{\infty} z^n P_n; \quad F(1) = 1$$

Many of the properties of the system can be computed from the generating function. For example, $L = F'(1)$, where the prime indicates differentiation by z. We can compute F directly from the equations of detailed balance (3.2), without first calculating the P's. We multiply the nth equation by (z^n/μ) and add them all:

$$0 = (-\rho P_0 + P_1) + z[\rho P_0 - (1+\rho)P_1 + P_2] + z^2[\rho P_1 - (1+\rho)P_2 + P_3] + \cdots$$

obtaining $\quad \rho z F(z) - (1+\rho)F(z) + P_0 + (1/z)F(z) - (1/z)P_0 = 0$

or $\qquad\qquad [\rho z^2 - (1+\rho)z + 1]F(z) = (1-z)P_0$

or $\qquad\qquad\qquad F(z) = P_0/(1-\rho z)$

Since $F(1) = 1$, we can immediately obtain the value of P_0. Therefore, the generating function for the single exponential channel is

$$F(z) = \frac{1-\rho}{1-\rho z} = (1-\rho)\sum_{n=0}^{\infty}(\rho z)^n \tag{7.6}$$

By the definition of F, the coefficient of the nth power of z in the series expansion of F is the state probability P_n, which of course checks with

Eq. 7.5. The first derivative of F with respect to z is

$$F'(z) = \frac{\rho(1-\rho)}{(1.-\rho z)^2}$$

so the average number of units in the system, $L = F'(1)$, can be obtained directly in its closed form.

The generating function is not of great additional help in the analysis of this simple system; in more complicated cases with infinite queues we will find it increasingly powerful.

Effect of Service-Time Distribution

Next let us consider the case of a single Erlang k service channel with Poisson arrivals. There are k "internal states" to the service for each value of n, the number of units in the service (except for $n=0$), so that the state is specified by n and s, where s runs from 1 to k. Each phase of the Erlang model has a rate $k\mu$, so that the mean rate of completion of all k phases is μ. Referring to Eqs. 5.3, we see that the equations of detailed balance for the steady-state conditions are

$$k\mu P_{1,1} - \lambda P_0 = 0; \quad k\mu P_{1,s+1} - (k\mu + \lambda)P_{1,s} = 0 \quad (1 \leq s < k)$$

$$k\mu P_{2,1} + \lambda P_0 - (k\mu + \lambda)P_{1,k} = 0$$

$$k\mu P_{n,s+1} + \lambda P_{n-1,s} - (k\mu + \lambda)P_{n,s} = 0 \quad (n > 1; \ 1 \leq s < k) \tag{7.7}$$

$$k\mu P_{n+1,1} + \lambda P_{n-1,k} - (k\mu + \lambda)P_{n,k} = 0 \quad (n > 1)$$

The last two equations are the queue equations, and the first three are the initial equations. As indicated earlier, we first obtain a general solution of the queue equations and then fit the coefficients so that the initial equations are satisfied. Setting $P_{n,s} = B_s w^n$, we have

$$wB_{s+1} - (1+\theta)wB_s + \theta B_s = 0 \qquad (1 \leq s < k)$$

$$w^2 B_1 - (1+\theta)wB_k + \theta B_k = 0; \quad \theta = (\rho/k) = (\lambda/k\mu)$$

or $\quad B_s = [1+\theta-(\theta/w)]^{s-1}B_1 \quad$ and $\quad wB_1 = [1+\theta-(\theta/w)]^k B_1$

From the last equation we can obtain the secular equation for w,

$$w^{k+1} - [w+\theta(w-1)]^k = 0 \tag{7.8}$$

which is to be solved to obtain the allowed values of w. It is obvious that one root is $w = 1$ (which must be discarded because the corresponding series of P's would not converge). We will see later that the other k roots are all less than unity.

In the present case, however, we can simplify our calculations considerably by noting that the B's are also related through coefficients which are just different powers of some quantity $1+\theta-(\theta/w)$. Calling this u, we have $B_s = u^{s-1}B_1$. Moreover, the secular equation shows that $u^k = w$. Therefore, for this one-channel case, we can set $P_{n,s} = Cu^{k(n-1)+s}$ in any of the queue equations and obtain the same equation for u:

$$u^{k+1} - (1+\theta)u^k + \theta = 0 \qquad (7.9)$$

which is the equation for the kth root of w. One of these roots is $u=1$. Dividing Eq. 7.9 by $(u-1)$ we obtain the equation

$$u^k - \theta(u^{k-1} + u^{k-2} + \cdots + u + 1) = 0 \qquad (7.10)$$

for the k roots we shall use. That all of these roots are smaller than unity in magnitude when $k\theta = \rho < 1$ can be shown as follows. If $|u| > 1$, then $|u^{k-1} + \cdots + 1| < k|u|^{k-1}$ so that $|u|^k < \rho|u|^{k-1}$, which involves a contradiction if $\rho < 1$; on the other hand, if $|u| < 1$, then $|u^{k-1} + \cdots + 1| < k$ so that $|u|^k < \rho$, which does not involve a contradiction; therefore, all k roots of Eq. 7.10 have magnitude less than unity if $\rho < 1$.

Here we can obtain several different generating functions:

$$F(z) = P_0 + \sum_{n=1}^{\infty} z^n \sum_{s=1}^{k} P_{n,s}; \quad H(x,y) = \sum_{n,s} x^n y^s P_{n,s}$$

$$F(z) = P_0 + H(z,1);$$

$$E(y) = \sum_{n,s} y^{k(n-1)+s} P_{n,s} + P_0 = P_0 + y^{-k} H(y^k, y) \qquad (7.11)$$

where we use F when we are interested in the number of units in the system, but E or H if we wish to distinguish between phases. Multiplying the first of Eqs. 7.7 by $(1/k\mu)$, the next k by $(y^s/k\mu)$, the third by $(y^k/k\mu)$, and so on, and adding them all, we obtain

$$(1/y)[E(y) - P_0] - (1+\theta)E(y) + P_0 + \theta y^k E(y) = 0$$

or

$$(1 - y - \theta y + \theta y^{k+1})E(y) = (1-y)P_0$$

or

$$E(y) = P_0/[1 - \theta(y + y^2 + \cdots + y^k)] \qquad (7.12)$$

Note that the values of y for which E is infinite are the reciprocals of the roots of Eq. 7.10. Since $E(1)$ must equal unity, setting $y=1$ on both sides and remembering that $k\theta = \rho$, we finally have $P_0 = 1 - \rho$, which is the same expression we got for the exponential $k=1$ case. Therefore, the probability that the single service channel is idle is *independent* of the type of service-time distribution, as long as arrivals are Poisson (refer to the discussion after Eq. 5.4). It is for this reason that $\rho = 1 - P_0 = (\lambda/\mu)$ is called the *utilization factor;* in a large number of cases it is the fraction of time the service is busy.

We can, if we wish, expand this function in a series of powers of y and obtain expressions for the other P's (which of course will depend on k). But, as before, we might as well compute some of the average values directly from the generating functions. The mean waiting time can be obtained from $E(y)$. For the mean time before entering service, of a unit which joins the queue when there are n in the system and the service is in the sth phase, is $[(n-1)k+s]/k\mu$. Multiplying this by $P_{n,s}$ and summing over all n and s should give the average wait W_q. But this sum is related to the derivative of E, so

$$W = \frac{1}{\mu} + \frac{1}{k\mu}\left[\frac{d}{dy} E(y)\right]_{y=1} = \frac{1}{\mu} + \frac{\rho(k+1)}{2k\mu(1-\rho)} = \frac{2k - \rho(k-1)}{2k\mu(1-\rho)} \qquad (7.13)$$

The mean wait in queue W_q is just $W - (1/\mu) = [\rho(k+1)/2k\mu(1-\rho)]$. Both of these check with Eqs. 7.5 for $k=1$ (as of course they should).

From the W's we could get the L's ($\lambda W = L$), but it might be more educational to obtain the L's from the generating function $F(z)$. First we obtain $H(x,y)$ by multiplying the (n,s)'th equation of Eqs. 7.7 by $x^n y^s$ and adding. After some algebra, we finally obtain

$$\left(1+\theta-\theta x-\frac{1}{y}\right)H(x,y)+\left(1-\frac{y^k}{x}\right)\sum_{n=1}^{\infty} x^n P_{n,1} + \theta y^k(1-x)P_0 = 0$$

Setting $y = (1+\theta-\theta x)^{-1}$ enables us to evaluate the summation

$$\sum_{n=1}^{\infty} x^n P_{n,1} = \frac{\theta x(1-x)P_0}{1 - x(1+\theta-\theta x)^k}$$

and therefore to determine H,

$$H(x,y) = \frac{\theta xy(1-x)P_0}{1 - y(1+\theta-\theta x)}\left[\frac{1 - y^k(1+\theta-\theta x)^k}{1 - x(1+\theta-\theta x)^k}\right] \qquad (7.14)$$

from which, by Eqs. 7.11, we can obtain $E(y)$ and also $F(z)$

$$F(z) = \frac{(1-z)(1-\rho)}{1 - z(1+\theta-\theta z)^k} = \sum_{n=0}^{\infty} z^n P_n \qquad (7.15)$$

where $P_n = P_{n,1} + P_{n,2} + \cdots + P_{n,k}$ is the probability that n units are in the system, and where we have set $P_0 = 1 - \rho$, as was determined earlier.

We note that the values of z for which F is infinite are the reciprocals of the roots of Eq. 7.8, the corresponding secular equation, an analogue to the statement about $E(y)$ made after Eq. 7.12. Note also that as $z \to 1$

$$F(z) \to 1 + (z-1)\rho \left[\frac{2k - (k-1)\rho}{2k(1-\rho)} \right]$$

$$+ (z-1)^2 \rho^2 (k+1) \left[\frac{6k - 4(k-1)\rho + (k-1)\rho^2}{12k^2(1-\rho)^2} \right] + \cdots \quad (7.16)$$

The mean number of units in the system is then

$$L = \sum_{n=1}^{\infty} n P_n = F'(1) = \frac{2k\rho - \rho^2(k-1)}{2k(1-\rho)} = \lambda W \quad (7.17)$$

and the mean number in the queue is

$$L_q = L - \rho = [\rho^2(k+1)/2k(1-\rho)] = \lambda W_q$$

We thus see that although the fraction of time the channel is idle and the behavior of the single-channel facility when no queue is allowed (see Eqs. 5.4) are independent of k (and thus, within the family of Erlang distributions, are independent of the shape of the service-time distribution), nevertheless the behavior of the system when a queue is allowed *does* depend on k. Specifically, increase in "orderliness" of the service process reduces the length of queue and the mean delay time. The greatest gain to be gotten, however, (as long as μ is not changed) is a factor of 2; the mean values of queues and delays in queue for the most random case ($k=1$) attain just twice the size they have for the constant service-time case ($k=\infty$).

Incidentally, we have now shown that in this case also the relation between mean number and mean delay is via the factor λ, the arrival rate: $L = \lambda W$ and $L_q = \lambda W_q$. We will find, in *all* the examples encountered in this chapter and the next, for a wide variety of service and arrival distributions, for one or for several channels, that this same relationship holds. Those readers who would like to experience for themselves the slipperiness of fundamental concepts in this field and the intractability of really general theorems, might try their hand at showing under what circumstances this simple relationship between L and W does *not* hold. See discussion following Eqs. 3.10.

The mean-square deviation of L is

$$(\Delta L)^2 = \sum_n (n-L)^2 P_n = F''(1) + L - L^2$$

$$= \frac{\rho}{(1-\rho)^2} - \frac{(k-1)\rho^2}{12k^2(1-\rho)}[(18k+12) - (10k-4)\rho + (k-5)\rho^2]$$

$$\qquad\qquad\qquad\qquad\qquad\qquad\qquad\qquad\qquad (7.18)$$

$$\to \frac{\rho}{(1-\rho)^2} \qquad\qquad\qquad (k\to 1)$$

$$\to \frac{\rho}{12(1-\rho)^2}(12 - 18\rho + 10\rho^2 - \rho^3) \qquad\qquad (k\to\infty)$$

indicating that as regularity of service timing is improved (k is increased) the amplitude of fluctuations in queue length decreases, but only by about in the same proportion as does L or L_q.

Details of the $k=2$ Case

This is about as far as we can go, using the generating functions by themselves. To go farther we must actually work out the individual probability functions, which usually means computing the roots of the secular equation (see Eq. 7.4). This is not difficult for $k=2$, but for larger values of k, solutions must usually be computed numerically. Let us look into the case $k=2$ somewhat further, for the results will be of interest in themselves, and will in addition cast some light on the methods of solving the cases for $k>2$.

The pertinent equations for $k=2$ are

$$P_{1,1} = \theta P_0; \quad P_{1,2} = (1+\theta)P_{1,1}; \quad \theta = \tfrac{1}{2}\rho = (\lambda/2\mu)$$

$$P_{2,1} = (1+\theta)P_{1,2} - \theta P_0; \quad P_{2,2} = (1+\theta)P_{2,1} - \theta P_{1,1}$$

$$P_{3,1} = (1+\theta)P_{2,2} - \theta P_{1,2}; \quad P_{3,2} = (1+\theta)P_{3,1} - \theta P_{2,1}; \quad \text{etc.}$$

$$E(y) = \frac{P_0}{1 - \theta y - \theta y^2}; \quad F(z) = \frac{P_0}{1 - (2\theta + \theta^2)z + \theta^2 z^2} \qquad (7.19)$$

$$P_0 = 1 - 2\theta$$

We can compute $P_{n,s}$ or P_n from the equations for the P's, or by expanding E or F and computing the coefficients of the powers of y or z, or else we can express the P's as powers of the roots w or u of the secular Eqs. 7.8 or 7.10. The most straightforward is to solve the equations for the P's successively. We thus obtain

$$P_0=1-2\theta; \quad P_{1,1}=\theta(1-2\theta); \quad P_{1,2}=(\theta^2+\theta)(1-2\theta)$$

$$P_{2,1}=(\theta^3+2\theta^2)(1-2\theta); \quad P_{2,2}=(\theta^4+3\theta^3+\theta^2)(1-2\theta)$$

$$P_{3,1}=(\theta^5+4\theta^4+3\theta^3)(1-2\theta)$$

$$P_{3,2}=(\theta^6+5\theta^5+6\theta^4+\theta^3)(1-2\theta) \tag{7.20}$$

$$P_{n,1}=\sum_{m=0}^{n-1}\frac{(n+m)!(1-2\theta)}{(2m+1)!(n-m-1)!}\theta^{n+m}$$

$$P_{n,2}=\sum_{m=0}^{n}\frac{(n+m)!(1-2\theta)}{(2m)!(n-m)!}\theta^{n+m}$$

$$P_n=P_{n,1}+P_{n,2}=\sum_{m=0}^{n}\frac{(n+m+1)!(1-2\theta)}{(2m+1)!(n-m)!}\theta^{n+m} \tag{7.21}$$

From these, by further summations, we can calculate the probability $Q_N=\sum_{n=N}^{\infty}P_n$ that there are N or more units in the system (that the queue has more than N units in it).

We can also use the P_n's to calculate the functions $G(T)$ that an arriving unit will spend more time than T in the system (before service on it is completed) and $G_q(T)$ that the arriving unit will spend more time than T in the queue (before it enters service). For if the unit arrives when there are n units ahead of it and the unit in service is in the sth stage, that is, when the system is in state $(n-1)k+s$, unless more than $nk+s-1$ phases of service are completed in time T the unit in question will still be in the system (either queue or service) at the end of time T, and unless more than $(n-1)k+s-1$ phases are completed the unit in question will still be in the queue after time T. Since these phases are each exponential, the probability that m or fewer phases are completed in time T is

$$\sum_{i=0}^{m}[(k\mu T)^i/i!]\,e^{-k\mu T}$$

This must then be multiplied by the state probability that the arriving unit finds the system with m phases still to complete.

Referring to Eqs. 7.9 and 7.10, we utilize the solutions of the secular equation to set up an appropriate group of expressions for the state probabilities. There are k roots of Eq. 7.10, all of which are less than unity in magnitude; call them $u_j(1\leq j\leq k)$. Therefore, the individual state probability $P_{n,s}$, and also the probability P_n that n units are in the system, should be expressible in terms of these roots:

$$P_{n,s} = \sum_{j=1}^{k} C_j u_j^{(n-1)k+s}$$

$$P_n = \sum_{s=1}^{k} P_{n,s} = (\lambda/k\mu) \sum_{j=1}^{k} C_j w_j^n u_j \tag{7.22}$$

where we have used Eq. 7.10 to simplify the double sum, and where $w_j = u_j^k$ is one of the roots of Eq. 7.8 that have magnitude less than unity.

The values of the C's can be obtained from the initial equations, the first three of Eqs. 7.7. These may be rewritten more obviously as initial

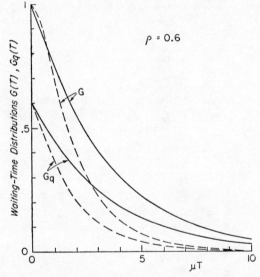

Fig. 7.1. Waiting-time distributions $G(T)$ and $G_q(T)$ for total time and for time in queue, as functions of μT for $\rho = 0.6$, for Poisson arrivals and for service-time distribution $k=1$ (solid lines) and $k=2$ (dashed lines). See Eqs. 7.5 and 7.28.

conditions by trying to make the initial equations correspond to the queue equations (the last two of Eqs. 7.7). For example, the third equation would correspond to the pattern of the last one if we would relabel P_0, calling it $P_{0,k}$. Also, the second of Eqs. 7.7 would correspond to the pattern of the fourth if we would invent a set of P's, $P_{0,s}$, all of which were zero, except for $s=k$. Finally, the first equation of Eqs. 7.7

would correspond to the pattern of the last if we invented a $P_{-1,k}$ which was equal to $(k\mu/\lambda)P_{0,k} = (k\mu/\lambda)P_0$. Consequently, the solutions of Eqs. 7.7, the state probabilities, are given by the combinations 7.22, with the values of the k coefficients C_j determined by the k *initial conditions*

$$P_{0,s} = \sum_{j=1}^{k} C_j u_j^{s-k} = 0 \qquad (1 \le s < k)$$

$$P_{0,k} = P_0 = 1 - (\lambda/\mu) = \sum_{j=1}^{k} C_j \tag{7.23}$$

When values of the roots u_j are known, the values of the C's may readily be computed.

Returning now to the time delays, we see that the probability $G(T)$ that the unit will have to stay longer than time T in the system is the probability $P_{n,s}$ that the incoming unit finds the system in state n,s, times the probability that $(n-1)k+s$ phases or fewer are completed in time T, the product then summed over n and s,

$$G(T) = \sum_{n,s} P_{n,s} \sum_{i=0}^{m+k-1} [(k\mu T)^i / i!] \, e^{-k\mu T} \quad (m = nk - k + s)$$

$$= \sum_{j=1}^{k} C_j \sum_{m=1-k}^{\infty} u_j^m \sum_{i=0}^{m+k-1} [(k\mu T)^i / i!] \, e^{-k\mu T}$$

$$= \sum_{j=1}^{k} C_j \sum_{i=0}^{\infty} [(k\mu T)^i / i!] \sum_{m=i+1-k}^{\infty} u_j^m \, e^{-k\mu T} \tag{7.24}$$

$$= \sum_{j=1}^{k} [C_j / u_j^{k-1}(1 - u_j)] \, e^{-k\mu(1-u_j)T}$$

where we have used Eqs. 7.23 and the expansion $\sum_{m=l}^{\infty} u^m = u^l/(1-u)$ to simplify the expressions. By a similar argument we find that $G_k(T)$, the probability that an arriving unit will spend longer than time T in the queue, to be

$$G_q(T) = \sum_{n,s} P_{n,s} \sum_{i=0}^{m-1} [(k\mu T)^i / i!] \, e^{-k\mu T}$$

$$= \sum_{i=1}^{k} [C_j u_j/(1 - u_j)] \, e^{-k\mu(1-u_j)T} \tag{7.25}$$

We note that (for $k>1$)

$$G(T)\to 1 \quad (T\to 0); \quad \to [C_k/u_k{}^{k-1}(1-u_k)]\,e^{-k\mu(1-u_k)T} \quad (T\to\infty)$$

$$G'(T)\to 0 \quad (T\to 0); \quad \to -k\mu(C_k/u_k{}^{k-1})\,e^{-k\mu(1-u_k)T} \quad (T\to\infty)$$

$$G_q(T)\to 1-P_0=\rho=(\lambda/\mu) \quad (T\to 0)$$

$$G_q'(T)\to -k\mu P_{1,1}=-\lambda P_0=-\lambda(1-\rho) \quad (T\to 0)$$

where u_k is the largest root of Eq. 7.10.

For the case $k=2$ (service-time distribution like curves b of Fig. 2.2 or 2.3) we can solve secular Eq. 7.10 algebraically:

$$u_1=-\tfrac{1}{2}\sqrt{\theta^2+4\theta}+\tfrac{1}{2}\theta$$

$$u_2=\tfrac{1}{2}\sqrt{\theta^2+4\theta}+\tfrac{1}{2}\theta; \quad \theta=(\rho/2)$$

The combination of roots which satisfies the initial conditions $P_{0,1}=0$, $P_{0,2}=P_0=1-2\theta$, is

$$P_{n,s}=\frac{1-2\theta}{\sqrt{\theta^2+4\theta}}(u_2{}^{2n+s-1}-u_1{}^{2n+s-1}) \quad (\theta=\lambda/2\mu)$$

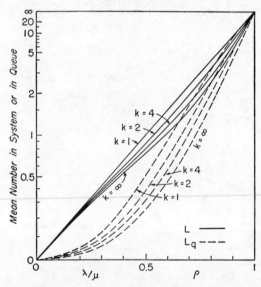

Fig. 7.2. Mean number in system L (solid lines) and mean queue length L_q (dashed lines) as function of ρ for Poisson arrivals at a single channel with different Erlang service-time distributions. See Eqs. 7.17 and 7.5. Vertical scale has been distorted to include the whole range of values.

and the probability that n units are in the system is then (see Eq. 7.22)

$$P_n = \frac{1-2\theta}{\theta\sqrt{\theta^2+4\theta}}\{[\tfrac{1}{2}(\theta^2+2\theta)+\tfrac{1}{2}\theta\sqrt{\theta^2+4\theta}]^{n+1}$$

$$-[\tfrac{1}{2}(\theta^2+2\theta)-\tfrac{1}{2}\theta\sqrt{\theta^2+4\theta}]^{n+1}\} \quad (7.26)$$

The probability that there are N or more units in the system (that there are more than $N-2$ units in the queue) is

$$Q_N = \sum_{n=N}^{\infty} P_n = \left[\frac{2-\theta}{2\sqrt{\theta^2+4\theta}}+\frac{1}{2}\right][\tfrac{1}{2}(\theta^2+2\theta)+\tfrac{1}{2}\theta\sqrt{\theta^2+4\theta}]^N$$

$$-\left[\frac{2-\theta}{2\sqrt{\theta^2+4\theta}}-\frac{1}{2}\right][\tfrac{1}{2}(\theta^2+2\theta)-\tfrac{1}{2}\theta\sqrt{\theta^2+4\theta}]^N \quad (7.27)$$

Finally the delay probabilities G and G_q, for this single-channel, $k=2$ Erlang service with Poisson arrivals, are

$$G(T) = \frac{1}{2}\left[\frac{2-\theta}{\sqrt{\theta^2+4\theta}}+1\right]e^{-\gamma_-T}-\frac{1}{2}\left[\frac{2-\theta}{\sqrt{\theta^2+4\theta}}-1\right]e^{-\gamma_+T}$$

$$(7.28)$$

$$G_q(T) = \left[\frac{\theta^2+\theta}{\sqrt{\theta^2+4\theta}}+\theta\right]e^{-\gamma_-T}-\left[\frac{\theta^2+\theta}{\sqrt{\theta^2+4\theta}}-\theta\right]e^{-\gamma_+T}$$

where
$$\gamma_+ = 2\mu-\tfrac{1}{2}\lambda+\sqrt{2\mu\lambda+\tfrac{1}{4}\lambda^2} = \mu[2-\theta+\sqrt{\theta^2+4\theta}]$$

and
$$\gamma_- = 2\mu-\tfrac{1}{2}\lambda-\sqrt{2\mu\lambda+\tfrac{1}{4}\lambda^2} = \mu[2-\theta-\sqrt{\theta^2+4\theta}]$$

The functions G and G_q are plotted as functions of μT for this $k=2$ case and also for the $k=1$ case (exponential service, see Eqs. 7.5) for $\rho=0.6$ in Fig. 7.1. Note that a short delay is a little more likely, a long delay much less likely, for $k=2$ than for $k=1$. This is not surprising; there are fewer long service times and fewer very short service times for $k=2$ than for $k=1$. The arriving unit is thus more likely to get delayed the "standard" amount, and is less likely to get a lucky or an unlucky break in delay.

Figure 7.2 shows comparative curves for mean length of queue L_q and mean number L, for the two cases, plotted as functions of the utilization factor $\rho=(\lambda/\mu)$. Note again that queue lengths are shorter for a given ρ for the more regular service ($k>1$); or, alternatively, utilization can be greater for a given mean queue length. The difference is still more noticeable if the service is still more regular (k greater than 2), until for constant service time ($k=\infty$, dashed curve of Fig. 2.2) L_q is only half the value it has for exponential service for the same value of ρ. Mean waits W are of course proportional to the L's, as indicated in Eq. 7.17.

Figure 7.3 compares the curves for Q_N, the probability that more than N units are in the queue, for the two cases $k=1$ and $k=2$, for

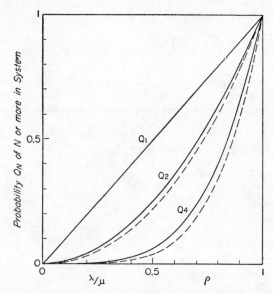

Fig. 7.3. Probability Q_N of N or more units in system as a function of ρ for $N=1$, 2, 4 for Poisson arrivals and for exponential service, $k=1$ (solid lines), and for $k=2$ service-time distributions (dashed lines). Curves are identical, $Q_1=\rho$, for $N=1$. See Eqs. 7.5 and 7.27.

different values of ρ and N. Here also the improvement is noticeable when service is made regular.

Hyper-Exponential Service

Next let us look at the behavior of a hyper-exponential service channel of the sort described by Eq. 5.15, subject to Poisson arrivals and with an infinite queue allowed. Arrivals join the queue and, when at the front of the line, enter one or the other of the alternate branches by some random choice, going to branch 1 (rate $2\sigma\mu$) a fraction σ of the time and to branch 2 (rate $2\mu-2\sigma\mu$) a fraction $(1-\sigma)$ of the time. Two subscripts are needed to describe the state of the system, the first (either 1 or 2) giving the branch the served unit is in, and the second (1 or 2 or 3, etc.) giving the number of units in service or in queue. In addition there is the state 0, with no unit present. The equations of detailed balance can be obtained by extension of Eqs. 5.17.

$$2\sigma\mu P_{11}+2(1-\sigma)\mu P_{21}-\lambda P_0=0$$

$$\sigma\lambda P_0+\sigma[2\sigma\mu P_{12}+2(1-\sigma)\mu P_{22}]-[\lambda+2\sigma\mu]P_{11}=0$$

$$(1-\sigma)\lambda P_0+(1-\sigma)[2\sigma\mu P_{12}+2(1-\sigma)\mu P_{22}]-[\lambda+2(1-\sigma)\mu]P_{21}=0$$

$$\lambda P_{1,n-1}+\sigma[2\sigma\mu P_{1,n+1}+2(1-\sigma)\mu P_{2,n+1}]-[\lambda+2\sigma\mu]P_{1n}=0 \qquad (7.29)$$

$$\lambda P_{2,n-1}+(1-\sigma)[2\sigma\mu P_{1,n+1}+2(1-\sigma)\mu P_{2,n+1}]$$

$$-[\lambda+2(1-\sigma)\mu]P_{2n}=0$$

To determine mean length of queue it is best to compute the generating functions $F_s(z)=\sum_{n=1}^{\infty}z^n P_{sn}$ $(s=1,2)$. Equations for these may be obtained by multiplying the second equation of Eqs. 7.29 by z, the fourth by z^n and adding

$$\left[\lambda z+\frac{2\sigma^2\mu}{z}-\lambda-2\sigma\mu\right]F_1+\frac{2\sigma(1-\sigma)\mu}{z}F_2=2\sigma^2\mu P_{11}+2\sigma(1-\sigma)\mu P_{21}-\sigma\lambda z P_0$$

Likewise, from the third and fifth equation of Eqs. 7.29 we obtain

$$\frac{2\sigma(1-\sigma)\mu}{z}F_1+\left[\lambda z+\frac{2(1-\sigma)^2\mu}{z}-\lambda-2(1-\sigma)\mu\right]F_2$$

$$=2\sigma(1-\sigma)\mu P_{11}+2(1-\sigma)^2\mu P_{21}-(1-\sigma)\lambda z P_0$$

Using the first of Eqs. 7.29 expresses P_{11} and P_{21} in these equations, in terms of P_0. The two can then be solved to obtain

$$F_1(z)=\sigma\rho z[2(1-\sigma)+\rho(1-z)]P_0/Q$$

$$F_2(z)=(1-\sigma)\rho z[2\sigma+\rho(1-z)]P_0/Q$$

$$F(z)=F_1+F_2=\rho z[4\sigma(1-\sigma)+\rho(1-z)]P_0/Q$$

where $\qquad Q=2\rho+4\sigma(1-\sigma)(1-\rho)-\rho(\rho+2)z+\rho^2 z^2$

Since $F(1)$ must equal $1-P_0$, the value of P_0 is soon found to be equal to $1-\rho$, just as for every other single-channel system with Poisson arrivals and infinite queue.

The mean number in the system is $F'(1)$, as before:

$$L = \frac{\rho^2 + \rho(1-\rho)4\sigma(1-\sigma)}{4\sigma(1-\sigma)(1-\rho)} \tag{7.30}$$

and
$$L_q = L - \rho = \rho^2/[4\sigma(1-\sigma)(1-\rho)]$$

Comparison with Eqs. 7.5 and 7.17 shows that increase in variability of service time beyond that of the exponential channel (Eq. 7.5 or the present case, $\sigma = \frac{1}{2}$) increases the length of queue, for L_q increases indefinitely as $\sigma \to 0$. This is not a surprising result, but the quantitative relation between the numerical value of L_q and the specific shape of the service distribution, given in Eq. 5.16, for a given value of σ is the important result of the analysis given here.

To obtain other operational measures for this case, we would have to solve Eqs. 7.29 to obtain values for the state probabilities, by the methods outlined at the beginning of this chapter. The expressions for the probabilities

$$P_{1,n} = B_1{}^+ w_+{}^n + B_1{}^- w_-{}^n; \quad P_{2,n} = B_2{}^+ w_+{}^n + B_2{}^- w_-{}^n$$

can be set into the queue equations to obtain the secular equation, the root $w = 1$ is discarded, and the two roots remaining are

$$w_\pm = \left(\frac{\rho}{2}\right)\left[\frac{\rho + 2 \pm \sqrt{\rho^2 + 4(2\sigma-1)^2(1-\rho)}}{\rho + 1 + 2(2\sigma-1)^2(1-\rho)}\right]$$

which can be substituted back in to get the ratios $(B_2{}^+/B_1{}^+)$ and $(B_2{}^-/B_1{}^-)$. The second and third of Eqs. 7.29 show that $P_{1,0} = \sigma P_0 = \sigma(1-\rho)$ and $P_{2,0} = (1-\sigma)(1-\rho)$, which suffices to determine the B's. Thus the probabilities $P_n = P_{1n} + P_{2n}$ that n units are in the system can all be computed, and from them, by methods we have already illustrated, can be obtained the functions $G(T)$, $G_q(T)$ and Q_N.

Non-Poisson Arrivals

Next we should investigate the effect of arrival-time distribution on the single service-channel, infinite-queue system. We first take the service channel to be exponential and the arrivals to be l-Erlang, corresponding to an arrival-timing channel with l phases (see Eq. 5.2). The units leave the storage depot in turn, traverse the arrival channel, then join the queue (if there is one), eventually are admitted to the service channel, are serviced and then depart. The phases in the arrival channel are numbered in order of occupancy by the arriving unit, $s = 1$ being the first one entered and $s=l$ being the last one, just prior to leaving the arrival-timing channel and joining the queue. In addition to s, the value of n, the number of units in the queue and service channel, is needed to specify the state completely. (Labelling of arrival phases here differs from that of p. 48.) Thus the state probabilities are $P_{s,n}$.

They are connected by the usual equations of detailed balance for the steady-state case. The rate of transition from one phase to the next in the arrival channel is $l\lambda$, in order to make the mean arrival rate λ; the service rate for the exponential service channel is μ. Then the equations for the P's are

$$\mu P_{11}-l\lambda P_{10}=0; \quad l\lambda P_{s-1,0}+\mu P_{s,1}-l\lambda P_{s,0}=0$$

$$l\lambda P_{l,n-1}+\mu P_{1,n+1}-(l\lambda+\mu)P_{1,n}=0 \qquad (n>0) \quad (7.31)$$

$$l\lambda P_{s-1,n}+\mu P_{s,n+1}-(l\lambda+\mu)P_{s,n}=0 \qquad (1<s\leq l)$$

where the last two equations are the queue equations and the first two are the initial equations.

Proceeding as suggested with Eq. 7.2, we set $P_{s,n}=B_s w^n$ and obtain the set of equations

$$(l\rho+1-w)B_s=l\rho B_{s-1} \qquad (1<s\leq l)$$

$$w(l\rho+1-w)B_1=l\rho B_l$$

from which we obtain the relations

$$B_s=\left[\frac{l\rho}{l\rho+1-w}\right]^{s-1}B_1; \quad w=\left[\frac{l\rho}{l\rho+1-w}\right]^l \qquad (7.32)$$

and thence the secular equation

$$w(1+l\rho-w)^l=(l\rho)^l \qquad (7.33)$$

which has, for one root, $w=1$.

Again we note that B_s can be expressed as a power of some quantity $u=[l\rho/(1+l\rho-w)]$ times a constant B_1 and that $u^l=w$. Consequently, we can express all the probabilities (at least for $n>0$) in terms of successive powers of u, $P_{s,n}=Au^{ln+s-1}$, and find an equation for u directly by substituting this in either of the queue equations

$$u^{l+1}-(1+l\rho)u+l\rho\equiv(u-1)(u^l+u^{l-1}+\cdots+u^2+u-l\rho)=0 \quad (7.34)$$

The root $u=1$ can be discarded. There is at least one root with magnitude less than unity (if $\rho<1$), for we can find a real positive quantity v, less than unity, such that $v^l+v^{l-1}+\cdots+v$ is equal to $l\rho<l$. But

there are no other roots less than unity. To show this, divide out the one small root, giving

$$(u-1)(u-v)[u^{l-1}+(1+v)u^{l-2}$$
$$+(1+v+v^2)u^{l-3}+\cdots+(1+v+v^2+\cdots+v^{l-1})]$$
$$\equiv(u-v)[u^l+vu^{l-1}+v^2u^{l-2}+\cdots+v^{l-1}u-(1+v+v^2+\cdots+v^{l-1})]=0$$

so that

$$1+v+v^2+\cdots+v^{l-1}=u^l+vu^{l-1}+\cdots+v^{l-1}u$$
$$\leq|u|^l+v|u|^{l-1}+\cdots+v^{l-1}|u|$$

This inequality will be satisfied only if u, the other $l-1$ roots, are all larger than unity.

Therefore, for $n>0$ the expression for the state probability is the simple one

$$P_{s,n}=Av^{ln+s-1} \qquad\qquad (1\leq s\leq l) \quad (7.35)$$

where v is that root of Eq. 7.34 which is less than unity. The probabilities for $n=0$ are obtained from the initial equations, the first two of Eqs. 7.31. Using the relations $v^m=(1+l\rho)v^{m-l}-l\rho v^{m-l-1}$ and $v^l=l\rho-v$ $-v^2-\cdots-v^{l-1}$, derived from Eq. 7.34, we obtain

$$P_{l,0}=(1/l\rho)[(1+l\rho)P_{1,1}-P_{1,2}]$$
$$=(A/l\rho)[(1+l\rho)v^l-v^{2l}]=Av^{l-1}$$
$$P_{l-1,0}=A[v^{l-1}-(v^{2l-1}/l\rho)]$$
$$=(A/l\rho)(l\rho v^{l-2}-v^{l-1})$$
$$P_{l-2,0}=(A/l\rho)(l\rho v^{l-2}-v^{l-1}-v^{2l-2})$$
$$=(A/l\rho)(l\rho v^{l-3}-v^{l-2}-v^{l-1})$$

$$\qquad\qquad\qquad\qquad\qquad\qquad (7.36)$$

$$\vdots$$

$$P_{2,0}=(A/l\rho)(l\rho v-v^2-v^3-\cdots-v^{l-1})$$
$$P_{1,0}=(A/l\rho)(l\rho-v-v^2-\cdots-v^{l-1})$$
$$=(Av^l/\rho l)=(P_{1,1}/l\rho)$$

the last equation checking with the first of Eqs. 7.31 and thus checking the whole sequence.

Here, even more than for the k-Erlang service, the individual phases in the arrival channel have very little real significance. What is important is the probability that n units are in the queue or in service. This is

$$P_n = \sum_{s=1}^{l} P_{s,n} = A(1-v^l)v^{nl}/(1-v)$$

for $n>0$. For the $n=0$ case, from Eqs. 7.36

$$P_0 = A \sum_{m=0}^{l-1} v^m - (A/l\rho) \sum_{m=1}^{l-1} mv^m$$

$$= A\left[\frac{1-v^l}{1-v}\right] - \frac{Av}{l\rho}\left[\frac{1-lv^{l-1}+(l-1)v^l}{(1-v)^2}\right]$$

$$= \frac{A}{l\rho} \frac{l\rho - l\rho v - l\rho v^l + l\rho v^{l+1} - v + lv^l - (l-1)v^{l+1}}{(1-v)^2}$$

$$= A\frac{(1-\rho)v^l}{\rho(1-v)}$$

where we have used Eq. 7.34 again in making the last step.

Now we can obtain the value of A, for

$$1 = \sum_{n=0}^{\infty} P_n = \frac{A(1-\rho)v^l}{\rho(1-v)} + \frac{Av^l}{1-v} = \frac{Av^l}{\rho(1-v)}$$

Consequently, the values of the probabilities are

$$P_0 = 1-\rho; \quad P_n = \rho(1-v^l)v^{(n-1)l} \qquad (n>0) \quad (7.37)$$

As with any single-channel, infinite-queue system, the probability that the system is empty is $1-\rho$, and the probability that the service channel is busy is ρ (which is why ρ is called the *utilization factor*). The mean number and the mean length of queue are

$$L = \frac{\rho}{1-v^l}; \quad L_q = \frac{\rho v^l}{1-v^l} \qquad (7.38)$$

Referring to the discussion after Eq. 5.11, we should not be surprised here to find that the probability P_n is *not* the probability that an arriving unit will find n in the system ahead of it. P_n is the probability that a *random* arrival would find n in the system; the point is that an l-Erlang arrival is *not a random arrival*. In fact, the probability that an *arriving unit* finds n in the system must be proportional to $P_{l,n}$, since the state

$s=l$ corresponds to the last phase in the arrival channel, from which the unit emerges to arrive at the queue. We could call this probability $P_{a,n} = CP_{l,n} = Bv^{ln}$. By summing over n we determine B (since the sum of all $P_{a,n}$'s must be unity) and thus obtain

$$P_{a,n} = (1-v^l)v^{ln} \tag{7.39}$$

We can now determine the probability that the unit spends more than time T in the system

$$G(T) = P_{a,0} e^{-\mu T} + P_{a,1}(1+\mu T) e^{-\mu T} + \cdots = e^{-\mu(1-v^l)T}$$
$$G_q(T) = v^l e^{-\mu(1-v^l)T} \tag{7.40}$$

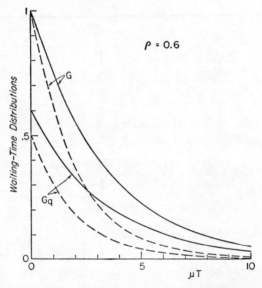

Fig. 7.4. Waiting-time distributions $G(T)$ and $G_q(T)$ for total time and for time in queue, as functions of μT for $\rho=0.6$ for exponential service and for arrival-time distributions $l=1$ (solid lines) and $l=2$ (dashed lines). See Eqs. 7.40 and 7.5. Also compare with Figs. 7.1 and 7.8.

Details of the l=2 Case

As an example, and because it is the type of arrival distribution more often encountered than any other except the Poisson distribution, we will work out the 2-Erlang arrival case ($l=2$) in detail. The secular equation $u^2+u-2\rho=0$ has one root, $v=-\frac{1}{2}+\sqrt{\frac{1}{4}+2\rho}$, which is less than unity in magnitude. The probabilities P_n that n units are in the system and those $P_{a,n}$ that the arriving unit finds n in the system are

$$P_0=1-\rho; \quad P_n=\rho[\tfrac{1}{2}-2\rho+\sqrt{\tfrac{1}{4}+2\rho}\,][\tfrac{1}{2}+2\rho-\sqrt{\tfrac{1}{4}+2\rho}\,]^{n-1}$$

(7.41)

$$P_{a,n}=[\tfrac{1}{2}-2\rho+\sqrt{\tfrac{1}{4}+2\rho}][\tfrac{1}{2}+2\rho-\sqrt{\tfrac{1}{4}+2\rho}\,]^{n}$$

The probability Q_N, that there are N or more units in the system and $Q_{a,N}$ that the arriving unit finds more than $N-1$ units in the system, can be determined from the P's by addition.

The mean number in the system and mean number in queue are

$$L=\frac{2\rho+\sqrt{\tfrac{1}{4}+2\rho}-\tfrac{1}{2}}{4(1-\rho)}\rightarrow\begin{cases}\rho & (\rho\rightarrow0)\\ \tfrac{3}{4}(1-\rho) & (\rho\rightarrow1)\end{cases}$$

(7.42)

$$L_q=\frac{4\rho^2+\sqrt{\tfrac{1}{4}+2\rho}-\tfrac{1}{2}-2\rho}{4(1-\rho)}\rightarrow\begin{cases}4\rho^3 & (\rho\rightarrow0)\\ \tfrac{3}{4}(1-\rho) & (\rho\rightarrow1)\end{cases}$$

Note the difference from Eq. 7.5, particularly for the limiting values of ρ.

The mean delays W and W_q are obtained, as before, by dividing the expressions for L and L_q by λ. This result should bear some scrutiny, however, for we have already noted that the average state displayed to an arriving unit is not the time-average state of the system *unless* arrivals are Poisson. Thus, we might wonder whether the mean time spent in the system by an arriving unit would be obtained by dividing the time-average number L by λ, which by Eq. 7.38 would be $W=1/\mu(1-v^l)$. To check this result, perhaps we should try to obtain W in some other way. For example, by an extension of the reasoning of Eq. 2.2 we can say that the mean time spent by the unit in the system should be

$$W=\int_0^\infty G(T)\,dT$$

(7.43)

But this, from Eq. 7.40, turns out to be just (L/λ).

Alternatively, we could compute W from Eq. 7.39. When the arriving unit finds n units ahead of it, it will take an average time (n/μ) to get through, so again

$$W=\sum_n (n/\mu)P_{a,n}=1/\mu(1-v^l)=(L/\lambda)$$

(7.44)

Consequently, even for non-Poisson arrivals we have $\lambda W=L$ and $\lambda W_q=L_q$.

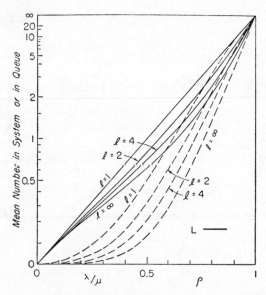

Fig. 7.5. Values of L (solid lines) or L_q (dashed lines) as a function of ρ for a single exponential service channel with different Erlang-type arrival distributions. See Eqs. 7.38 and 7.5. Compare with Figs. 7.2 and 7.9.

Returning to the specific case of $l = 2$ arrivals, the expressions for the delay-time distributions are

$$G(T) = e^{-\gamma T}; \quad G_q(T) = \left[\tfrac{1}{2} + 2\rho - \sqrt{\tfrac{1}{4} + 2\rho}\,\right] e^{-\gamma T} \qquad (7.45)$$

where $\quad \gamma = \mu\left[\tfrac{1}{2} + \sqrt{\tfrac{1}{4} + 2\rho} - 2\rho\right] = \tfrac{1}{2}\left[\mu + \sqrt{\mu^2 + 8\lambda\mu} - 4\lambda\right]$

Figures 7.4, 7.5 and 7.6 compare the values of the G's, the L's and the Q's, for various values of ρ, μT and N, for the single exponential service channel with mean service time μ, for several arrival distributions; the simple Poisson arrivals ($l = 1$) and the less random cases of $l > 1$. In Figs. 7.1, 7.2 and 7.3 we showed the effect of service-time distribution; here we show the effect of arrival-time distribution on the average behavior of the system. We see that changing the arrival statistics has a bit more effect on the G's, the delay-time distributions, than does changing the service characteristics when T is small. Values of L_q and Q_N are also more affected by change of l than by change of k.

Equations 7.17 gave values of L and L_q for all values of k, and showed that for the constant service-time case ($k \to \infty$) L_q reduced to only half the value it has for exponential service ($k = 1$). We should investi-

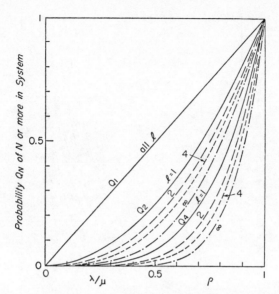

Fig. 7.6. Probability of N or more units in system, for $N=1,2,4$ for a single exponential ($k=1$) channel, for different arrival-time distributions, $l=1$ (Poisson), $l=2,4$, and ∞. Compare with Figs. 7.3 and 7.9.

gate the solutions for large values of l, to see what limit is reached when $l \to \infty$ (uniform arrivals). Referring to Eq. 7.34, we see that it can be written

$$u^l = \left(1+\frac{1}{l\rho}\right)^{-l}\left(1+\frac{u^{l+1}}{l\rho}\right)^l$$

As has been noted earlier, $[1+(x/l)]^l \to e^x$ as $l \to \infty$, so here our equation for the root with magnitude less than unity becomes

$$v^l \simeq e^{(v^l-1)/\rho}; \quad \text{or} \quad v^l \simeq 1-\rho \ln (1/v^l) \quad (l \to \infty) \quad (7.46)$$

Solutions of this equation can be obtained fairly easily by successive approximations:

$\rho=$ 0	0.2	0.3	0.4	0.5	0.6	0.7	0.8	0.9	1.0
$v^l=$ 0	.0070	.0409	.1074	.2032	.3242	.4669	.6285	.8065	1.0

When ρ is small, a good approximation is $v^l \simeq e^{-1/\rho}$; when ρ is near unity, a first approximation is $v^l \simeq 1-2\rho(1-\rho)$. Figure 7.7 gives curves of L and L_q for the cases of the Poisson exponential ($l=1$, $k=1$), the Poisson constant ($l=1$, $k \to \infty$) and the regular exponential ($l \to \infty$, $k=1$).

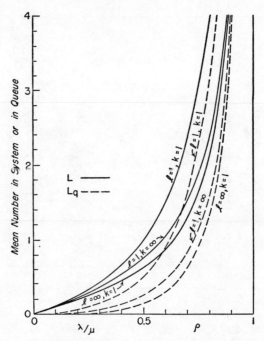

Fig. 7.7. Comparison, for single service channel, of L and L_q for Poisson arrival, exponential service ($l=1$, $k=1$); Poisson arrival, constant service ($l=1$, $k=\infty$); and regular arrival, exponential service ($l=\infty$, $k=1$).

Both Service and Arrivals Non-Exponential

Before we finish this section we should discuss the more complicated case where arrivals are l-Erlang and the service channel is k-Erlang. Here we use three subscripts to specify the state: s ($1 \le s \le l$) to specify the phase in the arrival-timing channel, m ($1 \le m \le k$) to specify the phase in the service channel, and n the number in the system. Remembering that the arrival channel is numbered in order of the unit's progress, whereas the service phases are numbered in reverse order, the equations of detailed balance are

$$k\mu P_{1,1,1} = l\lambda P_{1,0}; \quad l\lambda P_{s-1,0} + k\mu P_{s,1,1} = l\lambda P_{s,0}$$

$$(1 < s \le l)$$

$$l\lambda P_{l,0} + k\mu P_{1,1,2} = (l\lambda + k\mu)P_{1,k,1}$$

$$l\lambda P_{l,m,n-1} + k\mu P_{1,m+1,n} = (l\lambda + k\mu)P_{1,m,n}$$

$$(1 \le m < k; n > 1) \quad (7.47)$$

$$l\lambda P_{s-1,k,n} + k\mu P_{s,1,n+1} = (l\lambda + k\mu)P_{s,k,n}$$

$$(1 < s \le l; n > 0)$$

$$l\lambda P_{s-1,m,n} + k\mu P_{s,m+1,n} = (l\lambda + k\mu)P_{s,m,n}$$

$$(1 < s \le l; 1 \le m < k; n > 0)$$

The last three equations are the queue equations, the first three the initial equations. As before, we set $P_{s,m,n} = B_{s,m}w^n$ and obtain

$$\phi B_{s-1,m} + B_{s,m+1} - (1+\phi)B_{s,m} = 0 \quad (1 < s \le l; 1 \le m < k)$$

$$\phi B_{l,m} + w[B_{1,m+1} - (1+\phi)B_{1,m}] = 0 \qquad (1 \le m < k)$$

$$\phi B_{s-1,k} + wB_{s,1} - (1+\phi)B_{s,k} = 0 \qquad (1 < s \le l)$$

where $\phi = (l\lambda/k\mu) = (l\rho/k)$.

If we assume that $B_{s,m} = Cu^s v^m$, we can show, first of all, that if $u^l = w$ the second equation reduces to the first, and next, that if $v^k = w$, the third equation reduces to the first. Then if l and k are prime, we set $z = w^{(1/lk)} = u^{1/k} = v^{1/l}$, and obtain from any of the three equations the secular equation

$$\phi + z^{l+k} - (1+\phi)z^k = 0 \tag{7.48}$$

One root of this equation is $z = 1$, which is to be discarded. Dividing out by $(z-1)$ we obtain

$$kz^k(z^{l-1} + z^{l-2} + \cdots + z + 1) = l\rho(z^{k-1} + z^{k-2} + \cdots + z + 1) \tag{7.49}$$

which is a combination of Eqs. 7.10 and 7.34. Extending the discussion of the roots of these earlier equations, we can show that there are only k of the $l+k+1$ roots of this equation that have magnitude less than unity. Call them z_q ($q = 1, 2, \cdots, k$). Then the state probabilities for $n > 0$ are

$$P_{s,m,n} = \sum_{q=1}^{k} C_q z_q^{kln+sk+ml} \tag{7.50}$$

The values of the C's and of the P's for $n = 0$ must be determined from the initial equations.

When k and l are not mutually prime, this procedure can be simplified somewhat. For example, suppose $k=l$. A modification of Eq. 7.48 can be obtained by manipulation and substitution back for v:

$$\phi^l = [(1+\phi) - v]^l v^k \qquad (7.51)$$

when $l=k$, $u=v$ and Eq. 7.51 reduces to

$$v^2 - (1+\phi)v + \phi\, e^{2\pi i q/l} = 0 \quad (q=1,2,\cdots,l)$$

and the $k=l$ useful roots are the set

$$v_q = \tfrac{1}{2}(1+\phi) - \tfrac{1}{2}\sqrt{(1+\phi)^2 - 4\phi\, e^{2\pi i q/l}} \qquad (7.52)$$

for the k different values of q. When $k=l$, we note that $\phi=\rho$. The state probabilities are then

$$P_{s,m,n} = \sum_{q=1}^{k} C_q v_q^{\,nk+s+m} \qquad (n>0) \quad (7.53)$$

We shall carry out some of the computations for the case $l=k=2$ to show how the initial conditions work out. The two roots, in this case, are

$$v_1 = \tfrac{1}{2}(1+\rho) - \tfrac{1}{2}\sqrt{1+6\rho+\rho^2}; \quad v_2 = \rho \qquad (7.54)$$

and the higher state probabilities are

$$P_{s,m,n} = -C_1 v_1^{\,2n+s+m-4} + C_2 \rho^{\,2n+s+m-4}$$

Using the first three equations of Eqs. 7.47, we work backward through

$$P_{2,0} = C_1 + C_2; \quad P_{1,0} = (C_1/\rho)(\rho + v_1)$$

and finally $P_{1,0} = (-C_1 + C_2)/\rho$. From the last two we can determine C_2 in terms of C_1

$$C_2 = C_1(1+\rho+v_1) = \tfrac{1}{2}C_1[3(1+\rho) - \sqrt{1+6\rho+\rho^2}\,]$$

The probability that n units are in service or in queue is then

$$P_n = \sum_{s,m} P_{s,m,n} = C_1[-v_1^{\,2n-2}(1+v_1)^2 + (1+\rho+v_1)\rho^{2n-2}(1+\rho)^2]$$

$$P_0 = (C_1/\rho)[3\rho + \rho^2 + (1+\rho)v_1] \qquad (7.55)$$

Adding all these gives us an equation to determine C_1,

$$1 = C_1\left[3+\rho+\frac{1+\rho}{\rho}v_1 + (1+\rho+v_1)\frac{1+\rho}{1-\rho} - \frac{1+v_1}{1-v_1}\right]$$

and from this set of relations we can compute L, L_q, Q_N, G, G_q, W and W_q, if the need arises.

Hyper-Poisson Arrivals

To make complete this discussion of the effect of arrival distributions, we should work out the hyper-Poisson case discussed in Eq. 5.15 *et seq.* Here the state is labeled by the branch of the arrival-timing channel that is occupied (first subscript 1 if the $2\sigma\lambda$ branch is busy, 2 if the other is busy), and by the number n (second subscript on P) in the exponential service channel (rate μ) or in queue after having left the arrival-timing channel. The equations appropriate for this case are

$$\mu P_{11} - 2\sigma\lambda P_{10} = 0; \quad \mu P_{21} - 2(1-\sigma)\lambda P_{20} = 0$$

$$2\sigma^2\lambda P_{1,n-1} + 2\sigma(1-\sigma)\lambda P_{2,n-1} + \mu P_{1,n+1} - (\mu + 2\sigma\lambda)P_{1,n} = 0$$

$$2\sigma(1-\sigma)\lambda P_{1,n-1} + 2(1-\sigma)^2\lambda P_{2,n-1}$$

$$+ \mu P_{2,n+1} - [\mu + 2(1-\sigma)\lambda]P_{2,n} = 0$$

$$(7.56)$$

In the case of hyper-exponential service and Poisson arrival (Eq. 7.29 *et seq.*) we had only one state for $n=0$, so both generating functions could be expressed in terms of P_0 and the value of P_0 could be determined by the requirement that the sum of both generating functions (for $z=1$) plus P_0 must equal 1. Here there are two states for $n=0$, so it is necessary to evaluate both P_{10} and P_{20} before the generating functions can be used to compute L, which cannot be done from the single requirement that the sum of the P's is 1. On the other hand, for an exponential service channel the P's form a harmonic series, that is, there is only one root of the secular equation which can be used to generate the P's. Consequently, as with the l-Erlang arrivals, we turn here to the solution of the secular equation.

Setting $P_{s,n} = B_s w^{n-1}$, we see that the last two equations of Eqs. 7.56 become

$$[w^2 - (1+2\sigma\rho)w + 2\sigma^2\rho]B_1 + 2\sigma(1-\sigma)\rho B_2 = 0 \quad (\rho = \lambda/\mu)$$

$$2\sigma(1-\sigma)\rho B_1 + \{w^2 - [1 + 2(1-\sigma)\rho]w + 2(1-\sigma)^2\rho\}B_2 = 0$$

and the secular equation is

$$w(w-1)[w^2 - (1+2\rho)w + 2\rho - 4\sigma(1-\sigma)\rho(1-\rho)] = 0 \quad (7.57)$$

The root $w=1$ can be discarded, for the resulting series will not converge. The root $w=0$ cannot generate a series of P's, it simply indicates that $P_{s,0}$ is not a regular part of the series of P_{sn}'s. In fact the only root which is less than unity is

$$v = \tfrac{1}{2} + \rho - \sqrt{\tfrac{1}{4} - (2\sigma - 1)^2 \rho(1-\rho)} \rightarrow \begin{cases} (2 - 4\sigma + 4\sigma^2)\rho & (\rho \rightarrow 0) \\ 1 - 4\sigma(1-\sigma)(1-\rho) & (\rho \rightarrow 1) \end{cases} \quad (7.58)$$

for which
$$B_2 = \frac{v(1-v) + 2\sigma\rho(v-\sigma)}{2\sigma(1-\sigma)} B_1 = \frac{1 - \sigma + 2\sigma\rho - v}{\sigma} B_1$$

so that
$$P_{1,n} = B_1 v^{n-1}; \quad P_{2,n} = B_2 v^{n-1} \quad (n > 0)$$

The probabilities for $n = 0$ are

$$P_{10} = [B_1/2\sigma\rho]; \quad P_{20} = [B_2/2(1-\sigma)\rho]$$

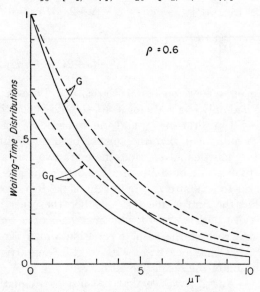

Fig. 7.8. Waiting-time distributions $G(T)$ and $G_q(T)$ for a single exponential service channel, for arrival-time distributions $j=1$ (Poisson) (solid lines) and $j=2$ ($\sigma = 0.2113$) (dashed lines). See Eqs. 7.61 and 7.5. Also compare with Figs. 7.1 and 7.4.

and the probabilities $P_n = P_{1n} + P_{2n}$ that there are n units in the queue and service-channel system are

$$P_0 = \frac{2 - 2\sigma + 2\sigma\rho - v}{2\sigma(1-\sigma)\rho} B_1$$

$$P_n = \frac{1 + 2\sigma\rho - v}{\sigma} B_1 v^{n-1}$$

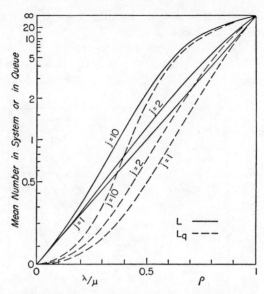

Fig. 7.9. Curves for L or L_q for a single exponential service channel with different hyper-Poisson arrival distributions. See Eqs. 7.5 and 7.60. Compare with Figs. 7.2 and 7.5.

Setting the sum of these equal to 1, we use the formulas $1+v+v^2+\cdots = 1/(1-v)$ and $(1-v)(2\rho-v)=4\sigma(1-\sigma)\rho(1-\rho)$ to find that

$$B_1 = \frac{2\sigma(1-\sigma)\rho(1-\rho)}{2-2\sigma+2\sigma\rho-v}$$

so that $\qquad P_0 = 1-\rho$

$$P_n = \frac{(1+2\sigma\rho-v)(1-v)(2\rho-v)}{2\sigma(2-2\sigma+2\sigma\rho-v)}v^{n-1} \qquad (7.59)$$

$$= (1-v)\rho v^{n-1}$$

Consequently, the expressions for L and L_q are

$$L = \frac{2\rho-v}{4\sigma(1-\sigma)(1-\rho)} = \frac{\rho}{1-v}; \quad L_q = \frac{\rho v}{1-v} \qquad (7.60)$$

The expressions for the probability that the delay is longer than T are

$$G(T) = e^{-\mu(1-v)T}; \quad G_q(T) = v\,e^{-\mu(1-v)T} \qquad (7.61)$$

and the probability that the queue length is $N-1$ or longer is $Q_N = \rho v^{N-1}$

for $N > 0$ (Q_0 is of course unity). In all of these formulas, we use the value of v given in Eq. 7.58.

Figures 7.7, 7.8 and 7.9 compare the curves of G, L and Q for this case of hyper-Poisson arrivals with those for Poisson arrivals. They should be compared to Figs. 7.4, 7.5 and 7.6 for "sub-Poisson" arrivals.

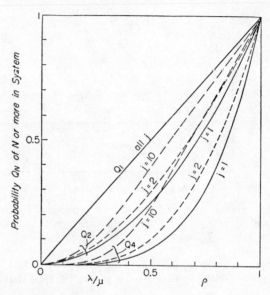

Fig. 7.10. Probability of N or more units in system, for $N = 1,2,4$ for a single exponential service channel, for Poisson and hyper-Poisson arrivals, $j = 1$ ($\sigma = 0.5$), $j = 2$ ($\sigma = 0.2113$), and $j = 10$ ($\sigma = 0.0477$). See Eq. 7.59. Compare with Figs. 7.3 and 7.6.

We note that as variability of arrivals increases, mean queue lengths and probabilities of delay are increased. We have again expressed this variability in terms of the parameter $j = [1/2\sigma(1-\sigma)] - 1 = (\lambda \Delta t_a)^2$ (see discussion following Eq. 5.15).

Incidentally, Eqs. 7.37 and 7.59 show that when the single service channel is exponential, state probabilities P_n form a geometric series (proportional to v^n) no matter what the arrival distribution may chance to be. The numerical magnitude of v depends on ρ and on the shape of the arrival distribution, but as long as the service distribution is exponential, P_n is proportional to v^n for a single channel.

Example of Service Line

Finally, we consider one example of a service line with two exponential stations, with no queue between the first and second station but with an infinite possible queue in front of the first. Referring to Eqs. 4.6, we first determine the possible states to be determined by (1) the number in the queue and (2) an index number indicating the state of affairs in the line. We shall label the three possible situations (when a queue is present) arbitrarily:

$(n,0)$ $n-1$ in the queue, 1 unit in the first station, none in the second
$(n,1)$ $n-1$ in the queue, 1 unit in the first station, 1 in the second, both being worked on
$(n,2)$ n in the queue, 1 unit in the second station, 1 blocked unit in the first, waiting for the second station to finish

In addition, there are the initial no-queue states:

$(0,0)$ no unit present in the system (00 of Eq. 4.6)
$(0,1)$ no unit in the first station, one in the second (01 of Eq. 4.6)
$(0,2)$ a unit in both stations, first station blocked ($b1$ of Eq. 4.6)
$(1,0)$ a unit in the first station, none in the second (10 of Eq. 4.6)
$(1,1)$ a unit in both stations, both stations working (11 of Eq. 4.6)

The equations of detailed balance are then

$$P_{0,1} = \rho P_{0,0}; \quad P_{1,0} + P_{0,2} = (1+\rho)P_{0,1}; \quad P_{1,1} = (1+\rho)P_{0,2}$$

$$\rho P_{n-1,0} + P_{n,1} = (1+\rho)P_{n,0}; \quad \rho P_{n-1,2} + P_{n+1,1} = (1+\rho)P_{n,2} \quad (7.62)$$

$$\rho P_{n-1,1} + P_{n+1,0} + P_{n,2} = (2+\rho)P_{n,1} \quad\quad\quad (n>0)$$

The last three equations are the queue equations. They may be solved by setting $P_{n,s} = B_s w^n$ and obtaining the equations

$$w[w(1+\rho) - \rho]B_0 = w^2 B_1 = [w(1+\rho) - \rho]B_2$$

$$[w(2+\rho) - \rho]B_1 = w^2 B_0 + w B_2 \quad\quad\quad (7.63)$$

$$[w(1+\rho) - \rho]^2[w(2+\rho) - \rho] - 2w^3[w(1+\rho) - \rho] = 0$$

The last equation is the secular equation; its roots are $w_1 = 1$,

$$w_2 = \rho/(1+\rho)$$

$$w_3 = \tfrac{1}{4}(\rho^2 + 3\rho) + \tfrac{1}{4}\sqrt{\rho^4 + 6\rho^3 + \rho^2}$$

$$w_4 = \tfrac{1}{4}(\rho^2 + 3\rho) - \tfrac{1}{4}\sqrt{\rho^4 + 6\rho^3 + \rho^2}$$

The first root is discarded, but we need the other three roots to fit the three initial equations. However, if ρ is larger than $\frac{2}{3}$, w_3 is larger than unity and thus cannot be used. Consequently, a divergent (non-stationary) situation will arise if the utilization factor ρ is as large as or larger than $\frac{2}{3}$. The lack of storage between stations 1 and 2 and the consequent blocking have reduced the capacity of the service channel to $\frac{2}{3}$ of the capacity of either station taken separately (note discussion after Eq. 4.7).

Substituting in Eqs. 7.63 for the w's enables us to calculate the B's for each root, and substituting these in the initial equations results in equations which may be solved for the B's. We eventually obtain

$$P_{n,0} = -QA\left(\frac{\rho}{1+\rho}\right)^n + (Q-\rho+1)\left(\frac{\rho}{4}\right)^n (\rho+3+Q)^n A$$

$$+ (Q+\rho-1)\left(\frac{\rho}{4}\right)^n (\rho+3-Q)^n A$$

$$P_{n,1} = \rho(\rho+3)A\left(\frac{\rho}{4}\right)^n (\rho+3+Q)^n - \rho(\rho+3)A\left(\frac{\rho}{4}\right)^n (\rho+3-Q)^n \qquad (7.64)$$

$$P_{n,2} = -QA\left(\frac{\rho}{1+\rho}\right)^{n+1} + \rho(Q-\rho+1)\left(\frac{\rho}{4}\right)^n (\rho+3+Q)^n A$$

$$+ \rho(Q+\rho-1)\left(\frac{\rho}{4}\right)^n (\rho+3-Q)^n A$$

where $Q = \sqrt{\rho^2+6\rho+1}$ and where A is a common coefficient having a value determined by the requirement that the sum of all the P's equals unity. From this we can compute values of L, L_q, etc.

But if we wish to compute only the mean number in the system or in the queue, we should use the generating function rather than the individual state probabilities. Suppose we define three generating functions:

$$F_s(z) = \sum_{n=0}^{\infty} z^{n+s} P_{n,s} \qquad (s=0,1,2) \quad (7.65)$$

We note that $\Sigma F_s(1) = 1$, that $\Sigma F_s'(1) = L$, and that L_q equals the derivative of $z^{-2}(zF_0+F_1+F_2)$ at $z=1$. Multiplying the equation with $(1+\rho)P_{n,0}$ in Eqs. 7.62 by z^n, that with $(2+\rho)P_{n,1}$ by z^{n+1} and so on, and making three separate sums, we get the following equations for the F's (using the first of Eqs. 7.62 several times to get rid of $P_{0,1}$).

$$(1+\rho-\rho z)F_0-(1/z)F_1=P_{00}$$

$$-F_0+(2+\rho-\rho z)F_1-(1/z)F_2=(\rho z-1)P_{00}$$

$$-F_1+(1+\rho-\rho z)F_2=-\rho z P_{00}$$

These equations can be solved to find the F's in terms of P_{00}; then the three F's can be added and P_{00} can be found by requiring that $\Sigma F_s=1$ for $z=1$. It turns out that $P_{00}=(2-3\rho)/(2+\rho)$ and that

$$F_0(z)=[2(1+\rho)-(3\rho+2\rho^2)z+\rho^2z^2]W$$

$$F_1=[2(\rho+\rho^2)z-(3\rho^2+\rho^3)z^2+\rho^3z^3]W \qquad (7.66)$$

$$F_2(z)=[(2\rho^2+\rho^3)z^2-\rho^3z^3]W$$

where $\qquad W=[(2-3\rho)/(2+\rho)(1+\rho-\rho z)(2-3\rho z-\rho^2z+\rho^2z^2)]$

The generating function for the system as a whole is

$$F(z)=\sum_{s=0}^{2}F_s(z)=(2+2\rho-\rho z)W$$

Differentiating this with respect to z and setting $z=1$ gives us a closed expression for the mean number in the system

$$L=[4\rho(2-\rho^2)/(2+\rho)(2-3\rho)] \qquad (7.67)$$

We note that this goes to infinity at $\rho=\frac{2}{3}$, as was pointed out before. Even for ρ small, this value of L is about twice as large as the expression $\rho/(1-\rho)$ for a single exponential station. Even if arrivals are sparse, each unit has to stay in each station, and on the average stays twice as long (for $\rho\ll1$), thus the mean number in the system at any time is about twice as large as for the one-station case. Of course, as ρ increases, the effect of blocking gets more important; L increases faster than the one-station case, until at $\rho=\frac{2}{3}$, the two-station line cannot handle any more. It can be shown that for a three-station line (no queues between the stations) the limit is even lower, for $\rho=22/39$; whereas (as we saw in Chapter 4) if we allow a queue of one between the two stations, the limiting value is raised to $\frac{3}{4}$.

Chapter 8

MULTIPLE CHANNELS, INFINITE QUEUES

INSTEAD OF INCREASING the service rate of the single service channel, we can improve the capacity of the service facility by adding channels in parallel. In some ways this procedure has advantages; it reduces the size of the queue in comparison to the number in the system, and thus in many cases reduces the mean delay in queue, or else it enables one to run the facility nearer full utilization (ρ nearer 1) before the queue gets too long. But it also has disadvantages; it does not speed up service in the individual channel, so that mean delays in service are *not* reduced. In other words, the advantages of multiple-channel service are chiefly to the service facility and the disadvantages are mostly to the customer, the arriving unit. As with single-channel facilities, there are cases for which the incoming units have to join the queue, no matter what its size, so it is profitable to examine the infinite-queue, multiple-channel system in some detail.

Exponential Channels

We have already (see Eq. 4.1) touched on the multiple exponential channel case. Reference to Eq. 4.2 shows that for M exponential channels, all alike, the state probabilities are

$$P_n = P_0(\rho M)^n/n! \qquad (0 \leq n \leq M)$$
$$= P_0\rho^n M^M/M! \qquad (n \geq M) \tag{8.1}$$

where $\rho = (\lambda/M\mu)$ is the utilization factor for the whole facility, the mean fraction of channels busy. Using the functions defined in Eq. 4.3 and given in the tables (see Appendix), we can easily show that for the infinite-queue case

$$P_0 = [(1-\rho)\, e^{-\rho M}/D_{M-1}(\rho M)] \rightarrow \begin{cases} 1-\rho M & (\rho M \ll 1) \\ (1-\rho)M!/M^M & (\rho \rightarrow 1) \end{cases}$$

$$L_q = \sum_{m=1}^{\infty} m P_{m+M} = [\rho\, e_M(\rho M)/(1-\rho)D_{M-1}(\rho M)]$$

$$\rightarrow \begin{cases} \rho(\rho M)^M/M & (\rho M \ll 1) \\ \rho/(1-\rho) & (\rho \rightarrow 1) \end{cases} \tag{8.2}$$

$$L = L_q + \rho M; \quad W_q = (L_q/\lambda); \quad W = (L/\lambda)$$

Figures 8.1 and 8.2 show curves of L and L_q (or of W and W_q) for various values of M. If the cost of service per channel is proportional to its rate of service, increasing the rate of service of a single channel

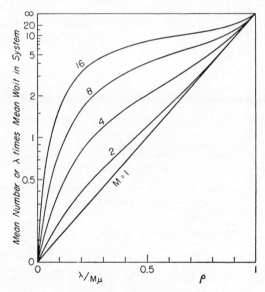

Fig. 8.1. Curves for $L = \lambda W$ as function of $\rho = (\lambda/M\mu)$ for Poisson arrivals, M exponential channels, single queue.

by a factor of M will cost the same amount as increasing the number of channels to M, keeping the rate of each unchanged; and different facilities, for different values of M, will have the same cost of operation if they have the same values of ρ (assuming arrival rates λ are the same). A comparison of the curves of Fig. 8.1 shows that, for a given value of ρ, increasing M *decreases* L_q but *increases* L. Therefore, *if* operating costs are proportional to rate of service, so that two slow channels cost as much as one twice as fast, whenever the most important requirement is to keep queue length down it is best to have many channels, even if each is slow; but whenever it is more important to keep *total* delay time W a minimum, it is better to have a single high-speed channel. If relationships between costs and M and ρ are more complicated than this, other conclusions may of course result.

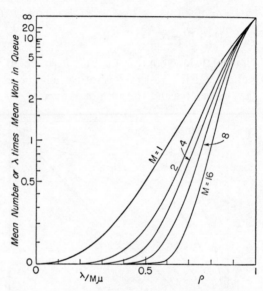

Fig. 8.2. Curves for $L_q = \lambda W_q$ as function of $\rho = (\lambda/M\mu)$ for Poisson arrivals, M exponential channels, single queue.

The probability that the queue is as long as or longer than a length N is

$$Q_{M+N} = \sum_{n=0}^{\infty} P_{M+N+n} = [\rho^N e_M(\rho M)/D_{M-1}(\rho M)] \qquad (8.3)$$

Values of this quantity may be obtained easily from Table VII, or else from Fig. 8.3, which displays curves of Q_M, the probability that all channels of the service facility are busy, as function of ρ for different values of M. Note that as M is increased, ρ can get nearer unity before the channels become saturated.

To find the delay-time distribution functions G and G_q, we first have to compute the probability that more than m units have their service completed in time t when all the channels are filled. The probability that not one of M exponential channels will complete service in time t

is $(e^{-\mu t})^M = e^{-M\mu t}$, where μ is the rate of each individual channel (this simple result comes about because, for Poisson arrivals, each service channel operates independently). The probability that just one service is completed in time t is the sum of the probabilities that just the first or just the second, etc., channel completed service, but no other,

$$\sum_{j=1}^{M} \mu t \, e^{-\mu t} (e^{-\mu t})^{M-1} = (M\mu t) \, e^{-M\mu t}$$

Likewise, the chance that just n units, neither more nor less, are ejected in time t turns out to be $[(M\mu t)^n/n!] \, e^{-M\mu t}$, so that the output from M

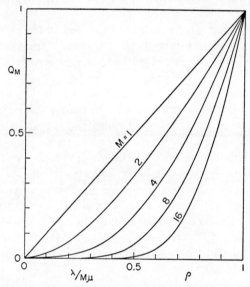

Fig. 8.3. Probability Q_M that all M channels are busy, as function of $\rho = (\lambda/M\mu)$ for Poisson arrivals, M exponential channels, single queue.

exponential channels, each of rate μ, continually filled, is Poisson, just like the output from a single exponential channel of rate $M\mu$.

Consequently, the chance that an arriving unit joins the system when there are m in the queue *and* that it is still in the queue after time T is

$$P_{M+m} \sum_{j=0}^{m} [(M\mu T)^j/j!] \, e^{-M\mu T}$$

the sum being over all numbers of units ejected *less* than the number $m+1$ which would allow the arriving unit to enter a service channel.

The average probability that an arriving unit, no matter when it arrives, will not yet be out of the queue after time T is then the sum over m.

$$
\begin{aligned}
G_q(T) &= \sum_{m=0}^{\infty} P_{M+m} \sum_{j=0}^{m} [(M\mu T)^j/j!] \ e^{-M\mu T} \\
&= P_0[(\rho M)^M/M!] \sum_{j=0}^{\infty} [(M\mu T)^j/j!] \ e^{-M\mu T} \sum_{m=j}^{\infty} \rho^m \\
&= Q_M \ e^{\mu M(\rho-1)T}
\end{aligned}
\tag{8.4}
$$

where $\qquad Q_M = [e_M(\rho M)/D_{M-1}(\rho M)] \qquad$ (See Table VII)

is the probability that all channels are busy and where $\rho = (\lambda/\mu M)$. We note again that W_q equals the integral of G_q over T from zero to infinity, in other words that G_q is related to W_q in the same way that S_0 is to T_s (see Eq. 2.2).

The distribution function for length of stay in the system (queue plus service) is a bit more complicated. In the first place the unit, once it is in a service channel, travels toward the exit at a mean rate μ, whereas it traveled at a mean rate $M\mu$ when it was in the queue. To find out the distribution in time for the whole process, we must combine the two processes. If the probability that an arriving unit will enter a service channel a time between y and $y+dy$ after it enters the queue is $g(y) \, dy = -[dG_q(y)/dy] \, dy$, and if the probability that a unit will complete its service at a time between x and $x+dx$, if it has started service at a time y, is $\mu \, e^{-\mu(x-y)} \, dx$, then the probability that a unit will enter the queue at $t=0$ and will emerge from the service channel a time between x and $x+dx$ later is

$$
\int_0^x g(y) \, dy \cdot \mu \, e^{-\mu(x-y)} \, dx
$$

and the probability that the unit will not yet have emerged from *the system* a time T after it enters *the queue* is

$$
\int_T^{\infty} dx \int_0^x g(y) \, dy \, \mu \, e^{-\mu(x-y)}
$$

But this is not $G(T)$, for there is a chance that an arriving unit does not find a queue to join, but can enter a service channel immediately. In fact, the probability that this occurs is $(1-Q_M)$, and the probability

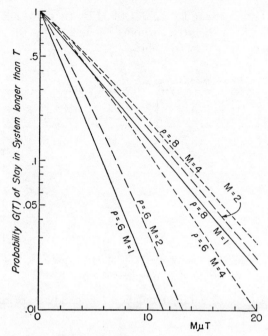

Fig. 8.4. Probability $G(T)$ of a delay longer than T, as a function of $M\mu T$, for different values of $\rho = (\lambda/M\mu)$ and M, for Poisson arrivals, M exponential channels.

that such a unit is not through with service after time T is $e^{-\mu T}$. Therefore,

$$G(T) = (1 - Q_M)\, e^{-\mu T} + \mu(\mu M - \lambda)Q_M \int_T^\infty dx\, e^{-\mu x} \int_0^x dy\, e^{[\lambda - (M-1)\mu]y} \qquad (8.5)$$

$$= \{[(M-1)\mu - \lambda + \mu Q_M]\, e^{-\mu T} - \mu Q_M\, e^{(\lambda - \mu M)T}\} / [(M-1)\mu - \lambda]$$

We note that the integral of $G(T)$ over T from 0 to ∞ is equal to W. Plots of $G(T)$ for a few values of ρ and M are given in Fig. 8.4.

Effects of Arrival-Time Distribution

We next should investigate the effect of arrival statistics on the results, by considering Erlang arrivals to a facility of M exponential channels, with an infinite queue allowed. The arrangement to simulate this case is diagrammed in Fig. 8.5, having an arrival-timing channel of l phases and M exponential service channels in parallel. The queue is joined by all arrivals, and the queue discipline is first-come-first-served.

The states of the system can be described by two integers (s,n), with s giving the phases of the arrival-timing channel and n the total number of units in queue and service facility.

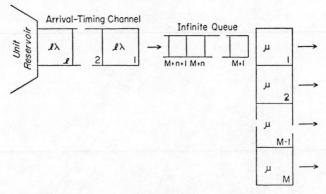

Fig. 8.5. Representation of a system of M exponential channels with l-Erlang arrivals, given in Eqs. 8.6.

The equations of detailed balance for steady-state operation are analogous to those of Eq. 7.31.

$$\mu P_{1,1} - l\lambda P_{1,0} = 0; \quad l\lambda P_{s-1,0} + \mu P_{s,1} - l\lambda P_{s,0} = 0$$

$$l\lambda P_{l,n-1} + (n+1)\mu P_{1,n+1} - (l\lambda + n\mu)P_{1,n} = 0$$
$$l\lambda P_{s-1,n} + (n+1)\mu P_{s,n+1} - (l\lambda + n\mu)P_{s,n} = 0 \qquad (0 < n < M) \quad (8.6)$$

$$l\lambda P_{l,n-1} + M\mu P_{1,n+1} - (l\lambda + M\mu)P_{1,n} = 0$$
$$l\lambda P_{s-1,n} + M\mu P_{s,n+1} - (l\lambda + M\mu)P_{s,n} = 0 \qquad (M \leq n)$$

The queue equations, the last two, can be solved by setting $P_{s,n} = u^{nl+s}B$, as in Chapter 7, and obtaining the secular equation

$$u^{l+1} - (l\rho+1)u + l\rho = 0; \quad \rho = (\lambda/M\mu)$$

which is factored into $u-1=0$ and

$$u^l + u^{l-1} + \cdots + u - l\rho = 0 \qquad (8.7)$$

which is the same as Eq. 7.34. Only one root of this equation is less than unity if $\rho < 1$. Call this root v. We then have

$$P_{s,n} = v^{(n-M)l+s}P_{l,M-1} \qquad (n \geq M) \quad (8.8)$$

The state probabilities for $n < M$ can then be determined from the initial equations, the first of Eqs. 8.6.

We will only solve in detail the case $l = M = 2$, to show how it goes. The single root less than unity here is

$$v = \sqrt{2\rho + \tfrac{1}{4}} - \tfrac{1}{2} \xrightarrow[\rho \to 0]{} 2\rho; \quad \xrightarrow[\rho \to 1]{} 1 - \tfrac{2}{3}(1-\rho)$$

so
$$P_{1,0} = \frac{v + \tfrac{1}{2}}{8\rho^2} P_{2,1}; \quad P_{1,1} = \frac{v + \tfrac{1}{2}}{2\rho} P_{2,1}$$

$$P_{1,n} = v^{2n-3} P_{2,1} \qquad\qquad (n > 1)$$

$$P_{2,0} = \frac{2\rho + \tfrac{1}{2} + v}{8\rho^2} P_{2,1}; \quad P_{2,n} = v^{2n-2} P_{2,1} \qquad (n \geq 1) \quad (8.9)$$

$$P_0 = \frac{\rho + \tfrac{1}{2} + v}{4\rho^2} P_{2,1}; \quad P_1 = \frac{2\rho + \tfrac{1}{2} + v}{2\rho} P_{2,1}$$

$$P_n = \frac{2\rho + 1 + v}{2\rho} v^{2n-2} P_{2,1} \qquad\qquad (n > 1)$$

where
$$P_{2,1} = \frac{8\rho^2(1 - v^2)}{8\rho^2 + 6\rho + 1 + v}$$

The constant $P_{2,1}$ is determined from the requirement that the sum of all the P's is equal to unity. The quantity P_n is the probability $P_{1,n} + P_{2,n}$ that there are n units in queue plus service, irrespective of the state of the arrival-timing channel.

The mean number in the system, L and the mean number in queue L_q (from which can be obtained the mean delay W and W_q on dividing by λ) are

$$L_q = \frac{4\rho^2[2\rho(2\rho - 1) + v]}{(1-\rho)[(4\rho + 1)(2\rho + 1) + v]} \to \begin{cases} 64\rho^5 & (\rho \to 0) \\ \tfrac{3}{4}(1-\rho)^{-1} & (\rho \to 1) \end{cases} \quad (8.10)$$

$$L = L_q + 2\rho$$

These formulas are to be compared with $L = 2\rho/(1 - \rho^2)$, $L_q = 2\rho^3/(1 - \rho^2)$ obtained from Eq. 8.2 for the same two-channel exponential service but with Poisson arrivals, and with Eqs. 7.42 for the single-channel $l = 2$ case. It is seen that the increased regularity of arrivals in the present example has reduced the values of L and L_q over most of the range of ρ. This is shown graphically in Fig. 8.6.

The delay-time distributions may be obtained by methods quite analogous to those used in obtaining Eqs. 7.40. We will not go through the details here.

The effect of hyper-Poisson arrivals may also be computed for the multiple-channel case, by using the techniques of Eq. 7.56 *et seq*. The results show that the increased irregularity of arrivals *increases* the

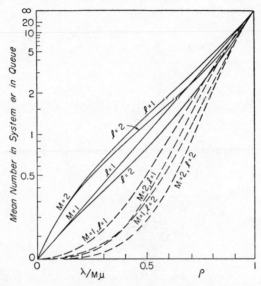

Fig. 8.6. Curves for L (solid lines) and L_q (dashed lines) as functions of $\rho = (\lambda/M\mu)$ for M exponential channels ($M = 1$ or 2) for two different arrival distributions, $l = 1$ (Poisson) and $l = 2$.

values of L and L_q over those of Eq. 8.2 for Poisson arrivals, in contrast to the results for a decrease in irregularity of arrivals, such as for Erlang ($k > 1$) arrivals.

Effects of Service-Time Distributions

We should also indicate how one computes the effect of varying *service-time* distribution in the multiple-channel case. To see what happens if the service times are more regular than for the exponential distribution, we can set up the equations for M channels, each with k phases (see Eq. 5.1) and of rate μ. As with the M exponential phases, the average service capacity is then $M\mu$ and the utilization factor is $\rho = (\lambda/M\mu)$. The state of the system is then given by the number n in the system (queue plus channels) plus the integers i_m, each giving the particular phase in which the unit in the mth channel happens to be, for m from 1 to M (we remember that phase k is the first phase entered by a unit coming into the channel, 1 the last phase before exit). The rate of service of each phase is $k\mu$, so that the mean rate for k in sequence is μ.

However each of the M channels is equivalent to any other, so we need not distinguish *which* channel has the unit in its fourth phase, for example; we need only note *how many* channels have a unit in the fourth phase, and so on. The state probabilities can be written $p(n;s_1,s_2,\cdots,s_k)$, with s_i being the number of channels having a unit in the ith phase, so that $\Sigma s_i = n$ if $n < M$ and $\Sigma s_i = M$ if $n \geq M$. Referring to the discussion preceding Eq. 5.5, we see that the equations of detailed balance for this system, for infinite possible queue, are

$$(1-\delta_{0s_k})\lambda p(n-1;s_1,\cdots,s_k-1)$$
$$+(s_1+1)k\mu\, p(n+1;s_1+1,s_2,\cdots,s_k)$$
$$+\sum_{i=1}^{k-1}(1-\delta_{0s_i})(s_{i+1}+1)k\mu\, p(n;s_1,\cdots,s_i-1,s_{i+1}+1,\cdots,s_k)$$
$$-(\lambda+nk\mu)p(n;s_1,\cdots,s_k)=0 \quad (M>n=\Sigma s_i)$$

$$(1-\delta_{0s_k})[\lambda p(M-1;s_1,\cdots,s_k-1)$$
$$+(s_1+1)k\mu\, p(M+1;s_1+1,s_2,\cdots,s_k-1)]$$
$$+\sum_{i=1}^{k-1}(1-\delta_{0s_i})(s_{i+1}+1)k\mu\, p(M;s_1,\cdots,s_i-1,s_{i+1}+1,\cdots,s_k) \quad (8.11)$$
$$-(\lambda+Mk\mu)p(n;s_1,\cdots,s_k)=0 \quad (M=n=\Sigma s_i)$$

$$\lambda p(n-1;s_1,\cdots,s_k)$$
$$+(1-\delta_{0s_k})(s_1+1)k\mu\, p(n+1;s_1+1,s_2,\cdots,s_{k-1},s_k-1)$$
$$+\sum_{i=1}^{k-1}(1-\delta_{0s_i})(s_{i+1}+1)k\mu\, p(n;s_1,\cdots,s_i-1,s_{i+1}+1,\cdots,s_k)$$
$$-(\lambda+Mk\mu)p(n;s_1,\cdots,s_k)=0 \quad (n>M=\Sigma s_i)$$

For large M or large k or both, these equations become quite tedious to solve algebraically; in fact, it usually is more convenient to solve the problem numerically on a digital computing machine. Some such methods will be discussed in a second monograph; at present we will content ourselves with working out the case of $M=2$, $k=2$ by the methods we have developed heretofore.

For $M=2$, $k=2$ the state probabilities $p(n;s_1,s_2)$ are characterized by three digits: n the number of units in the system (queue plus channel), s_1, and s_2 the number of channels having a unit in phase 1 or 2 respectively (s_1 and s_2 can have the values 0, 1 or 2). The set of equations for the p's is then

$$2\mu p(1;10) - \lambda p(0;00) = 0$$

$$2\mu p(1;01) + 4\mu p(2;20) - (\lambda+2\mu)p(1;10) = 0$$

$$\lambda p(0;00) + 2\mu p(2;11) - (\lambda+2\mu)p(1;01) = 0$$

$$2\mu p(2;11) - (\lambda+4\mu)p(2;20) = 0$$

$$\lambda p(1;10) + 4\mu p(3;20) + 4\mu p(2;02) - (\lambda+4\mu)p(2;11) = 0 \qquad (8.12)$$

$$\lambda p(1;01) + 2\mu p(3;11) - (\lambda+4\mu)p(2;02) = 0$$

$$\lambda p(n-1;20) + 2\mu p(n;11) - (\lambda+4\mu)p(n;20) = 0$$

$$\lambda p(n-1;11) + 4\mu p(n+1;20) + 4\mu p(n;02) - (\lambda+4\mu)p(n;11) = 0$$

$$\lambda p(n-1;02) + 2\mu p(n+1;11) - (\lambda+4\mu)p(n;02) = 0$$

We first obtain equations for the generating functions,

$$F_{20}(z) = \sum_{n=2}^{\infty} z^n p(n;20); \quad F_{11}(z) = zp(1;10) + \sum_{n=2}^{\infty} z^n p(n;11)$$

$$F_{02} = p(0;00) + zp(1;01) + \sum_{n=2}^{\infty} z^n p(n;02)$$

by multiplying the second, third, and fourth equation of Eqs. 8.12 by z, the last three equations by z^n, and adding one term in each trio together, giving

$$(1+\theta-\theta z)F_{20} + \tfrac{1}{2}F_{11} = -\tfrac{1}{2}zp(1;10)$$

$$-(1/z)F_{20} + (1+\theta-\theta z)F_{11} - F_{02} = \tfrac{1}{2}zp(1;10) - p(0;00) - \tfrac{1}{2}zp(1;01)$$

$$-(1/2z)F_{11} + (1+\theta-\theta z)F_{02} = p(0;00) + \tfrac{1}{2}zp(1;01)$$

where
$$\theta = (\lambda/4\mu) = (\rho/2)$$

These equations may be solved to obtain expressions for the three F's and, more useful, the sum of the three, the complete generating function $F(z)$

$$= F_{20} + F_{11} + F_{02}$$

$$= \frac{[1+(1+\theta)z-\theta z^2]p(1;10) + (4+2\theta-2\theta z)[p(0;00) + \tfrac{1}{2}zp(1;01)]}{4(1+\theta-\theta z)[1-(2\theta+\theta^2)z+\theta^2 z^2]} \qquad (8.13)$$

Since more than one initial p is involved in this expression, we cannot yet obtain their value by setting $F(1) = 1$. We have to use the first four equations of Eqs. 8.12 to enable us to express $p(1;10)$ and $p(1;01)$ in terms of $p(0;00)$ (which we might as well call P_0).

$$p(1;10) = 2\theta P_0; \quad p(1;01) = \frac{4\theta + 6\theta^2 + 4\theta^3}{2 + 3\theta} P_0 \qquad (8.14)$$

Substituting these into Eq. 8.13, setting $z = 1$ and requiring $F(1)$ to equal unity results in a determination of P_0:

$$P_0 = \frac{(2 + 3\theta)(1 - 2\theta)}{2 + 7\theta + 6\theta^2 + 2\theta^3} = p(0;00) \qquad (8.15)$$

We can now differentiate F with respect to z and then set $z = 1$, to obtain the mean number in the system and the mean queue length:

$$L = \frac{16\theta + 25\theta^2 - 14\theta^3 - 22\theta^4 - 8\theta^5}{2(1 - 2\theta)(2 + 7\theta + 6\theta^2 + 2\theta^3)} \quad (\theta = \lambda/4\mu = \rho/2)$$

$$\rightarrow 2\rho \quad (\rho \rightarrow 0); \quad \rightarrow \frac{3}{4(1 - \rho)} \quad (\rho \rightarrow 1) \qquad (8.16)$$

$$L_q = L - 4\theta; \quad W = (L/\lambda); \quad W_q = (L_q/\lambda)$$

which are to be compared with Eqs. 8.10 for Erlang arrivals. The greater regularity in service reduces queue length, as does greater regularity in arrivals. The comparison with two exponential channels is shown in Fig. 8.7.

To go much further, we must calculate the individual state probabilities. To obtain them we substitute

$$p(n;20) = B_{20} w^{n-1}; \quad p(n;11) = B_{11} w^{n-1}$$

$$p(n;02) = B_{02} w^{n-1}$$

into the last three equations of Eqs. 8.12, obtaining

$$(w\theta + w - \theta)B_{20} - \tfrac{1}{2}w B_{11} = 0$$

$$-w^2 B_{20} + (w\theta + w - \theta)B_{11} - w B_{02} = 0 \qquad (8.17)$$

$$\tfrac{1}{2}w^2 B_{11} + (w\theta + w - \theta)B_{02} = 0$$

and the secular equation

$$(w - 1)[w(1 + \theta) - \theta][w^2 - (2\theta + \theta^2)w + \theta^2] = 0 \qquad (8.18)$$

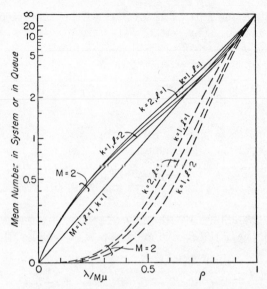

Fig. 8.7. Curves for L (solid lines) and L_q (dashed lines) against $\rho = (\lambda/M\mu)$ for $M = 2$ for different arrival and service distributions. Curve marked $M = 1$ is the curve for L for a single exponential channel for Poisson arrivals, for comparison. Compare also with Figs. 8.6, 8.1 and 8.2.

The three roots of this equation having magnitude smaller than unity (for $0 \le \theta < \tfrac{1}{2}$) are

$$w_0 = \theta/(1+\theta); \quad w_+ = \theta + \tfrac{1}{2}\theta^2 + \tfrac{1}{2}\sqrt{\theta^2 + 4\theta}$$

$$w_- = \theta + \tfrac{1}{2}\theta^2 - \tfrac{1}{2}\sqrt{\theta^2 + 4\theta}$$

(8.19)

Substituting these back into Eqs. 8.17, we obtain

$$p(n;20) = B_0 w_0{}^{n-1} + B_+ w_+{}^{n-1} + B_- w_-{}^{n-1}$$

$$p(n;11) = B_+\left(\frac{2w_+}{\theta} - 2\right)w_+{}^{n-1} + B_-\left(\frac{2w_-}{\theta} - 2\right)w_-{}^{n-1}$$

$$p(n;02) = B_0 w_0{}^n + B_+ w_+{}^n + B_- w_-{}^n \qquad (n > 1)$$

(8.20)

$$P_n = B_0(w_0+1)w_0{}^{n-1} + B_+\left(\frac{2+\theta}{\theta}w_+ - 1\right)w_+{}^{n-1}$$

$$+ B_-\left(\frac{2+\theta}{\theta}w_- - 1\right)w_-{}^{n-1}$$

where $P_n = p(n;20) + p(n;11) + p(n;02)$ is the probability that there are n units in the system (for $n > 1$).

By comparing with the second trio of equations in Eqs. 8.12, we see that they correspond to the third trio if we set

$$p(1;20) = 0; \quad p(1;11) = p(1;10); \quad p(1;02) = p(1;01)$$

and since values of $p(1;10)$ and $p(1;01)$ are known, we can consider these as initial equations to determine the values of B_0, B_+ and B_-. Thus we see that $B_0 = -B_+ - B_-$ and

$$\tfrac{1}{2}\theta p(1;10) = (w_+ - \theta)B_+ + (w_- - \theta)B_-$$

$$p(1;01) = \left(w_+ - \frac{\theta}{1+\theta}\right)B_+ + \left(w_- - \frac{\theta}{1+\theta}\right)B_-$$

so that

$$B_0 = \frac{1+\theta}{\theta^2}[\tfrac{1}{2}\theta p(1;10) - p(1;01)] = -\frac{(1+\theta)(2+\theta)^2}{\theta(2+3\theta)}P_0$$

$$B_+ = \frac{P_0}{2\theta(2+3\theta)}\left[(1+\theta)(2+\theta)^2 - \frac{4\theta^2(1+\theta) - \theta^4(1-\theta)}{\sqrt{\theta^2+4\theta}}\right] \quad (8.21)$$

$$B_- = \frac{P_0}{2\theta(2+3\theta)}\left[(1+\theta)(2+\theta)^2 + \frac{4\theta^2(1+\theta) - \theta^4(1-\theta)}{\sqrt{\theta^2+4\theta}}\right]$$

where we have already found the value of P_0 (see Eq. 8.15).

From these expressions it is possible to compute Q_N and the delay-time distribution functions G and G_q. The formulas are sufficiently complicated so that little is learned by setting them down. These functions, and the results for more channels and/or higher Erlang service distributions, are best computed numerically on a high-speed digital computer. Tables of L, Q and G for various values of M and k will be published in a later monograph.

Chapter **9**

QUEUE DISCIPLINE
AND PRIORITIES

[handwritten: Que Up First Come - First served]

HERETOFORE it has been assumed that when a unit is in the queue it stays in its place, behind the previous arrivals and ahead of the subsequent ones, until it comes to the head of the line, when it enters the service facility at the next opening. But actual queues do not always behave like this. If the arriving units are machines to be repaired, the service facility (repair crew) may have criteria for "first served" other than that of "first come." They may pick at random among those waiting, or at least pick without regard to when the unit entered the queue. If the arriving units are messages to be sent over a communication channel, some of the messages may be priority messages that are to be sent before any waiting, non-priority message is sent. In this section we will examine the effects of various rules of queue discipline on the general behavior of the system and on the delays suffered by various units.

In many cases the change in queue discipline does not change the overall dynamics of the system. The probability that n units are in the system is the same; the mean number of units present, regardless of priority, is the same, and so on. It is only the individual history of particular units which is affected, not the average behavior of all.

Single Channel, Random Access to Service

As a simple example, to introduce these ideas, we consider a single exponential service channel of rate μ and Poisson arrival distribution with rate λ, with every arriving unit staying in the queue until served. We analyzed this system earlier, assuming first-come-first-served discipline (see Eq. 7.5), and found that the probability that n units are in the system is $\rho^n(1-\rho)$, and that the mean number in the queue is

116

$\rho^2/(1-\rho)$ where $\rho = (\lambda/\mu)$. A little thought will convince one that these same state probabilities and mean numbers will still hold for other queue disciplines, as long as (1) all arrivals stay in the queue until served; (2) the service-time distribution of all classes of units is the same, with mean rate μ; (3) before it starts service on another, the service channel completes service on a unit received in service; and (4) the service channel always admits another unit, if *any* are waiting, as soon as it finishes with the previous one. If the service unit chooses its next unit for service by some rule other than first-come-first-served, the mean waits W and the waiting-time distributions G may differ from those of Eqs. 7.5, but the expressions for P_n and the L's will be the same as long as these four rules hold.

To show this, suppose that the service channel chose at random from the units in the queue, rather than picking the one at the front of the line. This model is more like the situation encountered in many retail stores, where those waiting for service have no place to "queue up," than is the assumption of first-come-first-served. It also corresponds fairly closely to a ticket reservation office where reservations are made by telephone, where if a person desiring a reservation finds the office's phone busy, he waits a while and tries again; if several people are trying, the one who happens to call first after the number is free is the next one served.

When the service facility picks at random from the queue in choosing the next unit to service, the four conditions mentioned two paragraphs back are satisfied, so the formulas for P_n and the L's given in Eqs. 7.5 are still valid, but we may need to work out new formulas for the W's and G's. To find them it is advisable to calculate the probability $q_n(t)$ that a given unit, which arrived when n other units were already in the queue, is still in the queue a time t after arrival. This is a conditional probability that must be computed from its equation for time dependence. Such an equation must be set up in a rather different way than Eq. 3.1, which has been the model for our equations of detailed balance. Here we are dealing with a specifically time-dependent probability, moreover one which is related to the state n at its initial instant, not throughout the interval t; n is the number of units in the queue *just before* the unit under study (let us call it the *tagged* unit) joins. If the tagged unit that joined the n others stays in the queue for a while, it certainly will not be in a queue of length $n+1$ for all of that while, and the chance that the queue meantime has changed to a length m is a quite messy thing to work out.

Luckily it is not necessary to work it out, for we can find the dependence of q_n on t by varying the *beginning* of the interval t rather than its end. Let us ask what q would become if the tagged unit joined the queue an instant dt later. The interval of time to the end would then be $t-dt$ instead of t. And in this instant dt, three things may happen (at least to the first order in dt): (1) another unit may arrive (transition probability λdt), in which case the chance for survival in the queue will be $q_{n+1}(t-dt)$; (2) a unit, *not the tagged one* (otherwise the tagged one would not be in the queue at the end of dt), may be taken into service (transition probability $\mu n/n+1$ corresponding to the randomness of choice), in which case the chance for survival is $q_{n-1}(t-dt)$; and (3) neither of these events will occur in dt (transition probability $1-\mu dt-\lambda dt$) in which case the chance for survival is $q_n(t-dt)$. The equation for the time dependence of the q's is then

$$q_n(t) = \mu dt \frac{n}{n+1} q_{n-1}(t-dt) + \lambda dt\, q_{n+1}(t-dt) + q_n(t-dt)(1-\mu dt-\lambda dt)$$

which becomes $\quad \dfrac{d}{dx} q_n = \dfrac{n}{n+1} q_{n-1} + \rho q_{n+1} - (1+\rho) q_n \qquad (9.1)$

where $x=\mu t$, and where for $n=0$ the term in q_{n-1} is not present. These simultaneous equations must be solved, subject to initial conditions.

The initial conditions, of course, are that $q_n(0)=1$; it is certain that if the tagged unit joins a queue, it will be in the queue after a zero-length interval of time. Also, since we are assuming the service facility is not·saturated, we can be sure the tagged unit will eventually get served; in other words $q_n(\infty)=0$. But since it will take longer for the arriving unit to get to service the longer the queue it joins, we can see that $q_n(x) \to 1$ as $n \to \infty$ for x not infinite.

If we can compute the q's, we can calculate the time-distribution of delay in queue for this random-service case. For $G_q(t)$ must be the sum of the probabilities $q_n(t)$ that the unit is still in the queue after time t, if it entered when n were in the queue, multiplied by the probability that the unit would find a queue of length n when it arrived, summed over n:

$$G_q(t) = (1-\rho) \sum_{n=0}^{\infty} \rho^{n+1} q_n(t)$$

and the mean stay in queue is the integral of G_q over the whole range of t from 0 to ∞. We have used the results of Eqs. 7.5 for the probability P_{n+1} that there are n units in the queue; we said earlier this was allowable.

The *mean* stay in queue can be obtained without knowing the specific dependence of G_q on t. For

$$W_q = \int_0^\infty G_q(t)\, dt = \frac{1-\rho}{\mu} \sum_{n=0}^\infty \rho^{n+1} W_{nq}; \quad W_{nq} = \int_0^\infty q_n\, dx$$

However, if we multiply Eq. 9.1 by $(n+1)\rho^{n+1}$, integrate both sides over x from 0 to ∞, and sum over n from 0 to ∞, we have

$$\sum_{n=0}^\infty (n+1)\rho^{n+1} \int_0^\infty dq_n = \sum_{n=0}^\infty (n+1)\rho^{n+2} W_{nq}$$

$$+ \sum_{n=1}^\infty n\rho^{n+1} W_{nq} - \sum_{n=0}^\infty (n+1)(1+\rho)\rho^{n+1} W_{nq}$$

$$= -\sum_{n=0}^\infty (n+1)\rho^{n+1} = \frac{-\rho}{(1-\rho)^2} = -\sum_{n=0}^\infty \rho^{n+1} W_{nq}$$

so that, as always,

$$W_q = \rho/\mu(1-\rho) = L_q/\lambda \tag{9.2}$$

Therefore, although $G_q(t)$ for random-exit queue is not equal to the corresponding function for delay in queue, given in Eqs. 7.5 for a first-come-first-served queue, nevertheless the *mean* wait W_q in queue has the same value for both kinds of queue discipline.

Computation of G_q is not simple. We can define the function

$$Q(t) = (1-\rho) \sum_{n=0}^\infty \rho^n q_n(t); \quad Q(0) = 1 \tag{9.3}$$

which is the probability that a unit, if it does have to join a queue, will be in the queue after time t, and from which, by multiplication by ρ in this one-channel case, we can obtain G_q. Successive differentiation of Eqs. 9.1 enables us to obtain eventually a power series in $x = \mu t$:

$$Q(t) \simeq 1 + x\left(\frac{1-\rho}{\rho}\right) \ln(1-\rho) + x^2(1-\rho)\left[1 + \left(\frac{1-\rho}{2\rho}\right) \ln(1-\rho)\right] - \cdots$$

but a more useful approximation, fairly accurate for all values of t when $\rho < 0.7$, is

$$Q(t) \simeq \tfrac{1}{2}\alpha\, e^{-\alpha(1-\rho)\mu t} + \tfrac{1}{2}\beta\, e^{-\beta(1-\rho)\mu t}$$

$$\alpha = 1 + \sqrt{\tfrac{1}{2}\rho}; \quad \beta = 1 - \sqrt{\tfrac{1}{2}\rho} \tag{9.4}$$

Comparison with the corresponding conditional probability $e^{-(1-\rho)\mu t}$ from Eqs. 7.5 shows that the $Q(t)$ for random service choice drops more rapidly at first, more slowly later, than does the $Q(t)$ for first-come-first-served queue discipline.

Figure 9.1 gives curves for $Q(t)$, calculated from more accurate formulas than Eq. 9.4, plotted on semilog scale to show the behavior for large t. The curve marked $\rho = 0$ is that for $Q = e^{-(1-\rho)\mu t}$, corresponding

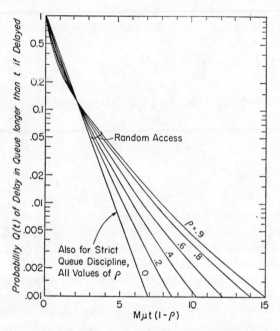

Fig. 9.1. Delay in queue for random access to service. Curves of $Q(t)$, probability of delay in queue longer than t if there is a delay at all, for M exponential channels, random access, as a function of $M\mu t(1-\rho)$ for various values of $\rho = (\lambda/M\mu)$. Curve marked $\rho = 0$ is also the curve for $Q(t)$ for strict queue discipline, for any value of ρ. Delay-time distribution in queue $G_q(t)$ equals $Q_M Q(t)$. See Eqs. 9.4, 8.4 and 7.5.

to Eq. 7.5, for strict queue discipline. Evidently if the system is near saturation (ρ near 1), an arriving unit at first has a *better* chance to get served if the service channel picks its next servee at random rather than first-in-line; but if the unit is not lucky enough to get picked soon and has to wait a while, its chance of getting served is soon *worse* than it would have been if queue discipline had been maintained. When mean queue lengths are long, breaking queue discipline shortens the wait of a few lucky ones but lengthens the wait of the unlucky ones, so that the *mean* wait is the same as if discipline had not been broken. Another way of saying this is that the mean variance of waiting times in queue is greater for random service choice than it is for strict queue discipline, though the mean value is the same.

It should be noted that our arguments about units arriving and being served, which led to Eqs. 9.1, would have been the same if the service facility had been multi-channel, as long as the M channels were exponential ones, except of course that the utilization factor ρ would be $(\lambda/M\mu)$ instead of (λ/μ). Consequently, the conditional probability $Q(t)$ plotted in Fig. 9.1 is suitable for a queue in front of a service facility of M similar exponential channels, each of service rate μ, if the ρ labeling the curves is set equal to $(\lambda/M\mu)$. The waiting-time distribution $G_q(t)$ is then obtained by multiplying Q by the probability Q_M that M or more units are in the system (that is, that all channels are busy). This result should be compared with Eqs. 8.4 for the first-come-first-served case.

Single Channel with Priorities

Next we turn to the effect of priorities. Suppose that a fraction α of the arriving units have the right to be served ahead of the remaining $(1-\alpha)$, though they do not have the right to displace a non-priority unit once it has gained the service facility. We assume again that arrivals are Poisson (rate $\alpha\lambda$ for priority units and rate $(1-\alpha)\lambda$ for non-priority); that the single service channel is exponential; and, to begin with, that the mean rate of service is the same, μ, for both priority and non-priority units. In this case Eqs. 7.5 hold for state probabilities and total numbers in the system, if we take no notice of priorities. As long as ρ is less than unity, there will be times when no priority units are in the system and the non-priority units can be served. We will find, however, that as ρ approaches unity, the mean number of non-priority units present increases much more rapidly than does the number of priority units. When the service rate is less than the total arrival rate but greater than the arrival rate of priority units, the system is saturated for the non-priority units but not for the priority ones; the number of priority units can still be in statistical equilibrium, though the number of non-priority units waiting for service will tend to increase indefinitely.

If we are to distinguish between the two types of arriving unit, our state probabilities must have three subscripts: the first denoting whether a priority (1) or a non-priority (2) unit is in service; the second, m, indicating how many priority units are in the system; and the third, n, giving the number of non-priority units in the system (there is also the state 0, corresponding to no units of any variety being present). Assuming that type 1 units are chosen by the service facility if any are present (therefore that the only way type 1 units can be present with a type 2 unit in service, is for the type 1 units to have arrived after service had started on the type 2 unit), and that first-come-first-served rules hold for each type of unit separately, the equations of detailed balance are

$$P_{110}+P_{201}=\rho P_0$$

$$\alpha \rho P_0+P_{120}+P_{211}=(\rho+1)P_{110}$$

$$(1-\alpha)\rho P_0+P_{111}+P_{202}-(\rho+1)P_{201}$$

$$\alpha \rho P_{1,m-1,0}+P_{1,m+1,0}+P_{2m1}=(\rho+1)P_{1m0}$$

$$(1-\alpha)\rho P_{2,0,n-1}+P_{11n}+P_{2,0,n+1}=(\rho+1)P_{20n}$$

$$(9.5)$$

$$(1-\alpha)\rho P_{1,1,n-1}+P_{12n}+P_{2,1,n+1}=(\rho+1)P_{11n}$$

$$\alpha \rho P_{2,n-1,1}=(\rho+1)P_{2m1}$$

$$\alpha \rho P_{1,m-1,n}+(1-\alpha)\rho P_{1,m,n-1}+P_{1,m+1,n}$$
$$+P_{2,m,n+1}=(\rho+1)P_{1mn} \quad (m>1;\ n>0)$$

$$\alpha \rho P_{2,m-1,n}+(1-\alpha)\rho P_{2,m,n-1}=(\rho+1)P_{2mn} \qquad (m>0;\ n>1)$$

We note that for P_{1mn}, m runs from 1 to ∞ and n from 0 to ∞, because the first subscript 1 indicates that a unit of type 1 (priority) is in service, and there must be at least one such unit present ($m>0$). The ranges are vice versa for P_{2mn}.

We already know something about these probabilities. In the first place, $P_0=1-\rho$, as indicated in Eq. 7.5. Just because we have labeled some units with a priority tag does not modify the fraction of times *no* unit is present. Also we have

$$\sum_{m=0}^{n-1}(P_{1,n-m,m}+P_{2,m,n-m})=(1-\rho)\rho^n \qquad (n>0) \quad (9.6)$$

But we are also sure, because the mean service rate is the same for both types of units, that the mean fraction of the time the service channel is working on priority items is proportional to the relative fraction α of priority arrivals and to the fraction ρ of time the channel is busy:

$$\sum_{m=1}^{\infty}\sum_{n=0}^{\infty}P_{1mn}=\alpha\rho; \quad \text{likewise} \quad \sum_{m=0}^{\infty}\sum_{n=1}^{\infty}P_{2mn}=(1-\alpha)\rho \qquad (9.7)$$

Unfortunately, to get further, even with this simple case, we must plow through a lot of algebra. The easiest approach is via the generating functions. These now are two-dimensional and can take several forms. Their definitions and properties are

$$F_{1m}(y) = \sum_{n=0}^{\infty} y^n P_{1mn}; \quad F_{2m}(y) = \sum_{n=1}^{\infty} y^n P_{2mn}$$

$$H_1(x,y) = \sum_{m=1}^{\infty} x^m F_{1m}(y); \quad H_1(1,1) = \alpha\rho$$

$$H_2(x,y) = \sum_{m=0}^{\infty} x^m F_{2m}(y); \quad H_2(1,1) = (1-\alpha)\rho$$

$$H(x,y) = H_1(x,y) + H_2(x,y) + P_0; \quad H(x,x) = \frac{P_0}{1-\rho x}; \quad H(1,1) = 1 \qquad (9.8)$$

$$\left[\frac{\partial}{\partial x} H(x,y)\right]_{x=y=1} = L_1 = L_{q1} + \alpha\rho = \alpha\lambda W_1$$

$$\left[\frac{\partial}{\partial y} H(x,y)\right]_{x=y=1} = L_2 = L_{q2} + (1-\alpha)\rho = (1-\alpha)\lambda W_2$$

$$L = L_1 + L_2 = L_q + \rho = \rho/(1-\rho); \quad P_0 = 1-\rho$$

where we have used Eqs. 9.6 and 9.7, and where we have defined the quantities L_1 and L_2 as the mean numbers of the respective units present in the system (with L_{q1} and L_{q2} as the corresponding mean numbers in the queue). The W's are the corresponding mean waits in the system.

We try going directly to the two functions H_1 and H_2. Multiplying the equations of Eqs. 9.5 by the appropriate powers of x and y and adding them in the proper ways, we finally obtain

$$\left[1 + \rho - \alpha\rho x - (1-\alpha)\rho y - \frac{1}{x}\right] H_1(x,y)$$

$$= \frac{1}{y} H_2(x,y) + \alpha\rho x P_0 - \left[F_{11}(y) + \frac{1}{y} F_{20}(y)\right]$$

$$[1 + \rho - \alpha\rho x - (1-\alpha)\rho y] H_2(x,y) = \left[F_{11}(y) + \frac{1}{y} F_{20}(y)\right] - [\rho - (1-\alpha)\rho y] P_0$$

Because of the presence of the partial sums F_{11} and F_{20}, we cannot determine H_1 and H_2 by means of the various limiting values given in

Eqs. 9.8. We can, however, by summing y^n times the equations in Eqs. 9.5 which involve $(1+\rho)P_{20n}$, obtain a relationship between F_{11} and F_{20}:

$$F_{11} = \left[1+\rho-(1-\alpha)\rho y - \frac{1}{y}\right]F_{20} + [\rho-(1-\alpha)\rho y]P_0$$

which enables us to determine H_1 and H_2 in terms of P_0 and $F_{20}(y)$.

$$[1+\rho-\alpha\rho x-(1-\alpha)\rho y]\left[1+\rho-\alpha\rho x-(1-\alpha)\rho y - \frac{1}{x}\right]H_1(x,y)$$

$$= -[1+\rho-\alpha\rho x-(1-\alpha)\rho y][\rho-\alpha\rho x-(1-\alpha)\rho y]P_0$$

$$-[1+\rho-(1-\alpha)\rho y]\left[1+\rho-\alpha\rho x-(1-\alpha)\rho y - \frac{1}{y}\right]F_{20}(y)$$

$$[1+\rho-\alpha\rho x-(1-\alpha)\rho y]H_2(x,y) = [1+\rho-(1-\alpha)\rho y]F_{20}(y) \tag{9.9}$$

$$H(x,y) = H_1+H_2+P_0 = \frac{(1-x)P_0}{1-x-\rho x(1-y-\alpha x-\alpha y)}$$

$$+ \frac{(1+\rho-\rho y+\alpha\rho y)(y-x)F_{20}(y)}{y[1+\rho-\alpha\rho x-(1-\alpha)\rho y][1-x-\rho x(1-y-\alpha x+\alpha y)]}$$

The second of these equations, when we set $y\to x\to 1$, enables us to determine that $F_{20}(1) = [(1-\alpha)\rho P_0/(1+\alpha\rho)(1-\rho)]$. When we set this and the relation $P_0 = 1-\rho$ into the third equation and again go to the limit $y\to x\to 1$, we find the whole right-hand side going to unity, as it should. We can find L_1 without knowing the dependence of F_{20} on y, and from it can find L_2 and the L_q's:

$$L_1 = \alpha\rho\frac{1+\rho-\alpha\rho}{1-\alpha\rho} \; ; \quad L_{q1} = \frac{\alpha\rho^2}{1-\alpha\rho} \; ; \quad W_{q1} = \frac{\lambda}{\mu(\mu-\alpha\lambda)}$$

$$L_2 = (1-\alpha)\rho\frac{1-\alpha\rho+\alpha\rho^2}{(1-\rho)(1-\alpha\rho)} \; ; \quad L_{q2} = \frac{(1-\alpha)\rho^2}{(1-\rho)(1-\alpha\rho)} \tag{9.10}$$

$$W_{q2} = \frac{\lambda}{(\mu-\lambda)(\mu-\alpha\lambda)}$$

Thus we can find out a great deal about the system without knowing the exact dependence of the H's on y. We might stop here to examine these results.

They are not surprising. A unit of priority 2 waits in queue longer than a unit of priority 1 by a ratio $\mu/(\mu-\lambda)$ (where λ is the *total* arrival rate and μ the common service rate). As λ approaches μ, L_2, L_{q2} and W_{q2} approach infinity, whereas the corresponding lengths and mean waits for the first priority units approach a finite limit. They go to infinity only when *their* arrival rate $\alpha\lambda$ approaches the service rate μ. This is the justification of the statements made several pages earlier. Fig. 9.2 shows typical curves for mean delay. The curves are not con-

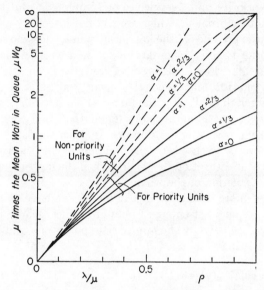

Fig. 9.2. Curves for μW_q for priority units (class 1, solid lines) and non-priority units (class 2, dashed lines) for different values of α, the mean ratio between priority and total arrivals, for a single exponential service channel with no differentiation in mean service time between class 1 and class 2 units. See Eqs. 9.10. The straight line is the curve for class 2 items with $\alpha=0$ (no class 1 unit arriving), and also for class 1 items with $\alpha=1$ (no class 2 units arriving).

tinued into the range $1<\lambda<1/\alpha$ because, although first-priority units are not yet piling up, second-priority units are accumulating continuously, so a steady state does not exist.

We also note that mean wait in queue, for the top-priority units, is longer than would obtain if *no* second-priority units were arriving. If only first-priority units were arriving, with arrival rate $\alpha\lambda$, then the mean wait in queue would be $\alpha\lambda/\mu(\mu-\alpha\lambda)$, which is smaller than the wait in the presence of second-priority units, by a factor α. The explanation is that first-priority units in the present model occasionally have to wait on a second-priority unit when it is in service. This occurs more and more often the more low-priority units are present (the smaller α is). The only way in which the first-priority units would not be delayed by the presence of lower-priority units would be if the first-priority units had *pre-emptive* priority; if an incoming high-priority unit found a lower-priority unit in service when it arrived, it would have the right to take this unit's place in service immediately, without waiting for the lower-priority unit's service to be completed. But this situation represents another problem, which we will not discuss.

Although the presence of the low-priority units does slow the progress of the high-priority units, they are not slowed as much as if they had no priority at all. For if all arriving units were treated alike (first-come-first-served for all), then the mean wait in queue would be $\lambda/\mu(\mu-\lambda)$, larger than W_{q1} by the factor $(1-\alpha\rho)/(1-\rho)$, which is near unity when $\rho \ll 1$ but is appreciably larger than unity when ρ is near unity and when α is smaller than unity. In other words, the assignment of priority appreciably speeds up the handling of the priority units when the system is near saturation ($\rho \to 1$) and when the units assigned priority are not a large fraction of the whole ($\alpha \ll 1$).

To get any more detail out of our model, we have to solve for the functions $F_{sm}(y)$, at least enough to obtain explicit solutions for $F_{20}(y)$. By multiplying Eqs. 9.5 by the appropriate power of y and then adding, we get the following:

$$[1+\rho-(1-\alpha)\rho y]F_{2,m}(y) = \alpha\rho F_{2,m-1}(y) \qquad (m>0)$$

$$\left[1+\rho-(1-\alpha)\rho y-\frac{1}{y}\right]F_{20}(y) = F_{11}(y)-[\rho-(1-\alpha)\rho y]P_0$$

$$-F_{12}(y)+[1+\rho-(1-\alpha)\rho y]F_{11}(y)-\alpha\rho P_0 = \frac{1}{y}F_{21}(y) \qquad (9.11)$$

$$-F_{1,m+1}(y)+[1+\rho-(1-\alpha)\rho y]F_{1m}(y)$$

$$-\alpha\rho F_{1,m-1}(y) = \frac{1}{y}F_{2m}(y) \qquad (m>1)$$

The first equation of this set indicates that $F_{2m}(y) = \{\alpha\rho/[1+\rho-(1-\alpha)\rho y]\}^m F_{20}(y)$. The last equation may be solved by setting $F_{1m} = Au^m + BF_{2m}$, where the second term corresponds to the particular solution and the first term corresponds to the solution of the homogeneous equation, without the F_{2m} term. The secular equation for u is

$$u^2 - [1+\rho-(1-\alpha)\rho y]u+\alpha\rho=0$$

This has two roots, one larger than unity (which is discarded), and the other

$$v(y) = \tfrac{1}{2}[1+\rho-(1-\alpha)\rho y] - \tfrac{1}{2}\sqrt{[1+\rho-(1-\alpha)\rho y]^2 - 4\alpha\rho}$$

$$\rightarrow \alpha\rho - \frac{\alpha(1-\alpha)\rho^2}{1-\alpha\rho}(1-y) \tag{9.12}$$

$$+\frac{\alpha(1-\alpha)\rho^3}{(1-\alpha\rho)^3}(1-y)^2 - \cdots \qquad (y\rightarrow 1)$$

Solving also for the particular solution, we have

$$F_{1m}(y) = Av^m - \frac{1}{y}F_{20}(y)\left[\frac{\alpha\rho}{1+\rho-(1-\alpha)\rho y}\right]^{m-1} \tag{9.13}$$

The second and third of Eqs. 9.11 are boundary conditions, enabling us to determine A and F_{20}. They are equivalent to saying that if there were functions $F_{1,0}$ and $F_{1,-1}$, expressible as above, then their values would have to be

$$F_{10}=P_0; \quad F_{1,-1}=(1/\alpha\rho)\{P_0-[1+\rho-(1-\alpha)\rho y]F_{20}\}$$

in order that the last of Eqs. 9.11 would hold for $m=1$ and 0 as well as for $m>1$. Setting these expressions into Eq. 9.13 enables us to obtain, after some algebraic gymnastics,

$$F_{20}(y) = \frac{\alpha\rho y[\rho-(1-\alpha)\rho y-v]P_0}{(v-\alpha\rho y)[1+\rho-(1-\alpha)\rho y]}$$

$$\xrightarrow[y\rightarrow 1]{} \frac{\rho(1-\alpha)P_0}{(1-\rho)(1+\alpha\rho)}\left[1-\frac{1-\alpha\rho+2\alpha\rho^3}{(1-\rho)(1-\alpha^2\rho^2)}(1-y)+\cdots\right] \tag{9.14}$$

$$A(y) = \frac{\rho(1-y)}{v-\alpha\rho y}P_0 \xrightarrow[y\rightarrow 1]{} \frac{(1-\alpha\rho)}{\alpha(1-\rho)}\left[1-\frac{(1-\alpha)\rho^2(1-y)}{(1-\rho)(1-\alpha\rho)^2}+\cdots\right]P_0$$

These expressions can then be substituted back in Eqs. 9.9 to obtain a complete expression for the combined generating function $H(x,y)$, from which, by expansion, one can obtain the state probabilities. We will not write them out explicitly, but only point out that even for this fairly simple priority situation the dependence of the individual state probabilities on ρ and m and n is not simple.

The Effect of Priorities on Average Delay

A more useful problem, but one somewhat more complicated, is the case where the type 1 units (priority) have mean service rate μ, as before, but where the type 2 units (non-priority) have mean service rate $\beta\mu$, where β can be less than or greater than unity. When β is not equal to unity, the system does not have the overall behavior of the simple system of Eq. 7.5, for we have two classes of units, with different service rates, even if priorities are not attached. In fact, in order to see the effect of priorities, we had better examine first the behavior of the system without priorities. If we do not give priorities to either type of unit, the service channel taking the μ or the $\beta\mu$ units as they come, the equations for the system are quite analogous to those of Eq. 7.29. The arrival rate for type 1 units is $\alpha\lambda$, and its service rate is μ; the arrival rate for type 2 units is $(1-\alpha)\lambda$, and its service rate is $\beta\mu$. If no priorities are attached, the equations are

$$P_{11}+\beta P_{21}=\rho P_0$$

$$\alpha\rho P_0+\alpha P_{10}+\alpha\beta P_{22}=(\rho+1)P_{11}$$

$$(1-\alpha)\rho P_0+(1-\alpha)P_{10}+(1-\alpha)\beta P_{22}=(\rho+\beta)P_{21} \qquad (9.15)$$

$$\rho P_{1,n-1}+\alpha P_{1,n+1}+\alpha\beta P_{2,n+1}=(\rho+1)P_{1n}$$

$$\rho P_{2,n-1}+(1-\alpha)P_{1,n+1}+(1-\alpha)\beta P_{2,n+1}=(\rho+\beta)P_{2n}$$

where the first subscript indicates which unit is in the service channel, and the second how many units of either sort are in the system. Note the close connection between these equations and Eqs. 7.29. Why?

A bit of ratiocination may be necessary to account for the terms $\alpha P_{1,n+1}+\alpha\beta P_{2,n+1}$ and $(1-\alpha)P_{1,n+1}+(1-\alpha)\beta P_{2,n+1}$ in these equations. These terms come from the transition from a previous state to the states $(1,n)$ or $(2,n)$ by the completion of a service. If the previous unit in service were a type 1 unit, its mean rate of completion would be μ; if the previous unit were type 2, its rate would be $\beta\mu$. In either case, when service is completed, the chance that a type 1 unit will be next in line, so that the next state will be $(1,n)$, is α; the chance that a type 2 unit is next in line is $1-\alpha$ (since the respective rates of arrival are $\alpha\lambda$ and $\lambda-\alpha\lambda$, on the average the type 1 units make up a fraction α of the queue and type 2 units make up a fraction $1-\alpha$). Therefore, the rate of transition from state $(1,n+1)$ to state $(1,n)$ is $\alpha\mu$; the rate from state $(2,n+1)$ to $(1,n)$ is $\alpha\beta\mu$; that from state $(1,n+1)$ to $(2,n)$ is $(1-\alpha)\mu$; and that from state $(2,n+1)$ to $(2,n)$ is $(1-\alpha)\beta\mu$. Since we have divided by μ to obtain Eqs. 9.15, the terms $\alpha P_{1,n+1}+\alpha\beta P_{2,n+1}$ and

$(1-\alpha)P_{1,n+1}+(1-\alpha)\beta P_{2,n+1}$ occur in the equations of detailed balance for states $(1,n)$ and $(2,n)$ respectively.

As with the solutions of Eq. 7.29, we solve for the generating functions $F_1(z)=\sum_{n=1}^{\infty}z^nP_{1n}$ and $F_2(z)=\sum_{n=1}^{\infty}z^nP_{2n}$ and obtain

$$F_1(z)=z\alpha\rho(\beta+\rho-\rho z)P_0/Q$$

$$F_2(z)=z(1-\alpha)\rho(1+\rho-\rho z)P_0/Q$$

(9.16)

where $Q=\rho(\beta+\alpha-\alpha\beta)+\beta-(\beta+1)\rho z+\rho^2 z(z-1)$, and where the probability the service channel is idle is $P_0=1-\alpha\rho-(1-\alpha)(\rho/\beta)$, an obvious generalization of the simple expression $1-\rho$ of Eqs. 7.5 for the simpler system.

By differentiating F_1, F_2 and F_1+F_2 with respect to z and setting $z=1$, we obtain the mean number in the system, the mean number in the queue, and the mean waits in queue:

$$L_1=\alpha\rho+L_{q1}; \quad L_{q1}=\alpha\rho^2\frac{1-(\beta-1)(1-\alpha)(\rho/\beta^2)}{1-\alpha\rho-(1-\alpha)(\rho/\beta)}$$

$$W_{q1}=(L_{q1}/\alpha\rho)$$

$$L_2=(1-\alpha)(\rho/\beta)+L_{q2}; \quad L_{q2}=(1-\alpha)\rho^2\frac{(1/\beta^2)+(\beta-1)\alpha(\rho/\beta^2)}{1-\alpha\rho-(1-\alpha)(\rho/\beta)}$$

(9.17)

$$L_q=\frac{\alpha\rho^2+(1-\alpha)(\rho^2/\beta^2)}{1-\alpha\rho-(1-\alpha)(\rho/\beta)} \; ; \quad W_q=(L_q/\lambda); \quad \rho=(\lambda/\mu)$$

These formulas go to the simple ones of Eqs. 7.5 when $\beta=1$, that is, when there is no difference in service between the two kinds of units. The true utilization factor, the fraction of times the service facility is busy, is not ρ but $\rho_{\text{eff}}=\rho[\alpha+(1-\alpha)(1/\beta)]$, which is greater than ρ if $\beta<1$ (if class 2 units are served slower than rate μ), is less than ρ if $\beta>1$ (if class 2 units are served faster than rate μ). In terms of the effective utilization factor, we have

$$L_q=\frac{\rho_{\text{eff}}^2}{1-\rho_{\text{eff}}}\frac{\alpha+(1-\alpha)(1/\beta^2)}{[\alpha+(1-\alpha)(1/\beta)]^2}$$

(9.18)

which has a minimum value $\rho^2/(1-\rho)$ (for constant ρ_{eff}, letting β vary) for $\beta=1$, as it should. For β less than or greater than 1, the mean number in the queue is larger for the same effective utilization factor. In other words, serving a mixed population of units cannot be as efficient as serving a uniform population.

We now wish to see whether imposing a priority on the system will improve the situation or not. We keep the same rates as above, $\alpha\lambda$ and μ for type 1 units, $(1-\alpha)\lambda$ and $\beta\mu$ for type 2 units, but now we require that the service channel take type 1 units from the queue as long as type 1 units are present. Then Eqs. 9.5 become

$$P_{110}+\beta P_{201}=\rho P_0$$

$$\alpha\rho P_0+P_{120}+\beta P_{211}=(\rho+1)P_{110}$$

$$(1-\alpha)\rho P_0+P_{111}+\beta P_{202}=(\rho+\beta)P_{201}$$

$$\alpha\rho P_{1,m-1,0}+P_{1,m+1,0}+\beta P_{2m1}=(\rho+1)P_{1m0}$$

$$(1-\alpha)\rho P_{2,0,n-1}+P_{11n}+\beta P_{2,0,n+1}=(\rho+\beta)P_{20n}$$

$$(1-\alpha)\rho P_{1,1,n-1}+P_{12n}+\beta P_{2,1,n+1}=(\rho+1)P_{11n} \tag{9.19}$$

$$\alpha\rho P_{2,m-1,1}=(\rho+\beta)P_{2m1}$$

$$\alpha\rho P_{1,m-1,n}+(1-\alpha)\rho P_{1,m,n-1}+P_{1,m+1,n}$$
$$+\beta P_{2,m,n+1}=(\rho+1)P_{1mn} \quad (m>1; n>0)$$

$$\alpha\rho P_{2,m-1,n}+(1-\alpha)\rho P_{2,m,n-1}=(\rho+\beta)P_{2mn} \quad (m>0; n>1)$$

From these we can obtain a set of equations, analogous to Eqs. 9.11, for the partial generating functions $F_{s,m}(y)$:

$$[\beta+\rho-(1-\alpha)\rho y]F_{2m}(y)=\alpha\rho F_{2,m-1}(y) \qquad (m>0)$$

$$\left[\beta+\rho-(1-\alpha)\rho y-\frac{\beta}{y}\right]F_{20}(y)=F_{11}(y)-[\rho-(1-\alpha)\rho y]P_0$$

$$-F_{12}(y)+[1+\rho-(1-\alpha)\rho y]F_{11}(y)-\alpha\rho P_0=\frac{\beta}{y}F_{21}(y) \qquad (9.20)$$

$$-F_{1,m+1}(y)+[1+\rho-(1-\alpha)\rho y]F_{1m}(y)$$
$$-\alpha\rho F_{1,m-1}(y)=\frac{\beta}{y}F_{2m}(y) \quad (m>1)$$

The relation between the successive F_{2m}'s

$$F_{2m}(y)=\{\alpha\rho/[\beta+\rho-(1-\alpha)\rho y]\}^m F_{20}(y) \tag{9.21}$$

differs from the solution of Eqs. 9.11 only in the presence of the β (instead of 1).

The last of Eqs. 9.16 can again be solved by setting $F_{1m}(y)=Au^m+BF_{2m}(y)$, where the secular equation for u is the same as for Eqs. 9.11

and the one root which can be used is the $v(y)$ given in Eq. 9.12. Therefore,

$$F_{1m}(y) = Av^m - \frac{\alpha\beta\rho F_{20}(y)}{\alpha\rho y + (\beta-1)y[\beta+\rho-(1-\alpha)\rho y]}\left[\frac{\alpha}{\beta+\rho-(1-\alpha)\rho y}\right]^{m-1}$$

The boundary conditions, in the form used before, are

$$F_{10} = P_0; \quad F_{1,-1} = (1/\alpha\rho)\{P_0 - [\beta+\rho-(1-\alpha)\rho y]F_{20}\}$$

From this we can find that

$$F_{20}(y) = y\frac{\alpha\rho + (\beta-1)[\beta+\rho-(1-\alpha)\rho y]}{[\beta+\rho-(1-\alpha)\rho y]}$$

$$\times\frac{[\rho-(1-\alpha)\rho y - v]P_0}{\beta v + \alpha\rho y + \beta(\beta-1) - (\beta-1)y[\beta+\rho-(1-\alpha)\rho y]}$$

$$A(y) = P_0 + \frac{\beta[\beta+\rho-(1-\alpha)\rho y]F_{20}}{\alpha\rho y + (\beta-1)y[\beta+\rho-(1-\alpha)\rho y]}$$

and that $P_0 = 1 - \alpha\rho - (1-\alpha)(\rho/\beta)$, as it is for the non-priorities case given in Eqs. 9.16 *et seq.* From these we can compute the expressions for all the F's and, by differentiation, obtain the individual state probabilities $P_{s,m,n}$, though the specific formulas would be quite complicated.

The probabilities that m units of type 1, no matter how many type 2 units are present, if a unit 1 or a unit 2 is in service, are

$$F_{1m}(1) = \frac{\beta(\beta+\alpha\rho-1)+\rho(1-\alpha)}{\beta(\beta+\alpha\rho-1)}(1-\alpha\rho)(\alpha\rho)^m$$

$$-\frac{\rho(1-\alpha)}{\beta+\alpha\rho-1}\left(\frac{\alpha\rho}{\beta+\alpha\rho}\right)^m \quad (9.22)$$

$$F_{2m}(1) = \frac{\rho(1-\alpha)}{\beta+\alpha\rho}\left(\frac{\alpha\rho}{\beta+\alpha\rho}\right)^m$$

From these, by summation, we can obtain the averages we wish. For example, the probability that a type 1 (priority) unit is in service is

$$\sum_{m=1}^{\infty} F_{1m}(1) = \alpha\rho$$

and

$$\sum_{m=0}^{\infty} F_{2m}(1) = (1-\alpha)\frac{\rho}{\beta}$$

is the probability of finding a type 2 (non-priority) unit in service. Both of these have the same value as if no priorities had been imposed (Eqs. 9.15). But the mean number in the system *is* changed by imposition of priorities. The mean number of type 1 units in the system is

$$\sum_{m=1}^{\infty} m[F_{1m}(1)+F_{2m}(1)] = \frac{\alpha\rho}{1-\alpha\rho}\left[1+\frac{(1-\alpha)\rho}{\beta^2}\right] = L_1$$

which is definitely different from the value given in Eq. 9.17 for the no-priority case. For one thing, the present L does not go to infinity when the effective utilization factor $\rho_{\text{eff}} = \rho[\alpha+(1-\alpha)(1/\beta)]$ goes to unity, but goes to infinity only when the factor $\alpha\rho$, having to do with arrivals and servicing of *only* type 1 units, goes to unity. This result corresponds to the results of Eqs. 9.10 for the same sort of priority arrangement, only for $\beta=1$ (no service-time difference between types of units). As mentioned there, as we approach saturation (as $\rho_{\text{eff}}\rightarrow 1$), priority units have more and more advantage over type 2 units, until at saturation, though type 2 units are piling up, saturation has not yet set in for type 1 units.

The mean number of type 2 units present may be obtained by differentiating the F's with respect to y and summing over m, or else by starting over again with the functions $G_{1n}(x) = \Sigma x^m P_{1mn}$, etc. By either method we finally obtain

$$L_1 = \alpha\rho + L_{q1}; \quad L_{q1} = \alpha\rho^2\frac{\alpha+(1-\alpha)(1/\beta^2)}{1-\alpha\rho}$$

$$L_2 = (1-\alpha)(\rho/\beta) + L_{q2}; \quad L_{q2} = \left[\frac{(1-\alpha)\rho^2}{1-\alpha\rho}\right]\frac{\alpha+(1-\alpha)(1/\beta^2)}{1-\alpha\rho-(1-\alpha)(\rho/\beta)}$$

$$L_q = L_{q1} + L_{q2} = \left[\frac{\alpha\rho^2+(1-\alpha)(\rho^2/\beta^2)}{1-\alpha\rho-(1-\alpha)(\rho/\beta)}\right]\frac{1-\alpha\rho[\alpha+(1-\alpha)(1/\beta)]}{1-\alpha\rho}$$

$$= \frac{\rho_{\text{eff}}^2}{1-\rho_{\text{eff}}}\frac{[\alpha+(1-\alpha)(1/\beta^2)]}{[\alpha+(1-\alpha)(1/\beta)]^2}\frac{1-\alpha\rho_{\text{eff}}}{1-\alpha\rho}; \quad W_{q1}=(L_{q1}/\alpha\lambda), \text{ etc.}$$

(9.23)

These should now be compared with the formulas of Eqs. 9.17, for the same system but with no priorities imposed. We see that L_{q2} in Eqs. 9.23 is larger than L_{q2} in Eqs. 9.17 for allowable values of α, β and ρ. In other words, imposition of priorities increases the mean number of non-priority units present and makes their average wait in line longer, whereas it usually shortens the queue and delay of the priority item. If the overriding requirement is to reduce delay for one particular class of unit, then this class should be given priority. This is particularly profitable if the non-urgent units (type 2) take longer to serve, on the average ($\beta < 1$).

On the other hand, it may not be important that one class of unit be favored over another; the criterion may simply be to cut down the total number of waiting units of either type, to reduce the *average wait in line of all units*. Comparison of the formulas for L_q in Eqs. 9.23 and 9.17 shows that giving priority to type 1 units changes L_q and W_q by the factor

$$\frac{1-\alpha\rho[\alpha+(1-\alpha)(1/\beta)]}{1-\alpha\rho}=\frac{1-\alpha\rho_{\text{eff}}}{1-\alpha\rho}$$

When this ratio is larger than unity, there is more waiting and more units are waiting if priorities are imposed than if no priorities are imposed; if it is less than unity, imposing priorities shortens the mean wait and reduces the mean number waiting. It is larger than unity when $\beta > 1$ (when the non-priority units can be served, on the average, *faster* than the priority units), and smaller than unity when $\beta < 1$ (when the non-priority units *take longer* to be served).

Consequently, when the desideratum is to *reduce the total number waiting* or to shorten the overall mean wait in line, then if there is any way of distinguishing, on the average, between units according to the prospective lengths of their service times, it helps to give priority to that class of units which *tends* to have the faster service rate, which has the *shorter mean service time* even if there is a wide spread in individual service times. This result is independent of the size of the ratio $\alpha/(1-\alpha)$ between the numbers of units of the two classes arriving, though of course the *degree* of advantage does depend on the value of $\alpha/(1-\alpha)$. The degree of reduction of mean wait obtained by imposing priorities depends on the numerical magnitude of $(1-\alpha\rho_{\text{eff}})/(1-\alpha\rho)$, whereas the fact that there *is* a reduction simply depends on whether the factor $(1-\alpha\rho_{\text{eff}})/(1-\alpha\rho)$ is less than unity or not.

Figure 9.3 shows how L_{q1}, L_{q2} and L_q vary with ρ, α and β. Solid lines correspond to priorities being given to type 1 units (Eqs. 9.23), whereas the dashed curves are for the same system with two classes of units with regard to service rate but with no priority distinction between them, corresponding to Eqs. 9.17. We see that the effect of priorities on length of queue is not very pronounced for these service and arrival distributions.

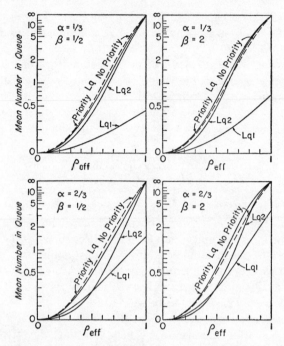

Fig. 9.3. Curves for mean total number in queue, L_q, and mean number in queue of units 1 or 2, L_{q1} and L_{q2}, for different fractional rates α of arrivals of type 1 units and for different ratios β between service rate of type 2 and that of type 1, as a function of $\rho_{eff} = (\lambda/\mu)[\alpha + (1-\alpha)(1/\beta)]$ (λ is mean total arrival rate, μ mean service rate of type 1 unit, and $\mu\beta$ service rate of type 2) when type 1 units are given priority of service. Dashed line gives L_q when no priority is imposed.

Multiple Channels, Single versus Multiple Queues

Other kinds of dependence on queue discipline are occasionally of interest. For example, suppose there are two similar exponential service channels, what queue discipline is most effective? There may be two separate queues, one in front of each channel, with no "switching lines" allowed and strict discipline required within each line. This is the case with lines of cars in front of toll booths when two are open, and it is often the case with lines in front of railway ticket windows. If arriving units (arriving at rate λ, with Poisson distribution) choose between the queues equally, at random, the system is really just two independent single-channel systems, each with arrival rate $\frac{1}{2}\lambda$ and service rate μ. The combined probability that m units are in system 1 and n in system 2 is the product of the separate probabilities, and

$$P_{mn}{}^{(2)} = (1-\rho)^2(\rho)^{m+n}; \quad L_1{}^{(2)} = L_2{}^{(2)} = \rho/(1-\rho) = \tfrac{1}{2}\lambda W^{(2)}$$

$$L^{(2)} = L_1{}^{(2)} + L_2{}^{(2)} = 2\rho/(1-\rho) \tag{9.24}$$

$$L_q{}^{(2)} = 2L_{q1}{}^{(2)} = 2\rho^2/(1-\rho) = \lambda W_q{}^{(2)}$$

where the utilization factor ρ is now $(\lambda/2\mu)$. The superscript 2 stands for the fact that there are 2 independent queues, one in front of each channel.

This is not a very efficient way of using the service facilities, for there is a chance that one channel is idle when there are units in the other queue; in fact, the probability of this occurring is $2\rho^2(1-\rho)$. These idle times can be eliminated whenever it is possible to operate a combined queue feeding from the front of a single line to whichever channel comes empty. This is the case considered in Chapter 8, and the formulas for the case of two exponential channels can be obtained from Eqs. 8.1 and 8.2:

$$P_0{}^{(1)} = (1-\rho)/(1+\rho)$$

$$P_n{}^{(1)} = 2\rho^n(1-\rho)/(1+\rho) \qquad (n>0)$$

$$L^{(1)} = 2\rho/(1-\rho^2) = \lambda W^{(1)} \tag{9.25}$$

$$L_q{}^{(1)} = 2\rho^3/(1-\rho^2) = \lambda W_q{}^{(1)} \qquad (\rho = \lambda/2\mu)$$

where we use the superscript 1 to denote the fact that there is one common queue for both channels. The mean number in queue in this case is $\rho/(1+\rho)$ times the mean number $L_q{}^{(2)}$ in the two independent queues, showing that the mean delay and the mean number waiting is less when a single common queue is used than when two independent queues are used. In fact, since the ratio $\rho/(1+\rho)$ is $\tfrac{1}{2}$ when $\rho \to 1$ and less than $\tfrac{1}{2}$ for $\rho < 1$, we see that with a common queue we have less than half the number waiting (and less than half the mean delay) than if two queues were used and the incoming units chose the queue they enter at random, regardless of the queue's length.

We note that the fraction of time a given queue is idle is $(1-\rho)$ in either case. However, the common queue arrangement enables the two channels to work more efficiently when they do work; the fraction of time *both* channels are empty simultaneously in the single-queue case $P_0{}^{(1)}$ is $(1-\rho)/(1+\rho)$, which is *larger* than the corresponding fraction $P_{00}{}^{(2)} = (1-\rho)^2$ for the two independent queues. But the fraction of time one channel is idle when the other is busy is $2\rho(1-\rho)/(1+\rho)$ for the common-queue system, which is *smaller* than the corresponding fraction $2\rho(1-\rho)$ for the two-queue system. And the fraction of time a channel is idle when a unit is waiting for service is zero in the common-queue case, whereas it is $2\rho^2(1-\rho)$ for the two-queue case, as we noted earlier.

There are, of course, many situations where it is not feasible to have a single common queue to feed two or more channels. In many cases it would necessitate more personnel to usher the queue members to the open channels, and for lines of automobiles it may take more linear space than is available. Nevertheless, when smallness of queue or shortness of delay is an important item, it may be worth both added space and personnel to reduce the numbers waiting and the duration of wait by a factor of two or more.

Other rules of queue discipline, for two or more service channels, can occur. For example, two queues may be set up, one in front of each channel (for the two-channel case), and the rule made that the arriving unit joins the *shorter* of the two queues, choosing at random only when the queues are equal in length. This case is intermediate between the two cases we have already discussed. It is not as efficient as the common-queue system, for it is still possible to have one channel idle and a queue in front of the other channel, a situation impossible with the common-queue system. On the other hand, it is more efficient than the system with two completely independent queues fed at random by arrivals, for if there is an idle channel and a queue, *all* the arrivals go to the idle channel, in the present case of two non-independent queues, and none join the queue, whereas the arrivals go half to each in the system corresponding to Eqs. 9.24. Consequently, the chance of having an idle channel and a queue present at the same time is about half as great for the non-independent queues as it is for independent queues. We would expect, therefore, that mean numbers waiting and mean delays with two queues, where arrivals go to the shorter queue, would be less than is the case where arrivals join the queues at random, but that the improvement would not be by the factor of two or more, which is possible when a common queue can be used.

Incidentally, the solution of the equations of detailed balance for the case where the arrival joins the shorter queue appears impossible to achieve in closed form, because of the essentially non-separable nature of the boundary conditions on the two-dimensional state probabilities P_{mn}.

Another choice of queue discipline, of course, is no discipline at all; the arriving units can mill around the two channels, being chosen at random when a channel is vacated. This is the situation discussed earlier in this chapter. There we saw that mean values turn out to be the same as for strict queue discipline, so that mean numbers and waits would be those given in Eqs. 9.25, but the delay-time distribution is different, more units having either short or very long delays than is the case for a common disciplined queue. Therefore, complete chaos in front of the queues produces mean delays and mean queue lengths smaller than for two independent queues and, indeed, as good as the single common disciplined queue, but the variance of the delay times is greater for the undisciplined case.

Chapter 10

PROBLEMS OF
INVENTORY CONTROL

THE FLOW OF SALABLE GOODS through a retail store or a warehouse is also an operation involving variable supply and demand, and thus some of its dynamics can be analyzed by means of the techniques of queuing theory, particularly those aspects which depend on the degree of variability of the demand or supply. Some of the characteristics of this type of operation require rather special models of queues, and some of these will be discussed in the following pages. This chapter, however, makes no pretense of being a complete treatise on inventory control; only those aspects are discussed wherein variability of demand or of supply is likely to be important.

The Effects of Variance of Demand and Supply

The characteristic of an inventory operation which sets it off from other queuing problems is that the primary "arrival," the individual customer or the order for withdrawal from inventory, produces a *decrease* in the amount of inventory rather than an increase in the size of the queue. The "service operation," from this point of view, is the process of replenishing this vacancy in the inventory, the process of re-ordering the missing item from the factory or wholesaler. And, of course, the "service time" is the time required to replace the item, the interval between the time when an item is sold or otherwise withdrawn from inventory and the time when a new item arrives to fill the vacancy caused by the earlier withdrawal.

Thus, the "queue" can sometimes be considered to be the number of unfilled orders, sent by the store possessing the inventory to the factory or wholesaler, for items to replace those sold. In the present chapter the word "order" will be used exclusively in this meaning, as an order on the factory for replacement stock. The act of withdrawing an item from inventory, the "arrival" in this system, will simply be called a sale, whether the withdrawal represents a true retail sale or simply a transfer to another part of the system. For the purposes of our analysis the item has been removed from inventory in either case, and eventually must be replaced. We shall be concerned here mainly with standard items having a fairly steady sale, which have to be kept continuously in stock; this whole monograph is concerned mainly with statistically steady-state conditions.

A very simple example can serve to illustrate some of the concepts and some of the special techniques useful with such problems. Suppose the items in inventory are bulky, expensive ones (automobiles or TV sets, for example), such that only a few are normally kept in inventory and such that each time a single unit is sold an order is issued to the factory for its replacement. In such cases a possible practice would be to keep on hand only a sample of the item for sale and to take orders for delivery later, forcing the customer to bear the burden of the delay in delivery. In many markets, however, the customer will not wait for delivery, and unless the store has the item on hand no sale is made, or at least the chance of a sale is drastically diminished. In such cases the store must stock the items in order to sell them, but it cannot stock too many, of course, because of the cost of carrying them in inventory. This is a situation reminiscent of the problems discussed in Chapter 4.

Re-order for Each Item Sold

As usual, we consider first the very simplest case. Suppose: (1) the store orders another unit from the factory as soon as one is sold, so that the sum of units on hand plus the unfilled replacement orders is a constant, which we will call the maximum inventory; (2) the management has decided to set the value of this maximum inventory to be M; (3) prospective customers arrive at a rate such that, as long as the item is in stock, sales have a Poisson distribution in time, with rate λ per week (or per month, whatever unit of time is used); (4) no sales are made when the item is out of stock, prospective customers being lost whenever the inventory is zero; (5) the distribution of time intervals, from the instant a re-order is made out until the replacement corresponding to *that particular re-order* has been added to the inventory, is one of the Erlang functions S_0 or A_0 shown in Fig. 5.1 and given in Eqs. 5.2, with a mean *replenishment* time $T = (1/\mu)$ ($l = \infty$ corresponds to constant replenishment time, $l = 1$ to exponential replacement-time distribution). These rules of operation lead to a model that is too simple to correspond adequately to most inventory situations, but will do to illustrate some of the general characteristics of the operation. We will later examine models in which one or more of these five conditions are altered.

The queuing situation corresponding to this model is that of an M-channel facility; an "idle" channel corresponds to an item in inventory, and a "busy" channel corresponds to an empty space on the shelf, to an unfilled replacement order; commencement of "service" corresponds to a sale consummated, and completion of "service" corresponds to the arrival of the replacement item back in stock. Thus, the model specified by the five rules given in the previous paragraph corresponds completely with the queuing situation shown in Fig. 5.3, with equations of detailed balance given in Eqs. 5.5 and solutions given in Eqs. 4.4. Redefining the terms to fit the present operational situation, we see that the probability that there are m items in stock ($M - m$ unfilled re-orders outstanding) is

$$P_m = [(\lambda T)^{M-m} e^{-\lambda T} / (M-m)! E_M(\lambda T)] \quad (M \geq m \geq 0) \quad (10.1)$$

where M is the maximum inventory, λ the mean sales rate *when items are in stock*, T is the mean replenishment time, and the functions $E_M(x)$ are defined in Eq. 4.3 and given in Table V. These, of course, represent steady-state probabilities when λ and T are independent of time, as long as the five rules hold. We note that the probabilities are the same *no matter what the distribution of replenishment time is* (constant or exponential or hyper-exponential), as long as the mean replenishment time is T.

From these probabilities we can compute the measures of effectiveness of the system:

Mean number replacement orders outstanding $= L = \sum_0^M n P_{M-n}$

$$= [\lambda T E_{M-1}(\lambda T) / E_M(\lambda T)]$$

Mean inventory $= I = M - L = M[D_{M-1}(\lambda T) / E_M(\lambda T)]$ \quad (10.2)

Probability of being out of stock $= P_0$

Mean number sales in replenishment time $T = L_s = \lambda T (1 - P_0) = L$

Curves for $I = M - L = M - L_s$ divided by M are given in Fig. 10.1, as functions of $(\lambda T/M)$, for different values of M. We note that when λT is much smaller than M, the mean inventory is near M and the mean sales L_s per replenishment time T are practically equal to the average sales λT that would be attained in that time if the store were never out of stock. On the other hand, if λT is considerably larger than M, mean inventory is small compared to M and mean sales per time T approach M (which is much smaller than λT in this case). In this case the store sells in a short time all the items it has, and then has to wait for replenishment.

It is not difficult to see whether a sales operation corresponds to this simple model. It must, of course, obey the first four rules for this example. The arrival rate λ can be determined by counting the average rate

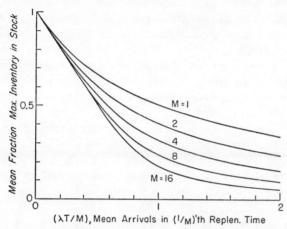

Fig. 10.1. Curves for (I/M), where I is mean inventory and M is maximum inventory, against $(\lambda T/M)$, where λ is mean rate of arrival of potential customers and T is mean replenishment time, for different values of M.

of sales *when the item is in stock* (leaving out the times when it is out of stock). The validity of the assumption of Poisson arrivals can be checked by seeing whether the mean inventory corresponds to that given by Eq. 10.2 or, in more detail, whether the fraction of time there are m items in stock is P_m.

Determination of Optimum Inventory

The appropriate value of M, the maximum inventory, must be determined by management according to some criterion. The usual method is to adjust it to yield greatest profit, so that not too many potential sales are lost because an item is out of stock too often, at the same time keeping inventory costs within reason. To work this balance out in a quantitative manner, we must know the values of the unit costs and profits involved. The sales price, the amount of money taken in by the store when an item is sold, is easily determined. The costs of handling items for sale are usually more difficult to separate out. This cost can, at least approximately, be separated into several parts: a part proportional to the number of items sold; a part proportional to the mean number of items carried in inventory; a part proportional to the number of orders for replenishment sent in to the factory, including the cost of shipping the order back from the factory (in the present simple model these costs would also be proportional to the number of items sold, but in other models, discussed later, the number of re-orders will not equal the number of items sold); and a fixed cost, independent of size of stock or number sold but occurring because the item in question is carried at all.

The size of the fixed cost does not enter into the determination of optimum size of inventory, though it certainly is pertinent to other management decisions, such as whether the item is to be carried at all. The part of the cost proportional to the number of units sold, divided by the number sold to obtain a per unit cost, is subtracted from the sales price to obtain a "gross profit" G per item sold. The part of the cost proportional to the number in inventory is a yearly cost, including some of the warehouse costs and the interest on capital tied up in inventory. This yearly cost, divided by the mean number in inventory, is C_I, the inventory cost per unit per year. For our purposes it is more useful to divide this quantity by T_y, the mean replenishment time in *fractions of a year* (if replenishment time is 1 week, T_y would be 1/52), to obtain $C_i = (C_I/T_y)$, the inventory cost per unit per replenishment time. The cost proportional to the number of re-orders, divided by the number of re-orders, is C_p, the cost per replenishment order.

The quantity useful in determining optimum inventory is the "net profit" per time T,

$$Pr = L_s G - C_i I - C_p R \qquad (10.3)$$

where R is the mean number of re-orders per time T. In the present model $R = L_s$, the number of sales per time T, so that here we can set $Pr = L_s g - C_i I$, where $g = G - C_p$. As noted, Pr does not include fixed charges, so it is not a useful figure for other calculations; it is the quantity which is useful for determination of inventory policy, and so it should not be called net profit without quotation marks. Perhaps it is better simply to call it Pr.

After these definitions of the quantities entering the calculation, we can now return to our determination of optimum inventory for the simple model under consideration. Management can fix the value of M by deciding to keep the probability of being out of stock less than some small value. In this case M must be adjusted so that P_0 is just smaller than this limit. On the other hand, if M is to be adjusted for maximum profit, we must work out the balance between sales profits and inventory costs.

Suppose the "gross profit" per sale, *not* including a charge-off for fixed costs or inventory costs, is $g = G - C_p$ as defined in the preceding paragraph, and suppose that the total cost of carrying one item in inventory for the replenishment time T is C_i as defined. Then the "net profit" in time T, the quantity which is to be maximized by varying M, is

$$Pr(M) = g(\text{mean number sales in time } T) - C_i(\text{mean number in stock})$$

$$= L_s g - C_i I = gM - (C_i + g)[M E_M(\lambda T) - \lambda T E_{M-1}(\lambda T)]/E_M(\lambda T)$$

For M small enough, we find that the value of gM, the first term in the formula, increases faster as M is increased than does the second term, the one with $(C_i + g)$. Consequently, profits will increase as M is increased, until the increase in the second term, as M is increased by unity, just equals the increase $g(M+1) - g(M) = g$ of the first term. Any choice of M larger than this optimum value M_0 will produce less profit again, so M_0 is the value of maximum inventory that will yield maximum net profit in time T, which will best balance the costs of large inventory against the losses of sales that occur when the item is out of stock.

Setting $Pr(M_0 + 1) - Pr(M_0) = 0$, we finally arrive at an equation for this optimum maximum inventory M_0:

$$\frac{C_i}{C_i + g} = \lambda T \left[\frac{E_M(\lambda T)}{E_{M+1}(\lambda T)} - \frac{E_{M-1}(\lambda T)}{E_M(\lambda T)} \right] \quad (M = M_0) \quad (10.4)$$

The value of M that most nearly satisfies this equation is the value M_0. But now we see that the term on the right is exactly the same function we defined in Eq. 4.5 and plotted in Fig. 4.3, in connection with the optimum number of channels in a multi-channel service facility. The variable marked $M\rho$ in Fig. 4.3 is now λT, the mean number of prospective customers arriving in replenishment time T. The quantity is now to be set equal to the fraction $C_i/(C_i + g)$, the fractional inventory cost. If this is large, if inventory costs are large compared to gross profits, then it is best to keep but few items in stock, even though this means a high percentage of lost sales; if $C_i/(C_i + g)$ is much smaller than unity, then M_0 should be large, so as not to lose sales by being out of stock.

The curves of Fig. 4.3 extend to $M\rho$ (now λT, the number of arrivals per replacement time) out only to 2. Figure 10.2 extends this range

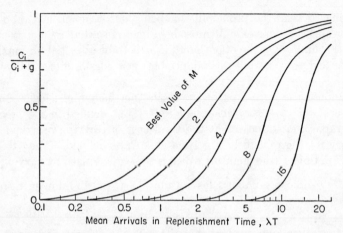

Fig. 10.2. Graphs for determining the optimum value of M, the maximum inventory, for various values of λT and of ratio of C_i, the cost of inventory, to $C_i + g$, cost of inventory plus mean profit per sale. See Eq. 10.4. See also Fig. 4.3.

somewhat. Approximate formulas valid for large values of M can be obtained from various limiting formulas for the E's. For example, for $C_i/(C_i + g)$ less than $\frac{1}{4}$ and λT larger than 10, we can use the formula

$$E_{m-1}(x) = 1 - e^{-x} \sum_{n=m}^{\infty} (x^n/n!) \qquad (x = \lambda T)$$

where when $x < m$ the second term is appreciably smaller than the first. In this case the right-hand side of Eq. 10.4 can be simplified. Using the Stirling approximation $m! \simeq \sqrt{2\pi m}\, m^m\, e^{-m}$ for m large, we obtain

$$\sqrt{2\pi}\, M^{M+\frac{1}{2}}\, e^{-M} \simeq \left(\frac{C_i + g}{C_i}\right) x^{M+1}\, e^{-x}\left(1 - \frac{x}{M+1}\right) \quad (x = \lambda T)$$

From this we can obtain the approximate formulas for optimum maximum inventory M_{op} and for mean actual inventory I_{op}.

$$M_{op} \simeq x - \tfrac{1}{6} + \{\tfrac{1}{3}x \ln [(2w^2/3x) \ln w]\}^{\frac{1}{2}}$$

$$I_{op} \simeq \frac{C_i}{C_i + g} - \tfrac{1}{6} + \{\tfrac{1}{3}x \ln [(2w^2/3x) \ln w]\}^{\frac{1}{2}}$$

$$(10.5)$$

$$w = \sqrt{\frac{x}{2\pi}\left(\frac{C_i + g}{C_i}\right)} \qquad \text{valid when } \left(\frac{C_i + g}{C_i}\right) \gg 1$$

where the symbol ln denotes the natural logarithm. The best value of M is the integer nearest to the value of the right-hand side of the equation. I_{op} is the corresponding average inventory of items actually in stock.

When $C_i/(C_i+g)$ is between $\frac{1}{2}$ and $\frac{3}{4}$ and $x=\lambda T \gg 1$, we can use another approximation for E_m:

$$E_m(x) = \int_x^\infty (y^m/m!)\, e^{-y}\, dy \simeq \frac{1}{2} - \frac{1}{\sqrt{2\pi m}} \int_m^x (y/m)^m\, e^{m-y}\, dy \quad (m \gg 1)$$

$$\simeq \frac{1}{2} - \frac{x-m}{\sqrt{2\pi m}}\left[1 - \frac{(x-m)^2}{6m} + \frac{(x-m)^4}{40m^2} - \cdots \right]$$

$$\text{when } |x-m| \ll \sqrt{m}$$

In this case the approximate formulas turn out to be

$$M_{op} \simeq x - 0.7 + 0.5(\sqrt{x} + 0.3)\left(0.68 - \frac{C_i}{C_i+g} \right); \quad x = \lambda T$$

$$I_{op} \simeq 0.5\left(1.8 - \frac{C_i}{C_i+g} \right)\sqrt{x} - 0.7 \tag{10.6}$$

$$\text{valid when } 0.5 < \left(\frac{C_i}{C_i+g} \right) < 0.75$$

When $C_i/(C_i+g)$ is between $\frac{3}{4}$ and 1, M_{op} is considerably smaller than λT, but such cases are not likely to be of interest; the margin of profit is so small that a small decrease in λ would put the operation into the red. Unless there are other reasons for having such items on hand, they should not be carried at all.

The curves of Fig. 10.2, and Eqs. 10.5 and 10.6, show that if the cost C_i of keeping an item in stock for the replenishment time T is a small fraction of the gross profit per sale, that is, when $C_i/(C_i+g)$ is much smaller than $\frac{1}{2}$, it pays to plan a maximum inventory M_0 somewhat larger than the mean number λT of possible sales in a replacement time, just to take care of the occasional times when more potential customers arrive than usual. If $C_i/(C_i+g)$ is larger, if the cost of carrying an item in stock begins to be appreciable, then M_0 should be reduced somewhat below λT because the extra sales gained in the occasional buying peaks do not repay the cost of keeping the additional stock. The adjustment is not great, however, if $\lambda T \gg 1$, and the mean number actually in stock does not reduce by much, going from about $1.1\sqrt{\lambda T}$ (for $\lambda T \simeq 25$) to about $0.7\sqrt{\lambda T}$ as $C_i/(C_i+g)$ is changed from 0.1 to 0.6.

Next let us examine the effect of modifying some of the five rules we imposed on our simple model. Taking No. 4 first, we see what will occur if some customers (say a fraction γ of them) are willing to order an item even if it is not in stock. In this case the probabilities for m items in stock are

$$P_m = \{(\lambda T)^{M-m}\, e^{-\lambda T}/(M-m)!\,[\gamma+(1-\gamma)E_M(\lambda T)]\}$$

$$(0 \leq m \leq M)$$

$$= \gamma\{(\lambda T)^{M-m}\, e^{-\lambda T}/(M-m)!\,[\gamma+(1-\gamma)F_M(\lambda T)]\}$$

$$(0 > m)$$

$$(10.7)$$

where negative values of m, of course, denote orders placed for customers who were willing to buy even if no item were on hand, and were willing to wait the full time T, if necessary, to get one.

In general, the less impatient the customers (the nearer γ gets to unity), the less important it is to keep a large inventory. For $\gamma = 1$ (all customers willing to wait) M_0 can be zero; no inventory is necessary. If we can determine the fraction γ of customers who could be induced (by the granting of a discount, for example) to wait the re-order time T for their purchase, it is possible to work out an optimum solution for this more complex system.

Re-order When Out of Stock

Alternatively we can see what happens if we relax rule 1, if we order replacements in batches. First let us go to the opposite extreme, where a re-order for M items is sent in each time the inventory goes to zero. Obviously, this procedure will produce more lost sales, for each time the store sends in a replacement order it is out of stock for the whole replenishment time. But in cases where the items are not bulky or expensive the cost of sending through individual replacement orders may be the controlling factor. We first look at this opposite extreme, where rule 1 is replaced by: (1a) as soon as the item is out of stock, the store orders another M units. We will investigate some intermediate cases later.

It again turns out that the results are independent of the replenishment-time distribution (as long as arrivals are Poisson). The simple argument is as follows: the mean time between purchases is $(1/\lambda)$, so on the average the store will be out of stock in time (M/λ) after it started with M items; it will stay out of stock a time T and then start a new cycle. Consequently, if this simple reasoning is valid, the probability of having m items in inventory is

$$P_m = 1/(M+\lambda T) \qquad (0 < m \leq M)$$
$$P_0 = \lambda T/(M+\lambda T)$$

$$(10.8)$$

When the replenishment time has an exponential distribution, we can use a more rigorous derivation to obtain the same formula. We use the model represented in Fig. 5.2, with no queue and with M phases. Each phase represents an item in stock, each sale a transition from one phase to the next (rate λ in this case), and the transition from state 0 to state M is exponential with rate $\mu = (1/T)$. The equations of detailed balance are

$$0 = \lambda P_{n+1} - \lambda P_n \qquad (M > n > 0)$$
$$= \lambda P_1 - \mu P_0$$
$$= \mu P_0 - \lambda P_M$$

The solutions are the ones given in Eqs. 10.8. Detailed consideration of the case of constant replenishment time yields the same equations; indeed, Eqs. 10.8 result, for this model, from any distribution of replenishment time.

We can now use again our method of obtaining Eq. 10.4, to obtain a formula for maximum inventory that will minimize the average difference between gross profits from sales and cost of inventory plus cost of re-ordering. First we compute the measures of effectiveness:

$$\text{Mean inventory} = I = \sum_0^M nP_n = M(M+1)/2(M+\lambda T)$$

$$\text{Mean sales per time } T = L_s = \lambda T(1-P_0) = \lambda TM/(M+\lambda T)$$

$$(10.9)$$

$$\text{Replacement orders issued per time } T = P_0 = \lambda T/(M+\lambda T)$$

If now is g the gross profit per sale, C_i the cost of carrying one item in inventory for a time T, and C_p the cost of sending in one replacement order and receiving the resulting shipment (as defined earlier in this section), then from Eq. 10.3 net returns in time T are (we assume $M \gg 1$)

$$Pr(M) = gL_s - C_i I - C_p P_0$$
$$= [g\lambda TM - \tfrac{1}{2}C_i M^2 - \lambda TC_p]/(M+\lambda T)$$

And if M is large enough to be considered continuous variable, we can find the maximum by setting the differential of Pr with respect to

M equal to zero, giving the following equation

$$M^2 + 2\lambda TM - [2\lambda T(G+C_p)/C_i] = 0; \quad G = g\lambda T$$

$$M_{op} \simeq \lambda T\{\sqrt{[2(G+C_p)/\lambda TC_i] + 1} - 1\} \qquad (10.10)$$

$$\rightarrow \sqrt{2(G+C_p)\lambda T/C_i} \quad (G+C_p \gg \lambda TC_i)$$

$$\rightarrow (G+C_p)/C_i \qquad\qquad (G+C_p \ll \lambda TC_i)$$

where the optimum value of M is the integer nearest M_{op}.

These expressions can be given in terms of annual rates and costs. We express λ as λ_y, the number of prospective sales per year; then the actual number of items sold per year, S, is $\lambda_y(1-P_0)$, so we can compute λ_y by first obtaining from the records the fraction of the year the store was *not* out of stock $(1-P_0)$, and then by dividing total units sold per year by $(1-P_0)$. If we also express the mean replenishment time T in units of a year (call this fraction T_y), the cost of one unit inventory per year, C_I, is equal to C_i/T_y. Then Eqs. 10.10 become

$$M_{op} \simeq \lambda_y T_y\{\sqrt{[2(G+C_p)/\lambda_y T_y{}^2 C_I] + 1} - 1\}$$

$$\rightarrow (G+C_p)/T_y C_I \qquad (G+C_p \ll \lambda_y T_y{}^2 C_I)$$

$$\rightarrow \sqrt{2(G+C_p)\lambda_y/C_I} \quad (G+C_p \gg \lambda_y T_y{}^2 C_I)$$

The last limiting formula is a variant of the classical Wilson formula for optimum re-order quantity. We can see under what conditions it is valid: (*a*) the rules of the simple model given earlier; (*b*) re-order time is short compared to the mean time interval between sales, or profits per sale and/or cost of re-ordering is very large compared to inventory cost per unit per replenishment time.

Advisability of a Buffer Stock

It is not a very sensible arrangement, of course, to wait until one is out of stock before re-ordering; when stock is down to a certain minimum level, enough should be re-ordered to last, on the average, till the re-order is filled. This suggests a somewhat more complicated model: maximum inventory is $M = Q + D$; when the inventory is Q items below this (when inventory is equal to a "buffer supply" D), a re-order for Q items is sent in; if by any chance the store is bought out before this order comes back, another order for D items is sent to the factory. If we assume that replenishment time is exponentially distributed, with mean rate $\mu = (1/T)$, we can use the now familiar procedure to determine state probabilities. There are $M+1$ possible states, which can be labeled by the size m of the inventory for the state. Each state m changes to state $m-1$ at the consummation of an additional sale; if the order for Q items arrives, the state changes from m to $m+Q$; if the order for D items arrives, the transition is from 0 to $0+D$ (the order for D items is not sent *unless* the store is out of stock). The equations for detailed balance are

$$\mu P_{M-Q} - \lambda P_M = 0; \quad \lambda P_{n+1} + \mu P_{n-Q} - \lambda P_n = 0 \quad (M > n \geq Q)$$

$$\lambda P_{n+1} - \lambda P_n = 0 \qquad\qquad\qquad\qquad (Q > n > D)$$

$$\lambda P_{D+1} + \mu P_0 - (\lambda + \mu) P_D = 0 \qquad\qquad\qquad (10.11)$$

$$\lambda P_{n+1} - (\lambda + \mu) P_n = 0 \qquad\qquad\qquad (D > n > 0)$$

$$\lambda P_1 - 2\mu P_0 = 0$$

where $M = Q+D$, where λ is the mean rate of sales when stock is on hand, where $T = (1/\mu)$ is the mean replenishment time, and where we have assumed that $Q > D$.

The solutions of this set of equations are

$$P_n = (2/\lambda T)[(\lambda T + 1)/\lambda T]^{n-1} P_0 \qquad (0 < n \leq D)$$

$$= (2/\lambda T)\left[\left(\frac{\lambda T+1}{\lambda T}\right)^D - \frac{1}{2}\right] P_0 \qquad (D < n \leq Q)$$

$$\qquad\qquad\qquad\qquad\qquad\qquad\qquad\qquad (10.12)$$

$$= (2/\lambda T)\left[\left(\frac{\lambda T+1}{\lambda T}\right)^D - \left(\frac{\lambda T+1}{\lambda T}\right)^{n-Q-1}\right] P_0$$

$$(Q < n \leq M = Q+D)$$

where $\qquad P_0 = \dfrac{(\lambda T)^{D+1}}{2Q(1+\lambda T)^D + (\lambda T + D - Q)(\lambda T)^D}$

The measures of effectiveness for this system can be worked out. The mean number R of re-orders (either for Q or for D items) sent out in time T, the mean inventory I, and the mean number of sales L_s made in replenishment time T are

$$R = 2P_0 + \sum_{n=1}^{D} P_n = \frac{2\lambda T(1+\lambda T)^D}{2Q(1+\lambda T)^D + (\lambda T + D - Q)(\lambda T)^D}$$

$$L_s = \lambda T(1-P_0) = (\lambda T)\frac{2Q(1+\lambda T)^D + (D-Q)(\lambda T)^D}{2Q(1+\lambda T)^D + (\lambda T + D - Q)(\lambda T)^D} \qquad (10.13)$$

$$I = \sum_{n=1}^{M} nP_n = \frac{\left\{ \begin{array}{c} Q(Q+2D+1-2\lambda T)(1+\lambda T)^D \\ +\frac{1}{2}(D^2+4\lambda TQ - Q^2 + D - Q)(\lambda T)^D \end{array} \right\}}{2Q(1+\lambda T)^D + (\lambda T + D - Q)(\lambda T)^D}$$

These results should be compared with those of Eq. 10.9, for the case where $D=0$ (no buffer stock on hand at time of re-order) and $Q=M$. We see that when there are a moderate number of sales per replenishment time (λT not very large compared to 1), the presence of a buffer stock (the practice of re-ordering before stock runs completely out) appreciably reduces P_0, the chance of being out of stock, and therefore increases the average sales L_s. Whether this increase is worth the added cost of carrying the buffer stock is something we will have to work out. (In the limiting case of $D \to 0$, the formula for R, the number of orders issued for time T, of Eqs. 10.13 comes out twice that of Eqs. 10.9, because our new rules would specify two simultaneous re-orders being issued in the limit of $D=0$; aside from this, the formulas for L_s and I reduce to those of Eqs. 10.9 as $D \to 0$.) All of these qualitative results are not surprising; we could probably have figured them out without the mathematics. What the equations will give us, however, is the *quantitative* aspect, the *amount* of the effect.

When λT is much larger than unity (when there are many sales in a replenishment time), D must be appreciably larger than unity to make an appreciable change in L_s and P_0. After all, when λT is large it would be reasonable to have a larger buffer stock. But D does not necessarily have to be as large as λT, for we can see that the effect of buffer stock on P_0 and L_s is chiefly through the *power* of the ratio $\lambda T/(\lambda T+1)$, that is, an exponential effect. For example, when D is large enough so that $[\lambda T/(1+\lambda T)]^D$ is small compared to unity, we have

$$R \simeq (\lambda T/Q) - \frac{Q-D-\lambda T}{2Q}x^D; \quad x = \left(\frac{\lambda T}{\lambda T+1}\right)$$

$$L_s \simeq \lambda T[1 - (\lambda T/2Q)x^D]; \qquad P_0 \simeq (\lambda T/2Q)x^D \qquad (10.14)$$

$$I \simeq D - \lambda T + \tfrac{1}{2}Q + \tfrac{1}{4}\left(\frac{\lambda T+D}{Q}\right)\left(\frac{Q+2\lambda T-2D}{Q-2\lambda T+2D}\right)x^D$$

where x^D goes exponentially to zero as D increases. Therefore, even if $x=[\lambda T/(\lambda T+1)]$ is not very much smaller than unity, D does not need to be very large in order that P_0 be small. In fact, D has a much greater effect on P_0 than does Q. On the other hand, Q has the predominating effect on R, the rate of issuing re-orders (as long as x^D is small).

We are now ready to consider how the operating parameters Q and D are to be fixed. If the desideratum is that the chance of being out of stock should be no larger than some amount $P_{\min}$, we must have

$$D \simeq \frac{\ln (\lambda T/2QP_{\min})}{\ln [1+(1/\lambda T)]} \tag{10.15}$$

where, as before, ln denotes the natural logarithm. But we have not yet determined the optimal value of Q. Presumably this can be obtained by a procedure analogous to those which led to Eqs. 10.4 and 10.10.

If, as before, G is the gross profit per sale, C_i the cost of carrying an item in inventory for a replenishment time T, and C_p the cost of sending out a re-order and getting in the called-for shipment (as noted, C_p is that part of the cost of making the order and of getting the replenishment back which is *independent* of the size of the order; the part proportional to the size of the order should be charged to the cost per item, which is to be subtracted from the sales price to obtain G), the net receipts per replenishment time are

$$
\begin{aligned}
Pr(Q,D) =\ & GL_s - C_i I - C_p R \\
\simeq\ & G\lambda T - C_p(\lambda T/Q) - C_i(D - \lambda T + \tfrac{1}{2}Q) \\
& - \frac{x^D}{Q}\Big\{ \tfrac{1}{2}G(\lambda T)^2 - \tfrac{1}{2}C_p(Q - D - \lambda T) \\
& + \tfrac{1}{4}C_i(\lambda T + D)\Big[\frac{Q + 2\lambda T - 2D}{Q - 2\lambda T + 2D}\Big]\Big\}
\end{aligned}
\tag{10.16}
$$

By differentiating with respect to Q and setting the result equal to zero, we can find the value of the re-order quantity Q_{op} which makes Pr a maximum:

$$Q_{\mathrm{op}}(D) \simeq q + \tfrac{1}{2}qx^D\Big[\frac{G\lambda T}{2C_p} + \frac{1}{2}\frac{\lambda T + D}{\lambda T}\Big]; \quad q^2 = (2\lambda T C_p/C_i) \tag{10.17}$$

where $x=[\lambda T/(\lambda T+1)]$ as before, and where we have assumed that $C_i \ll C_p$ (which is usually the case).

Comparison with Eq. 10.10 shows again that the optimal re-order quantity, even in this more complicated model, depends most strongly on the "Wilson number" $q = \sqrt{2\lambda T C_p/C_i}$. In general the second term, the one in x^D, is a small correction. This correction, on the other hand, depends most strongly on the size of the buffer stock D. If the value of D is to be determined by fixing P_0, its value is given by Eq. 10.15. But it may be more appropriate to give D that value which will maximize Pr; in other words, we can also adjust D so that the lost sales are as low as is compatible with the cost of keeping the extra inventory.

Differentiating Pr with respect to D this time, letting $(dx^D/dD) = x^{D+1} - x^D = -(x^{D+1}/\lambda T)$ (since D is actually an integer and since $x = \lambda T/\lambda T + 1$) and setting the result again equal to zero, we eventually obtain for the optimal size of buffer stock D_{op}, and for the corresponding value of P_0 the probability of being out of stock:

$$D_{op} + 1 \simeq \frac{\ln[(G\lambda^2 T^2 - qC_p)/2\lambda TqC_i]}{\ln[1 + (1/\lambda T)]}$$

(10.18)

$$\text{and} \quad x^{D_{op}} \simeq \left(1 + \frac{1}{\lambda T}\right)\frac{2qC_i}{[\lambda TG - (q/\lambda T)C_p]} \;; \quad P_0 \simeq \frac{(\lambda T+1)C_i}{\lambda TG - (q/\lambda T)C_p}$$

If P_0 is larger than this optimal value, too many sales will be lost by being out of stock too often; if P_0 is smaller, too much will be spent on keeping inventory; in either case a proper balance will not have been reached. If this value of D_{op} is the one used, then the corresponding value of Q_{op} and the expected net receipts per replenishment time Pr are

$$Q_{op}(D_{op}) \simeq q + (\lambda T + 1)\frac{G\lambda T + C_p}{\lambda TG - (q/\lambda T)C_p} \;; \quad q^2 = \left(\frac{2\lambda TC_p}{C_i}\right)$$

(10.19)

$$Pr(Q_{op}, D_{op}) \simeq \lambda TG - C_i\left[q + D_{op} + \tfrac{1}{2}\left(1 + \frac{1}{\lambda T}\right)\frac{C_i(\lambda T + D_{op} + 1)}{\lambda TG - (q/\lambda T)C_p}\right]$$

If D_{op}, from Eqs. 10.18, comes out small or negative, it means that costs are such that it is not worthwhile to reduce P_0 by keeping a buffer stock, and the system leading to Eqs. 10.10 should be used (or else another criterion determining D should be developed).

These results are not surprising, in their general form. The optimal "net profit" (which, as pointed out before, does not include fixed costs) is equal to the amount which would be gained in replenishment time T if inventory automatically stayed at maximum value $(Q+D)$ (so that all possible sales λT were consummated and no re-order costs were incurred) minus a correction term, corresponding to the last term in the square brackets in the expression for Pr. The optimal re-order quantity Q_{op} is equal to the "Wilson number" q plus a small correction. The optimal size of the "buffer" inventory D_{op} is proportional to the natural logarithm of this same correction term (since the probability P_0 of being out of stock depends exponentially on D, it is not surprising that D_{op} comes out in terms of natural logarithms).

Each of these correction terms arises from the compromise we have made between loss of sales and costs of making a replenishment order and of inventory. This is indicated by the fact that the denominator of each term is the difference between λTG, the "gross profits" which would be made in time T if all sales were consummated, and $(q/\lambda T)C_p$ $\simeq (Q/\lambda T)C_p$, the re-order costs which would be incurred in time T if all λT sales were made and the store were never out of stock (no orders for D items were ever sent in), and by the fact that the numerators of some of the correction terms contain C_i. Incidentally, we should note that all these quantities depend on λT; if we can reduce the length of replenishment time T, we can reduce both D and Q. The fact that Pr also gets smaller does not matter; Pr is the profit per replenishment time T; profit per month or year would not be reduced by reducing T.

Re-order by Batches

Sometimes other operational criteria influence our choice of the re-order quantity Q. For example, warehouse limitations, manufacturing practice or shipping requirements may make it cheaper to order in integral multiples of a lot size Q which bears no relationship to the Q_{op} of Eqs. 10.19. In this case our maximum inventory M will presumably be an integral multiple of Q, and we will need to know *which* multiple is optimum. In other words, our maximum inventory M is lQ, where l is some integer and Q is the re-order lot size which has already been determined by some other operational criterion. Whenever the inventory goes from $mQ+1$ to $mQ(l>m\geq 0)$, we send in an order for Q more items; so that if the inventory is in the range from $(l-n)Q$ to $(l-n-1)Q+1$, inclusive, there are n replenishment orders outstanding, each for Q items.

Assuming that replenishment time has an exponential distribution (since the results do not depend strongly on the form of this distribution—indeed, it made no difference at all in the models of Eqs. 10.4 and 10.10—we may as well take the distribution which is easiest to work out) and that sales are Poisson as usual, our equations for detailed balance are

$$P_1 = lxP_0; \quad P_M = xP_{M-Q}; \quad M = lQ$$

$$P_{n+1} + (l-m)xP_{n-Q} - [1+(l-m-1)x]P_n = 0$$

$$(mQ < n \leq mQ + Q; \; l > m > 0) \quad (10.20)$$

$$P_{Q+1} + lxP_0 - [1+(l-1)x]P_Q = 0; \quad x = (1/\lambda T)$$

$$P_{n+1} - [1+(l-1)x]P_n = 0 \qquad (Q > n > 0)$$

where the mean rate of sale of items when inventory is *not* zero is λ, where no sales are made when inventory is zero, and where T is the mean replenishment time. The quantity P_n is the probability that there are n items in stock at any given time.

The solution of this set of equations involves a certain amount of algebraic juggling, to get the results in a form which can be handled. Some of the expressions for the probabilities are

$$P_1 = lxP_0; \quad x = (1/\lambda T)$$

$$(P_n/P_1) = [1+(l-1)x]^{n-1} \qquad (0 < n \leq Q)$$

$$= [1+(l-2)x]^{n-Q-1}\{[1+(l-1)x]^Q + (l-2)\}$$

$$- (l-1)[1+(l-1)x]^{n-Q-1} \quad (Q < n \leq 2Q)$$

$$= [1+(l-3)x]^{n-2Q-1}\{[1+(l-1)x]^Q + (l-2)\} \cdot$$

$$\cdot \{[1+(l-2)x]^Q - 1\}$$

$$+ \tfrac{1}{2}(l-1)(l-2)[1+(l-3)x]^{n-2Q-1}$$

$$- (l-2)[1+(l-2)x]^{n-2Q-1}\{[1+(l-1)x]^Q + (l-2)\}$$

$$+ \tfrac{1}{2}(l-1)(l-2)[1+(l-1)x]^{n-2Q-1}$$

$$(2Q < n \leq 3Q)$$

$$= [1+(l-4)x]^{n-3Q-1}\{[1+(l-1)x]^Q + (l-2)\} \cdot \qquad (10.21)$$

$$\cdot \{[1+(l-2)x]^Q - 1\}\{[1+(l-3)x]^Q - 1\}$$

$$+ \tfrac{1}{2}(l-1)(l-2)[1+(l-4)x]^{n-3Q-1} \cdot$$

$$\cdot \{[1+(l-3)x]^Q + \tfrac{1}{3}(l-6)\}$$

$$- (l-3)[1+(l-3)x]^{n-3Q-1} \cdot$$

$$\cdot \{[1+(l-1)x]^Q + (l-2)\}\{[1+(l-2)x]^Q - 1\}$$

$$+ \tfrac{1}{2}(l-1)(l-2)(l-3)[1+(l-3)x]^{n-3Q-1}$$

$$+ \tfrac{1}{2}(l-2)(l-3)[1+(l-2)x]^{n-3Q-1} \cdot$$

$$\cdot \{[1+(l-1)x]^Q + (l-2)\}$$

$$- \tfrac{1}{6}(l-1)(l-2)(l-3)[1+(l-1)x]^{n-3Q-1}$$

$$(3Q < n \leq 4Q)$$

From these expressions for the probabilities, we can compute the measures of effectiveness: the probability P_0 of being out of stock; the mean number of sales L_s made per replenishment time T; the mean number R of orders for Q items sent back to the factory in time T; and I the average inventory. The algebraic form of these quantities will vary with the value of l, the integral ratio between M (the maximum inventory) and Q (the re-order quantity). Expressions for $l=1$ (re-order only when out of stock) have been given in Eqs. 10.9. Expressions for $l=2$ (re-order when half out of stock and again when out of stock) are

$$l=2; \quad P_0 = \frac{(\lambda T)^{Q+1}}{(\lambda T)^{Q+1}+M(\lambda T+1)^Q} ; \quad M=2Q$$

$$L_s = \frac{\lambda T M(\lambda T+1)^Q}{(\lambda T)^{Q+1}+M(\lambda T+1)^Q} = QR \qquad (10.22)$$

$$I = \tfrac{1}{2}M\frac{(3Q+1-2\lambda T)(\lambda T+1)^Q+2(\lambda T)^{Q+1}}{2Q(\lambda T+1)^Q+(\lambda T)^{Q+1}}$$

The corresponding expressions for $l=3$ ($M=3Q$) (re-order when $\tfrac{1}{3}$ or $\tfrac{2}{3}$ or completely out of stock) are more complicated:

$$P_0 = \frac{(\lambda T)^{2Q+1}}{(M+\lambda T)(\lambda T)^{2Q}+M[(\lambda T+2)^Q+(\lambda T)^Q][(\lambda T+1)^Q-(\lambda T)^Q]}$$

$$L_s = \lambda T M \frac{(\lambda T)^{2Q}+[(\lambda T+2)^Q+(\lambda T)^Q][(\lambda T+1)^Q-(\lambda T)^Q]}{\left\{ \begin{array}{l} (M+\lambda T)(\lambda T)^{2Q} \\ \quad +M[(\lambda T+2)^Q+(\lambda T)^Q][(\lambda T+1)^Q-(\lambda T)^Q] \end{array} \right\}} = QR \qquad (10.23)$$

$$I = \tfrac{1}{2}M \frac{\left\{ \begin{array}{l} (5Q+1)(\lambda T)^{2Q}+(5Q+1-2\lambda T) \\ \quad \times[(\lambda T+2)^Q+(\lambda T)^Q][(\lambda T+1)^Q-(\lambda T)^Q] \end{array} \right\}}{\left\{ \begin{array}{l} (M+\lambda T)(\lambda T)^{2Q} \\ \quad +M[(\lambda T+2)^Q+(\lambda T)^Q][(\lambda T+1)^Q-(\lambda T)^Q] \end{array} \right\}}$$

Likewise the expression for $l=4$ ($M=4Q$) (re-order when stock passes each quarter-value) turn out to be

$$P_0 = \frac{(\lambda T)^{3Q+1}}{(\lambda T)^{2Q}\{3M[1]+(\lambda T+M)(\lambda T)^Q\}+M[3][2][1]}$$

$$L_s = \lambda TM \frac{(\lambda T)^{2Q}\{3[1]+(\lambda T)^Q\}+[3][2][1]}{(\lambda T)^{2Q}\{3M[1]+(\lambda T+M)(\lambda T)^Q\}+M[3][2][1]} = QR \quad (10.24)$$

$$I = \tfrac{1}{2}M \frac{(7Q+1)(\lambda T)^{3Q}+(7Q+1-2\lambda T)[1]\{3(\lambda T)^{2Q}+[3][2]\}}{(M+\lambda T)(\lambda T)^{3Q}+M[1]\{3(\lambda T)^{2Q}+[3][2]\}}$$

where $[1]=[(\lambda T+1)^Q-(\lambda T)^Q]$; $[2]=[(\lambda T+2)^Q-(\lambda T)^Q]$; $[3]=[(\lambda T+3)^Q +(\lambda T)^Q]$. Formulas for larger values of l can be obtained if required.

These formulas may be used to obtain the optimal value of l. If Q is already fixed in value by other considerations, we can calculate the "net profit" per replenishment time

$$Pr(Q,l,\lambda T) = GL_s - C_iI - C_pR$$

$$= [G-(C_p/Q)]L_s - C_iI$$

for different values of l, for the appropriate values of Q and λT. The value of l which gives the largest value of Pr is the best value to use, as long as Q and λT cannot be varied. Sample calculations will not be given here, for the simplifying approximations depend considerably on the relative sizes of the various quantities. In such a case it is perhaps appropriate to leave the details as "an exercise for the reader."

Chapter 11

MAINTENANCE OF EQUIPMENT

T HE REPAIR AND MAINTENANCE of machinery is another operation which exhibits the variability of demand and of service which is characteristic of the processes we are studying. Equipment breaks down from time to time, needing the service of repair crews to put it back in running order; both breakdowns, which are the analogues of *arrivals*, and completions of repair, which correspond to *service*, are variable in occurrence. Two considerations make the maintenance operation worthy of separate study: (1) the possibility of *preventive maintenance*, the possibility of cutting down on the irregularity of arrivals (breakdowns) by carrying out regularly scheduled repairs *before* the machine breaks down; (2) the fact that in this operation there is a limited population of units which can "arrive," and when they are all in the system (being repaired or waiting for repair), no more can arrive. In most other operations where the queuing model is appropriate, the population of potential arrivals can be considered to be effectively limitless. Even in telephone operations the number of potential users of the exchange facilities is usually large enough that the likelihood of an appreciable fraction of them all wanting service at once is extremely small. But in maintenance problems it is often all too possible that an appreciable fraction of the machines of a given type are simultaneously out of order.

Breakdown-Time Distribution

The statistical distribution of the events important to our model may be described in the same general terms as given in Chapter 2. A plot similar to Fig. 2.1 can be made of the distribution of lengths of time between the completion of last repair (or preventive maintenance) and the next breakdown. From this we can obtain a distribution (which might as well be called A_0, as before) of times to breakdown (analogous to arrival times), the probability that the machine will still be running a time t after its last servicing. By differentiation, we can then obtain $a(t)$, the probability density of breakdown a time t after last service, and by integration we can obtain $U_0(t)$, the probability that a given machine will be running continuously, without need of repair, during the whole of a time interval t chosen at random. And from these we can also compute T_a, the *mean running life* of a machine, between repairs, and its reciprocal $\lambda = (1/T_a)$.

Actual breakdown distributions have quite a variety of shapes. Some machines, presumably those which have a few moving parts subject to wear, tend to break down a more or less constant time after last repair, so their breakdown distributions will resemble curve c of Fig. 2.2. Others, those which have a variety of moving parts or which depend on adjustments that may be destroyed by random causes, have breakdown distributions nearly of the exponential type, curve a of Fig. 2.2. And still others may have hyper-exponential breakdown distributions (curve d of Fig. 2.2, for example), perhaps because the machine's ability to do its job depends on one or more fine adjustments, which if done just right will stay right for a long time, but if not done quite right may soon need readjustment. We will see later that the utility of preventive maintenance depends quite markedly on the shape of the breakdown distribution curve.

Similarly, we can determine from the data on lengths of time for repair the repair-time distribution $S_0(t)$, the probability that the repair is not yet finished in time t, and its derivative density function $s(t)$, its integral function $V_0(x)$ and the mean duration of repair $T_s = (1/\mu)$. Here again, the shape of the S_0 curves varies considerably from operation to operation, depending on the nature and the complexity of the repair task.

Function S_0 is the distribution of repair times for genuine repairs, those operating on units which have actually broken down. In addition, there may be a time distribution for preventive maintenance operations, $M_0(t)$, the probability that the maintenance operation being done on a machine not yet broken down is not yet finished after time t, and a corresponding density function $m(t)$, integral function $W_0(t)$ and mean duration $T_m = (1/\sigma)$. In general T_m, the mean duration for a preventive maintenance task, is smaller than T_s, the average length of time taken to repair a machine which has actually broken down. Also, since the preventive maintenance operation can be planned in more detail than a repair operation, it is more likely to be nearly constant in duration (its curve is more like curve c of Fig. 2.2) than is the true repair job.

Because of the wide variety of the distributions encountered and because of the great differences in operational procedures, it is even less feasible than with other queuing situations to set up a "standard model" of a typical maintenance operation, the results of which would be applicable to many cases encountered in practice. Rather, we shall have to discuss some of the special problems which turn up and, by means of simple examples, show how the techniques may be used to obtain formulas to fit the needs of the particular practical case.

Single Machine, Optimum Repair Effort

As before, we consider the very simplest case first; that of a single machine with breakdown distribution function $A_0(t)$, and a single repair crew with distribution of repair times $S_0(t)$. The corresponding mean times, the reciprocals of the "mean rates," equal to the integral of A_0 or S_0 respectively (see Eq. 2.2) are $T_a = (1/\lambda)$ and $T_s = (1/\mu)$. Then it is not difficult, by use of the formulas of Chapter 2, to show that

Probability that the machine is working $= [T_a/(T_a+T_s)]$

$$= \text{fraction of time repair crew is idle}$$

Probability that machine is being repaired $= [T_s/(T_a+T_s)]$

$$= \text{fraction of time repair crew is busy}$$

(11.1)

This assumes, of course, that as soon as the machine breaks down the crew gets to work repairing it, and that as soon as the repair is finished the machine is used again.

A possibility for optimization of repair operations will occur if the cost of the machine crew and its equipment is somehow proportional to the speed of their repair activities, so that the monthly cost of maintenance is $C_m\mu = (C_m/T_s)$, where C_m is a constant, dependent on the nature of the machine. Suppose the monthly output of the machine, if it worked full time, would bring an income G; then the size of the repair crew which will maximize the income from the machine minus the repair crew cost can be obtained from the following:

$$0 = \frac{d}{dT_s}\left[\frac{GT_a}{T_a+T_s} - \frac{C_m}{T_s}\right] = -\frac{GT_a}{(T_a+T_s)^2} + \frac{C_m}{T_s^2} \quad \text{or}$$

$$T_s^2 GT_a = C_m(T_a+T_s)^2 \quad \text{or} \quad T_s = T_a[\sqrt{GT_a/C_m} - 1]^{-1} \quad \text{and}$$

Fraction of time machine is working $= 1 - \sqrt{C_m/GT_a}$

Monthly value of machine output $= G - \sqrt{GC_m/T_a}$

(11.2)

Monthly cost of repair crew $= \sqrt{GC_m/T_a} - (C_m/T_a)$

We note that if the repair cost is high enough so that $(C_m/T_a) > G$, there is no maximum and the machine had better not be used to turn out so unrewarding a product (or else a better machine should be bought).

Preventive Maintenance

Next suppose the repair crew also carries out preventive maintenance on the machine, going over it after the machine has been running without breakdown for a time T_p, spending a time T_m (on the average, see earlier discussion) getting it into shape and then letting it go again. Of course, if the machine breaks down before time T_p, the crew will repair it, though it will take an average time T_s to get it repaired, which is often longer than T_m (perhaps because a breakdown is more serious than a preventive maintenance, or perhaps because a breakdown comes at an unplanned time and thus involves additional delays). We can thus divide the sequence of events into two kinds of cycles, both starting when the machine is just put into running order and both ending when the machine is next ready to go into production. The "usual" cycle is for the machine to run without breakdown until the end of the time T_p, when the repair crew gives it a preventive maintenance going over, taking a time T_m on the average, after which the machine is ready to start another cycle. The relative frequency of this sort of cycle is equal to the probability $A_0(T_p)$ that the machine will run the whole interval T_p without breakdown, as defined earlier. The mean fraction of time the machine will be in operation, with this kind of cycle, is $T_p/(T_p+T_m)$.

The "unusual" cycle involves the machine breaking down some time *before* T_p, in which case it will have to be repaired, which will take time T_s on the average. The probability that such a cycle occurs is $1-A_0(T_p)$, and the mean time the machine is productive before breakdown, *if* a breakdown does occur before T_p, is

$$T_b = [1-A_0(T_p)]^{-1} \int_0^{T_p} ta(t)\,dt = [1-A_0]^{-1}\left\{\int_0^{T_p} A_0\,dt - [tA_0]_0^{T_p}\right\} \quad (11.3)$$

$$= [T_a - T_a U_0(T_p) - T_p A_0(T_p)][1-A_0(T_p)]^{-1}$$

where (see Eq. 2.8)

$$U_0(t) = (1/T_a)\int_t^{\infty} A_0(x)\,dx; \quad T_a = \int_0^{\infty} A_0(x)\,dx$$

In this case (when breakdowns occur before T_p) the mean fraction of time the machine is productive is $T_b/(T_b+T_s)$.

We now assume that the repair job is statistically as good as the maintenance job, that from the behavior of the machine during a cycle it is impossible to distinguish whether the previous cycle had been a repair cycle or a maintenance cycle. This may not be the case in practice, but if it is not, one of the jobs is not as effective as the other in

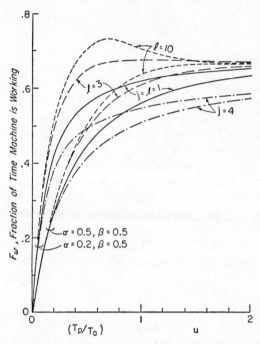

Fig. 11.1. Fraction of time F_w the machine is working, as a function of $u = (T_p/T_a)$, the ratio between preventive maintenance period and machine breakdown time, where $\beta = (T_s/T_a)$ and $\alpha = (T_m/T_a)$, for different kinds of machine-breakdown distributions. Solid curves for $j = l = 1$ are for exponential breakdown distributions, dashed lines and dotted lines for Erlang distributions $l = 3$ and $l = 10$ (see Fig. 5.1), and dot-dash curves are for hyper-exponential distribution $j = 4$ (see Fig. 5.6), according to Eqs. 11.4.

getting the machine back into running condition, and an effort should be made to improve it to make the two equivalent. If they are indistinguishable in their effects on the machine, each cycle is independent of the previous cycle and we can add their effects in a simple manner.

The mean length of a cycle is then

$$(T_p + T_m)A_0(T_p) + (T_b + T_s)[1 - A_0(T_p)]$$
$$= T_a[1 - U_0(T_p) + \alpha A_0(T_p) + \beta - \beta A_0(T_p)]$$

where $\alpha = (T_m/T_a)$, $\beta = (T_s/T_a)$ and the functions A_0 and U_0 are functions of the quantity $u = (T_p/T_a)$. All time intervals are thus in terms of the mean running life T_a of the machine. Therefore, the fraction of time F_w the machine is in working condition, and the mean fractions F_m and F_s of time the machine is in preventive maintenance and in repair, respectively, are

$$F_w = \left[1 + \alpha \frac{A_0}{1 - U_0} + \beta \frac{1 - A_0}{1 - U_0} \right]^{-1}$$

$$F_m = \alpha \frac{A_0}{1 - U_0} F_w; \quad F_s = \beta \frac{1 - A_0}{1 - U_0} F_w$$

(11.4)

where U_0 and A_0 are functions of $u = (T_p/T_a)$ and where u, α and β are scheduled intervals T_p between preventive maintenance, mean durations T_m of preventive maintenance and T_s of repair services, respectively, measured in units T_a of mean duration of machine operation before breakdown. Functions A_0 and U_0 are functions of u; if the machine breakdown-time distribution is similar to one of the curves of Fig. 5.1, they equal $E_{l-1}(lu)$ and $D_{l-1}(lu)$ of Eqs. 5.2 and Table V, with $\lambda t = u$; if the distribution resembles one of the hyper-exponential curves of Fig. 5.6, A_0 and U_0 are equal to the S_0 and V_0 of Eqs. 5.16 and Table VI, with $\mu t = u$ (we note that the $l = 1$ case of Eqs. 5.2 and the $j = 1$, $\sigma = \frac{1}{2}$ case of Eqs. 5.6 are both equal to the simple case of exponential breakdown where $A_0 = U_0 = e^{-u}$).

Typical curves for F_w, F_s and F_m, as functions of u, the relative time between preventive maintenance, are given in Figs. 11.1, 11.2 and 11.3, for sample values of α, β, l and j (curves marked $j = l = 1$ are for exponential breakdown, either $l = 1$ or $j = 1$). The values of α and β are chosen to exaggerate the characteristics of the curves, not because they are typical of actual cases. In actual cases both α and β are usually considerably smaller than 0.1 (times for maintenance or for repair less than one tenth of the mean time between breakdowns). However, the curves for the larger values of α and β show more clearly what is going on.

We note, first, from the curves of Fig. 11.1, that the value of preventive maintenance is much more clear-cut when the breakdown-time distribution displays small variability (l large, Fig. 5.1) than when there is wide variability in breakdown times (j large, Fig. 5.6), with the exponential case intermediate. For $l = 10$, for example, there is a value of u between 0.6 and 0.8 (scheduled preventive maintenance interval between 0.6 and 0.8 of the mean time between breakdowns), for which there is a pronounced maximum value of F_w, the fraction of time the machine is productive. Any shortening of the time between preventive maintenance actions puts the machine too often out of service for maintenance; any lengthening of this time would increase the chance of machine breakdown enough to reduce again the mean productive time of the machine.

We also see that the amount of the advantage obtained by preventive maintenance depends on the difference between the times taken to

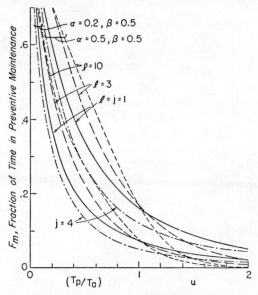

Fig. 11.2. Fraction of time F_m the machine is in preventive maintenance, for the conditions depicted in Fig. 11.1.

perform preventive maintenance and that taken, on the average, to repair a breakdown (that is, on the difference between α and β). If preventive maintenance takes as long to carry out as does repair, there is no particular gain in trying to fix the machine before it breaks down; if maintenance is considerably shorter than repair, productive machine time is gained by substituting maintenance for repair (by reducing u to a value somewhat less than 1 but not so small as to overdo the maintenance).

That we are more able to substitute maintenance for service when the variability of breakdown time is small (l large) than when it is large (j large) is shown in Fig. 11.3. For the case of $l = 10$, the value of F_s, the fraction of time the machine is in repair, is quite small when u is less than about 0.6, rising to near its limiting value only as u gets larger than 1. In this case of low variability in breakdown time, if preventive maintenance is scheduled sooner than the average breakdown time, it will forestall most breakdowns and the repair operation will have to be used only seldom (F_s small). On the other hand, if breakdown time has great variability (j large), the maintenance cycle would have to be inefficiently short in order to forestall a large majority of breakdowns (F_s

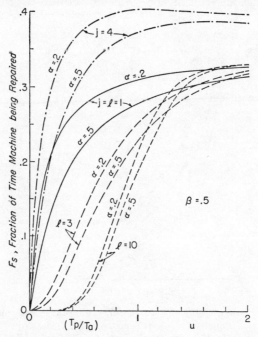

Fig. 11.3. Fraction of time F_s the machine is undergoing repair after breakdown, corresponding to the curves of Figs. 11.1 and 11.2 for F_w and F_m.

becomes small only when u is very small). In fact, for very large variability (the $j=4$ curves) the interposition of preventive maintenance actually increases (slightly) the amount of repair necessary (F_s is larger for $u \simeq 1$ than for $u \to \infty$). In this case tinkering with the machine before it breaks down is likely to *increase* the chance that the machine gets out of adjustment soon (see earlier discussion). As usual, the exponential case ($l = j = 1$) is intermediate between these two extremes.

The quantitative determination of the optimum maintenance cycle (and whether, indeed, to use preventive maintenance) depends, as usual, on the exact nature of the operational criterion imposed by management. If repair is no more objectionable than maintenance, and if the chief requirement is just to have the machine in productive condition as much of the time as possible, the curves of F_w will provide the criterion. Then if variability of breakdown time is small (l large), preventive maintenance will be worthwhile; if variability is large (l small or j large), a preventive maintenance system will not be worthwhile.

In fact, as long as the criterion to be optimized depends linearly on F_w, F_s and F_m, preventive maintenance will only be a clear advantage for machines with less variability of breakdown time than the exponential ($l > 1$). The basic reason is not hard to seek: for exponential breakdown-time distributions, breakdowns occur at a constant rate whenever the machine is operating, being just as likely to happen just after repair or maintenance is completed as later. Consequently, *the only way* to reduce the number of breakdowns per month (say) is to run the machine *less often per month;* preventive maintenance *only reduces* breakdowns by reducing running time, in this case. This tendency is even more pronounced for machines with larger variability of breakdown time ($j > 1$); here breakdowns are frequent *just after* the machine has been repaired, and if the machine survives these, it will run a long time (as explained earlier, this can be because the cause of breakdown is in some fine adjustment which, when right, stays right, but when a little off, goes bad soon). In this case preventive maintenance will usually *increase* the mean number of breakdowns per running time of the machine.

When Preventive Maintenance Is Advisable

For machines with less than exponential variability of breakdown-time ($l > 1$) we can develop a general formula for determining optimum preventive maintenance scheduling. Usually α and β are small compared to 1 and/or u (mean times to complete maintenance or repair are much less than mean interval between breakdowns and/or scheduled maintenance jobs). Consequently, we can use the simpler approximate formulas

$$F_w \simeq 1 - \alpha \frac{A_0}{1 - U_0} - \beta \frac{1 - A_0}{1 - U_0}$$

(11.5)

$$F_m \simeq \alpha \frac{A_0}{1 - U_0} \; ; \quad F_s \simeq \beta \frac{1 - A_0}{1 - U_0}$$

If the value of the output of the machine is G dollars per unit of productive time (per hour, for example), and if C_m is the cost per hour of maintenance service and C_s the cost of repair service (including the average cost of material destroyed during a breakdown, if appropriate), the formula for the net income from the machine per hour (or whatever unit is chosen) is

$$G - \alpha(G + C_m)\frac{A_0(T_p)}{1 - U_0(T_p)} - \beta(G + C_s)\frac{1 - A_0(T_p)}{1 - U_0(T_p)}$$

The optimum value of $u = (T_p/T_a)$ is that which makes the derivative of this, with respect to u, zero. If we remember that

$$(dA_0/du) = -(1/\lambda)a(T_p); \quad (dU_0/du) = -A_0(T_p); \quad (1/\lambda) = T_a$$

we see that for optimum operation of the preventive maintenance cycle we must have

$$\frac{T_m(G + C_m)}{T_s(G + C_s)} = \frac{(a/\lambda)(1 - U_0) - A_0(1 - A_0)}{(a/\lambda)(1 - U_0) + A_0^2} \tag{11.6}$$

Curves for the quantity on the right-hand side of Eq. 11.6, as a function of $u = (T_p/T_a)$, for different values of l (see corresponding dis-

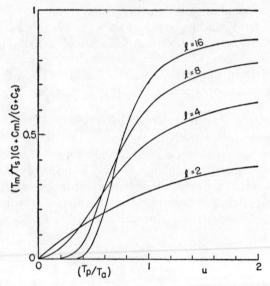

Fig. 11.4. Curves for determining the optimum period T_p for preventive maintenance for different degrees of variability of breakdown-time distribution (see Fig. 5.1) and for different values of the ratio $[T_m(G + C_m)/T_s(G + C_s)]$ explained in the text. See Eq. 11.6.

tributions of breakdown times in Fig. 5.1) are given in Fig. 11.4. As soon as the value of l appropriate for the machine is determined and the values of T_m, T_s, G, C_m and C_s are obtained, the value of u satisfying

Eq. 11.6 can be read off the curves. As noted earlier, machines with breakdown-time variance greater than the ones shown ($l=1$ or $j \geq 1$) have no solution for this equation; either preventive maintenance is not appropriate for these machines, or some other criterion is being imposed by management.

Many Machines, Single Repair Crew

Next we turn to the problems which arise when several similar machines are to be serviced, problems which are more related to the usual queuing situations. Suppose there are K machines and one repair crew (single service channel). At first suppose that the breakdown-time distribution is exponential, with mean time interval $T_a = (K/\lambda)$ (so that preventive maintenance is probably not appropriate) and that repair time is also exponentially distributed, with mean time for repair $T_s = (1/\mu)$. Then if there are $K - n$ machines still running (n either being repaired or waiting for repair), the rate at which machines break down is $(K-n)(\lambda/K)$. The state of the system may be designated by the value of n, the number of machines out of order, and the equations of detailed balance for a steady state are

$$\mu P_1 - \lambda P_0 = 0$$

$$\mu P_{n+1} + (K-n+1)\frac{\lambda}{K}P_{n-1} - \left[\mu + (K-n)\frac{\lambda}{K}\right]P_n = 0 \quad (0<n<K) \quad (11.7)$$

$$(\lambda/K)P_{K-1} - \mu P_K = 0$$

We have chosen to set T_a equal to (K/λ) in order to have λ equal the rate of breakdown for all K machines, rather than the rate per machine.

Solutions of this set of equations, in terms of the functions E_m and D_m or Eqs. 4.3 and 5.2 and Table V, are

Probability that n machines are out of commission

$$= P_n = [x^{K-n} e^{-x}/(K-n)! E_K(x)]$$

$$\rightarrow \left(1 - \frac{K}{x}\right)\sqrt{\frac{K}{K-n}}\left(\frac{K-n}{x}\right)^n \quad (x \gg K-n \gg 1) \quad (11.8)$$

Mean number of machines out of commission

$$= L = [K D_{K-1}(x)/E_K(x)] \rightarrow K/(x-K) \quad (x \gg K)$$

Mean number of machines in commission

$$= K - L = [x E_{K-1}(x)/E_K(x)] \rightarrow K(x-K-1)/(x-K) \quad (x \gg K)$$

where $x = (K\mu/\lambda) = (T_a/T_s)$.   Curves of $K-L$, the mean number of machines in commission, as a function of $x = (T_a/T_s)$, the ratio between the mean running life of a machine and the mean duration of the repair service, for different values of K, are shown in Fig. 11.5.   We note that

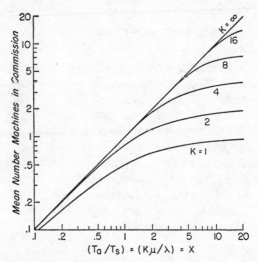

Fig. 11.5.   Mean number of machines in operation for a shop of K machines with exponential breakdown distribution and mean time T_a between breakdowns, as a function of $x = (T_a/T_s)$ (T_s being mean repair time) for different values of K.

the curves rise more or less linearly with x for x less than K, and that they approach asymptotically the value K when x is larger than K. Evidently, if there is to be a single repair crew, its efficiency needs to be great enough (the value of T_s needs to be small enough) so that x is about equal to K. If x is much smaller than K, the repair crew cannot get through its jobs fast enough to keep most of the machines in repair. On the other hand, there is no need to make the repair crew so efficient (T_s so small) that x is very much larger than K; the additional efficiency merely means the crew is idle more of the time and very few more machines are in commission as a result.

All this could have been reasoned out qualitatively without recourse to the equations.   By use of the equations, however, we can ensure quantitatively that we use the repair facilities in an optimum manner. For example, suppose we wish to balance the cost of the repair crew against the net productivity of the machines in commission.   Suppose that the net value of the product turned out per machine per month (or year, or week) is G, and the cost of the repair crew is proportional to their efficiency (inversely proportional to the mean time T_s to repair a machine), being (C_m/T_s) per month (or year, or week). We wish then to maximize the net return $G(K-L) - (C_m x/T_a)$, where $x = (T_a/T_s)$. Differentiating this with respect to x and equating to zero gives us eventually

$$\left(\frac{C_m}{GT_a}\right) = \left(\frac{1}{E_K{}^2}\right)[E_K E_{K-1} + x e_K E_{K-1} - x e_{K-1} E_K]$$

$$= \left[\frac{1}{E_K(x)}\right]^2 [E_K(x)E_{K-1}(x) - K e_K(x) D_{K-1}(x)] \tag{11.9}$$

where the functions e_K, E_K and D_K are those defined and tabulated in Table V.

The function on the right-hand side is plotted against x for different values of K in Fig. 11.6. To find the optimum maintenance effort for

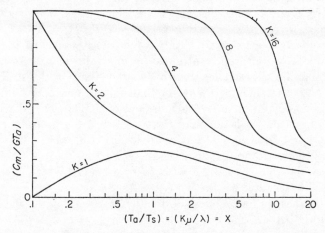

Fig. 11.6. Curves for optimizing repair crew size for a set of K machines, each with exponential breakdown distribution and mean time T_a between breakdowns for each machine. G is net value of machine product, and (C_m/T_s) is cost of repair crew, with T_s being the mean time to repair a machine. Variable x is (T_a/T_s), and appropriate cost of repair crew is (xC_m/T_a), with the value of x read from the curve for the appropriate value of K.

a given value of K, we find the x for which the appropriate curve has a value equal to (C_m/GT_a). Call this optimum value x_0. Then the appropriate monthly cost of maintenance is $(C_m x_0/T_a)$ and the corresponding value of $K-L$, the mean number of machines in operative condition, can be read from Fig. 11.5 for the appropriate value of K and the optimal value x_0. These optimal values of x_0 are not far from K itself, as we indicated from our earlier qualitative discussion, but we see that if the cost of maintenance is high (C_m/T_aG near unity), x should have a somewhat smaller value to save on maintenance at the expense of production; whereas if (C_m/T_aG) is quite small, x should be rather larger than K so as to keep the machines as near full production as possible, even if the relatively inexpensive repair crew is idle a good fraction of the time. We also note, for $K=1$ only, that an optimum is impossible if (C_m/GT_a) is too large. This is true only for exponential breakdown.

Imposing other operational requirements upon the system will, of course, result in different criteria for the level of repair activity.

Equations 11.8 do not look very much like Eqs. 7.5, but as K gets larger and larger the system should behave more and more like a system with an inexhaustible supply of arriving units, which is the case represented by Eqs. 7.5. The differences can be reconciled, however. In the first place, we are now using the variable $x=(T_a/T_s)=(K\mu/\lambda)$, whereas in Chapter 7 we used the utilization factor $\rho=(\lambda/\mu)$. In the second place, a steady state can be attained for *any* value of x or ρ when K is finite in size: if x is smaller than K (ρ larger than 1), the steady-state condition corresponds to P_K larger than P_0 (all machines out of commission more likely than no machines out of commission); if x is larger than K ($\rho<1$), P_0 is larger than P_K. But when K goes to infinity, the case $\rho>1$ ($x<K$) is not a steady state, for it would take an infinite time to get all the machines out of order; therefore, the steady-state situation will only describe the system with $K\to\infty$ when $x>K$ or $\rho<1$, as was indicated in Chapter 7. For $x>K$ ($\rho<1$) the formulas of Eqs. 11.8 do reduce to those of Eqs. 7.5, as substitution of $x=(K/\rho)$ into the limiting forms for $x\gg K$ will show.

We note also that $\rho=(\lambda/\mu)=(KT_s/T_a)$ is equal to the mean fraction of time the repair crew is busy *only* when ρ is less than unity and K is large enough so that the formulas of Eqs. 7.5 are valid. Figure 11.7 shows plots of the mean fraction of time the crew is busy,

$$1-P_0=[E_{K-1}(K/\rho)/E_K(K/\rho)]\to\rho \quad (\rho<1; K\gg\rho) \quad (11.10)$$

for different values of K and ρ. The curve marked $K\to\infty$ is the one corresponding to Eqs. 7.5. Wherever the curve for a finite value of K does not differ appreciably from the curve for $K\to\infty$, we can use the formulas of Eqs. 7.5 and treat the system as though it were essentially

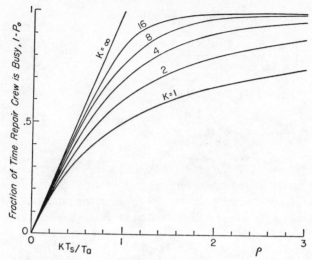

Fig. 11.7. Mean fraction of time the repair crew is busy in a shop with K machines each having exponential breakdown and mean working life T_a as a function of $\rho=(\lambda/\mu)=(KT_s/T_a)$ (where T_s is the mean repair time) for different values of K. For range of values of $(\rho<1)$, for which the curve for proper K is near to the curve marked $K\to\infty$, simple formulas of Eq. 7.5 may be used. See Fig. 4.2.

infinite. Wherever the two curves differ appreciably or when $\rho>1$, we must use the exact expressions of Eqs. 11.8.

Many Machines, More Than One Repair Crew

Next we can consider the situation with more than one repair crew. Suppose there are M crews, each of which has the same exponential distribution of repair times, with mean repair time T_s, and suppose there are K machines, each with exponential breakdown characteristics and with mean time T_a between breakdowns. If the breakdowns are handled on a first-come-first-served basis, each crew, when it finishes one repair, starting on the machine which has been out of commission the longest, then the equations of detailed balance become (if $K>M$):

$$xP_1-KP_0=0$$

$$(K-n+1)P_{n-1}+(n+1)xP_{n+1}-(K-n+nx)P_n=0$$

$$(0<n<M)$$

$$(K-n+1)P_{n-1}+MxP_{n+1}-(K-n+Mx)P_n=0 \qquad (11.11)$$

$$(M<n<K)$$

$$P_{K-1}-MxP_K=0; \quad x=(T_a/T_s)=(K\mu/\lambda)$$

and the solutions and related mean values are

$$P_n = \left[\frac{e_n(M)e_{K-n}(Mx)}{e_M(M)Q_{K,M}(Mx)} \right] \qquad (0 \leq n \leq M)$$

$$= [e_{K-n}(Mx)/Q_{K,M}(Mx)] \qquad (M \leq n \leq K) \quad (11.12)$$

$$L = \left\{ KD_{K-1}(Mx) + \sum_{n=0}^{M-1} ne_{K-n}(Mx) \left[\frac{e_n(M)}{e_M(M)} - 1 \right] \right\} \frac{1}{Q_{K,M}}$$

where, as before, P_n is the probability that n machines are not in working order and L is the mean number out of order at any time, either being repaired or waiting to be repaired, where the functions e, E and D are defined in Appendix 2 and tabulated in Table V, and where

$$Q_{K,M}(Mx) = E_K(Mx) + \sum_{n=0}^{M-1} e_{K-n}(Mx) \left[\frac{e_n(M)}{e_M(M)} - 1 \right]$$

Comparison with Eqs. 11.8 for the single-repair-crew case shows that the difference between the results obtained with M separate repair crews and those obtained with a single large crew with M times the repair speed lies in the second term in the expression for $Q_{K,m}$. For example, in a certain factory having K machines, one might have two repair crews each with mean repair time T_s, or one might have one repair crew with mean repair time $\frac{1}{2}T_s$. In the first case the mean number of machines out of commission is

$$KD_{K-1}(2x)/[E_K(2x) - \tfrac{1}{2}e_K(2x)] \quad (x = T_a/T_s)$$

and in the second case (single faster team) the mean number in need of repair is

$$[KD_{K-1}(2x)/E_K(2x)]$$

which is smaller than the previous expression.

Therefore, *if* it costs no more to have a single team with a given repair speed than it does to have two teams, each with half the repair speed, and *if* a reduction of machine time lost to maintenance is the sole criterion, then one should choose the single fast crew rather than the pair of slower ones. It is not usually true, of course, that a crew of twice the size (or cost) will carry out repairs just twice as fast, so the choice between multiple crews and combined crews is usually not so clean-cut.

More Than One Repair Crew **173**

Sample curves for L plotted against Mx, compared for different values of K and M, are shown in Fig. 11.8 to indicate the magnitude of this difference and the range of Mx for which it is important.

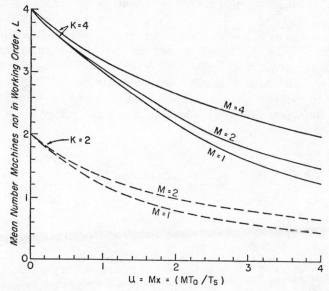

Fig. 11.8. Mean number of machines out of order in a shop with K exponential breakdown machines and M repair crews, as a function of $Mx = (MT_a/T_s)$, T_a being the mean time between breakdowns for each machine, and $T_s = MT_1$ being the mean repair time per repair for each of the M crews.

A limiting case, not often encountered, is the one where there is a maintenance crew for each machine, $M = K$. In this case

$$P_n = \frac{K!}{n!(K-n)!} \frac{x^{K-n}}{(1+x)^K}$$

$$L = \frac{-x^{K-1}}{(1+x)^K}\left[\frac{d}{dy}\left(1+\frac{y}{x}\right)^K\right]_{y=1} = \frac{K}{1+x} = \frac{KT_s}{T_a+T_s}$$

(11.13)

which is, of course, an obvious extension of Eqs. 11.1, derived for one machine and one repair crew. The formula for P_n is the standard binomial expression for $K-n$ "successes" in K "trials." A little thought will convince one that this should be true.

Many other special problems could be worked out for various special maintenance situations: the effect of different breakdown-time distributions on the results given in Eqs. 11.8 and 11.12, the advantages or disadvantages of a system of priorities in choice of the next machine to repair, and so on. But perhaps enough has already been given of the methods of setting up such problems so that the reader can work out his own solutions.

In fact, the time has now come to repeat what was said in the Introduction. The goal of this monograph is to provide understanding and familiarity with techniques, so that the reader may be able to set up his own mathematical model to fit his particular operational problem, and to compute his own formulas to fit his particular management criterion for optimization. May he now be able and willing to work out more and better queuing models!

GLOSSARY OF SYMBOLS USED

Numbers in parentheses refer to the equations first defining the symbol or where the symbol is first used. If the function is tabulated, reference to the table number is also given. Only those symbols used consistently in several sections are listed here.

$A_0(t)$ — Arrival time distribution (2.7), Tables V and VI.

$A_n(t)$ — Probability that n more arrivals will occur within a time t after last arrival (2.12, 5.2, 5.16).

$a(t)$ — Probability density of arrivals (2.7), Tables IV and VI.

C — Cost of unit being idle in queue (3.11).

C_i — Inventory cost (10.3); C_p, re-order cost (10.3); C_m, cost of maintenance (11.2).

D — Cost of service parameter (3.11); size of buffer stock (10.11).

$D_m(x)$ — Poisson integral function (4.3, 5.2), Table V.

E — Cost of service parameter (3.9).

$E_m(x)$ — Poisson distribution function (4.3, 5.2), Table V.

e — 2.71828, base of natural logarithms.

$e_m(x)$ — $x^m e^{-x}/m!$, Poisson density function (4.4), Table V.

$F(z)$ — $\sum_{n=0}^{\infty} z^n P_n$, generating function (7.6).

G — Net profit per customer (3.9).

$G(t)$ — Waiting-time distribution (7.5).

$G_q(t)$ — Delay-in-queue distribution (7.5).

$H(x,y)$ — Two-dimensional generating function (7.11).

I — Mean inventory (10.2).

j — Parameter in hyper-exponential distribution (5.15), Table VI.

K — Number of machines to be serviced (11.7).

k — Number of stages in service operation (5.1).

L — Total number in system, average value (3.6).

L_q — Mean number in queue (3.7).

L_s	Mean number of sales made per replenishment time (10.2).
l	Number of stages in arrival-timing channel (5.7); number of re-order batches in maximum inventory (10.20).
M	Number of service channels (4.1); maximum inventory (10.1).
N	Maximum number allowed in system (3.5).
n	Number of units present (3.1).
P_n	State probability (3.1).
Q	Re-order quantity (10.11).
Q_N	Probability of N or more being in system (7.4).
$Q(t)$	Distribution of waits in queue for random access to service (9.3).
$Q_M(\rho M)$	(8.4), Table VII.
R	Mean number of re-orders per replenishment time (10.3).
$S_0(t)$	Service-time distribution (2.1, 5.1), Tables V and VI.
$S_n(t)$	Probability that n more services are complete in time t after last service completion (5.2, 5.16).
$s(t)$	Probability density of service completion (2.1, 5.1), Tables IV and VI.
T_a	Mean time between arrivals (2.9); mean time between machine breakdowns (11.1).
T_m	Mean time to carry out preventive maintenance (11.4).
T_s	Mean duration of repair operation (11.1).
t	Time.
$U_n(t)$	Probability of n arrivals in interval t, randomly chosen (2.8), Tables V and VI.
u	Root of secular equation (7.9).
$V_n(t)$	Probability of n service completions in time t, randomly chosen (2.5), Tables V and VI.
v	Root of secular equation less than unity (7.35).
W	Mean waiting time, total.
W_q	Mean wait in queue.
w	Root of secular equation (7.2).
x	$(K\mu/\lambda)=(T_a/T_s)$, repair activity parameter (11.8).
δ_{mn}	$1(m=n)$ $=0(m\neq n)$, the Kroneker delta symbol.
Δt_a	Variance of arrival times (2.11).
Δt_s	Variance of service times (2.4, 5.1).
ΔL	Variance of number in system (3.10).
θ	$(\lambda/k\mu)$, (7.8).
λ	$(1/T_a)$, mean arrival rate (2.9).
μ	$(1/T_s)$, mean service rate (2.6).
ρ	Utilization parameter, $=(\lambda/\mu)$, (3.3); $=(\lambda/M\mu)$, (4.2).
σ	Parameter in hyper-exponential distribution (5.15), Table VI.
$\sum$	Summation symbol.
ϕ	$(l\lambda/k\mu)$, (7.48).

DEFINITIONS AND PROPERTIES
OF FUNCTIONS TABULATED

Functions Related to the Erlang Distribution

(See Eqs. 4.3 and 5.2.)

$$e_n(x) = x^n\, e^{-x}/n!\,; \quad E_m(x) = \sum_{n=0}^{m} e_n(x)\,; \quad D_m(x) = \frac{1}{m+1} \sum_{n=0}^{m} E_n(x)$$

For a k-Erlang arrival or service distribution:

$$[a(t)/\lambda] \quad \text{or} \quad [s(t)/\mu] = k e_{k-1}(kx), \quad \text{where } x = \lambda t \quad \text{or} \quad \mu t$$
$$A_0(t) \quad \text{or} \quad S_0(t) = E_{k-1}(kx), \quad U_0(t) \quad \text{or} \quad V_0(t) = D_{k-1}(kx)$$

Mean variance of distribution, $(\Delta t)^2 = (1/k\lambda^2)$ or $(1/k\mu^2)$
(See Eqs. 2.1, 2.5 and 5.2. See Tables IV and V.)

Properties of these functions:

$$E_m(x) = \int_x^{\infty} e_m(y)\, dy\,; \quad E_{m+1}(x) = E_m(x) + e_{m+1}(x)$$

$$\frac{d}{dx}\, E_m(x) = E_{m-1}(x) - E_m(x)\,; \quad \frac{d}{dx}\, [e^x E_m(x)] = e^x E_{m-1}(x)$$

$$D_m(x) = \frac{1}{m+1} \int_x^{\infty} E_m(y)\, dy = \sum_{n=0}^{m} \left(1 - \frac{n}{m+1}\right) e_n(x)$$

$$(m+1) D_m(x) = m D_{m-1}(x) - (m+1) E_m(x)$$

$$m E_m(x) = m D_{m-1}(x) + x E_{m-1}(x)$$

$$(m+1)\frac{d}{dx}\, D_m(x) = m D_{m-1}(x) - (m+1) D_m(x)$$

$$(m+1)\frac{d}{dx}\, [e^x D_m(x)] = m e^x D_{m-1}(x)$$

$$e_m(0) = E_m(0) = D_m(0) = 1\,; \quad e_0(x) = E_0(x) = D_0(x) = e^{-x}$$

177

When $m \gg 1$, $m! \simeq \sqrt{2\pi m}\, e^{-m} m^m$.

If, in addition, $x \ll m$, then

$$e_m(x) \simeq (x^m/m!)(1 - x + \tfrac{1}{2}x^2 - \tfrac{1}{6}x^3 + \cdots)$$

$$E_m(x) \simeq 1 - [x^{m+1}/(m+1)!]\left[1 - \frac{m+1}{m+2}x + \frac{m+1}{m+3}\frac{x^2}{2} - \cdots\right]$$

$$D_m(x) \simeq 1 - \frac{x}{m+1} + \frac{x^{m+2}}{(m+2)!}\left[\frac{1}{m+1} - \frac{x}{m+2} + \frac{m+1}{m+3}\frac{x^2}{2} - \cdots\right]$$

However, if $|x - m| \ll \sqrt{m}$, then

$$e_m(x) \simeq \frac{1}{\sqrt{2\pi m}}\left[1 - \frac{(x-m)^2}{2m} + \frac{(x-m)^3}{3m^2} + \cdots\right]$$

$$E_m(x) \simeq \frac{1}{2} - \frac{1}{\sqrt{2\pi m}}\left[(x-m) - \frac{(x-m)^3}{6m} + \frac{(x-m)^4}{12m^2} + \cdots\right]$$

$$D_m(x) \simeq \frac{1}{\sqrt{2\pi m}}\left[1 - \frac{2}{3m} + \frac{17}{30m^2} - \cdots\right] + \frac{1}{2(m+1)} + \cdots$$

$$- (x-m)\left[\frac{1}{2(m+1)} - \cdots\right] + \frac{(x-m)^2}{2(m+1)\sqrt{2\pi m}} - \cdots$$

and if $x \gg m$,

$$e_m(x) \simeq (x/m)^m[e^{m-x}/\sqrt{2\pi m}]$$

$$E_m(x) \simeq e_m(x)\left[1 + \frac{m}{x} + \frac{m(m-1)}{x^2} + \frac{m(m-1)(m-2)}{x^3} + \cdots\right]$$

$$D_m(x) \simeq [e_m(x)/(m+1)]\left[1 + \frac{2m}{x} + \frac{3m(m-1)}{x^2} + \frac{4m(m-1)(m-2)}{x^3} + \cdots\right]$$

Thus, for $m \gg 1$, we have

for $x \gg 1$, $\qquad Q_m \equiv \dfrac{e_m(mx)}{D_{m-1}(mx)} \simeq mx - 2(m-1) + \dfrac{(m-1)(m+2)}{mx} - \cdots$

for $|x - 1| \ll \dfrac{1}{\sqrt{m}}$, $\quad Q_m \simeq 1 + (\sqrt{2\pi m} - 3)\dfrac{(x-1)}{2} + (\pi-3)m\dfrac{(x-1)^2}{2} + \cdots$

and for $x \ll 1$, $\qquad Q_m \simeq \dfrac{(mx)^m}{m!}[1 - (m-1)x + \tfrac{1}{2}m^2 x^2 - \cdots]$

(See Eqs. 8.2 and 8.4 and Table VII.)

Functions for Hyper-Exponential Arrival or Service Distributions

$$[a(t)/\lambda] \quad \text{or} \quad [s(t)/\mu] = 2\sigma^2 \, e^{-2\sigma x} + 2(1-\sigma)^2 \, e^{-2(1-\sigma)x}$$

where $x = \lambda t$ or μt.

$$A_0(t) \quad \text{or} \quad S_0(t) = \sigma \, e^{-2\sigma x} + (1-\sigma) \, e^{-2(1-\sigma)x}$$

$$U_0(t) \quad \text{or} \quad V_0(t) = \tfrac{1}{2} \, e^{-2\sigma x} + \tfrac{1}{2} \, e^{-2(1-\sigma)x}$$

Mean variance of distribution, $(\Delta t)^2 = (j/\lambda^2)$ or (j/μ^2), where $j = [(1 - 2\sigma + 2\sigma^2)/2\sigma(1-\sigma)]$.

(See Eqs. 5.16 and Table VI.)

TABLES

TABLE I

Values of ρ^n

(ρ^n equals given fraction divided by ten to the power given in parentheses)

ρ	$n=1$	2	3	4	5
0.05	0.05	0.0025	0.125 (3)	0.625 (5)	0.3125 (6)
.10	.10	.01	.001	.0001	.00001
.15	.15	.225 (1)	.3375 (2)	.50625(3)	.75937(4)
.20	.20	.04	.008	.0016	.00032
.25	.25	.625 (1)	.15625(1)	.39062(2)	.97656(3)
.30	.30	.09	.027	.0081	.00243
.35	.35	.1225	.42875(1)	.15006(1)	.52522(2)
.40	.40	.16	.064	.0256	.01024
.45	.45	.2025	.91125(1)	.41006(1)	.18453(1)
.50	.50	.25	.125	.0625	.03125
.55	.55	.3025	.16637	.91506(1)	.50328(1)
.60	.60	.36	.216	.1296	.07776
.65	.65	.4225	.27462	.17851	.11603
.70	.70	.49	.343	.2401	.16807
.75	.75	.5625	.42187	.31641	.23730
.80	.80	.64	.512	.4096	.32768
.85	.85	.7225	.61412	.52201	.44371
.90	.90	.81	.729	.6561	.59049
.95	.95	.9025	.85737	.81451	.77378

ρ	$n=6$	7	8	9	10
0.05	0.15625(7)	0.78125(9)	0.39062(10)	0.19531(11)	0.97656(13)
.10	.1 (5)	.1 (6)	.1 (7)	.1 (8)	.1 (9)
.15	.11391(4)	.17086(5)	.25629(6)	.38443(7)	.57665(8)
.20	.64 (4)	.128 (4)	.256 (5)	.512 (6)	.1024 (6)
.25	.24414(3)	.61035(4)	.15259(4)	.38147(5)	.95367(6)
.30	.729 (3)	.2187 (3)	.6561 (4)	.19683(4)	.59049(5)
.35	.18383(2)	.64339(3)	.22519(3)	.78816(4)	.27585(4)
.40	.4096 (2)	.16384(2)	.65536(3)	.26214(3)	.10486(3)
.45	.83038(2)	.37367(2)	.16815(2)	.75668(3)	.34051(3)
.50	.15625(1)	.78125(2)	.39062(2)	.19531(2)	.97656(3)
.55	.27681(1)	.15224(1)	.83734(2)	.46054(2)	.25330(2)
.60	.46656(1)	.27994(1)	.16796(1)	.10078(1)	.60466(2)
.65	.75419(1)	.49022(1)	.31864(1)	.20712(1)	.13463(1)
.70	.11765	.82354(1)	.57648(1)	.40354(1)	.28248(1)
.75	.17798	.13348	.10011	.75085(1)	.56314(1)
.80	.26214	.20972	.16777	.13422	.10737
.85	.37715	.32058	.27249	.23162	.19687
.90	.53144	.47830	.43047	.38742	.34868
.95	.73509	.69834	.66342	.63025	.59874

(Continued)

Appendix 3

TABLE I (*Continued*)

ρ	$n=11$	12	13	14	15
0.05	0.48828(14)	0.24414(15)	0.12207(16)	0.61035(17)	0.30518(19)
.10	.1 (10)	.1 (11)	.1 (12)	.1 (13)	.1 (14)
.15	.86498(9)	.12975(9)	.19462(10)	.29193(11)	.43789(12)
.20	.2048 (7)	.4096 (8)	.8192 (9)	.16384(9)	.32768(10)
.25	.23842(6)	.59604(7)	.14901(7)	.37252(8)	.93132(9)
.30	.17715(5)	.53144(6)	.15943(6)	.47830(7)	.14349(7)
.35	.96549(5)	.33792(5)	.11827(5)	.41395(6)	.14488(6)
.40	.41943(4)	.16777(4)	.67109(5)	.26844(5)	.10737(5)
.45	.15323(3)	.68952(4)	.31029(4)	.13963(4)	.62833(5)
.50	.48828(3)	.24414(3)	.12207(3)	.61035(4)	.30518(4)
.55	.13931(2)	.76622(3)	.42141(3)	.23178(3)	.12748(3)
.60	.36280(2)	.21768(2)	.13061(2)	.78364(3)	.47019(3)
.65	.87508(2)	.56880(2)	.36971(2)	.24032(2)	.15621(2)
.70	.19773(1)	.13841(1)	.96889(2)	.67822(2)	.47476(2)
.75	.42235(1)	.31676(1)	.23757(1)	.17818(1)	.13363(1)
.80	.85899(1)	.68719(1)	.54975(1)	.43980(1)	.35184(1)
.85	.16734	.14224	.12090	.10277	.87355(1)
.90	.31381	.28243	.25419	.22877	.20589
.95	.56880	.54036	.51334	.48768	.46329

ρ	$n=16$	17	18	19	20
0.05	0.15259(20)	0.76294(22)	0.38146(23)	0.19073(24)	0.95367(26)
.10	.1 (15)	.1 (16)	.1 (17)	.1 (18)	.1 (19)
.15	.65684(13)	.98526(14)	.14779(14)	.22168(15)	.33253(16)
.20	.65536(11)	.13107(11)	.26214(12)	.52429(13)	.10486(13)
.25	.23283(9)	.58207(10)	.14552(10)	.36380(11)	.90949(12)
.30	.43047(8)	.12914(8)	.38742(9)	.11623(9)	.34868(10)
.35	.50710(7)	.17748(7)	.62120(8)	.21742(8)	.76095(9)
.40	.42950(6)	.17180(6)	.68720(7)	.27487(7)	.10995(7)
.45	.28275(5)	.12724(5)	.57256(6)	.25765(6)	.11595(6)
.50	.15259(4)	.76294(5)	.38146(5)	.19073(5)	.95367(6)
.55	.70115(4)	.38562(4)	.21209(4)	.11665(4)	.64158(5)
.60	.28211(3)	.16927(3)	.10156(3)	.60936(4)	.36561(4)
.65	.10153(2)	.65997(3)	.42898(3)	.27884(3)	.18125(3)
.70	.33233(2)	.23263(2)	.16284(2)	.11399(2)	.79792(3)
.75	.10023(1)	.75169(2)	.56377(2)	.42283(2)	.31712(2)
.80	.28147(1)	.22518(1)	.18014(1)	.14412(1)	.11529(1)
.85	.74251(1)	.63114(1)	.53646(1)	.45600(1)	.38759(1)
.90	.18530	.16677	.15010	.13509	.12158
.95	.44013	.41812	.39721	.37735	.35849

TABLE II

FACTORIALS OF INTEGERS

(*n*! equals number given multiplied by ten to the power given in parentheses)

n	*n*!	*n*	*n*!	*n*	*n*!
		20	243290(13)	40	815915(42)
1	1	21	510909(14)	41	334525(44)
2	2	22	112400(16)	42	140501(46)
3	6	23	258520(17)	43	604153(47)
4	24	24	620448(18)	44	265827(49)
5	120	25	155112(20)	45	119622(51)
6	720	26	403291(21)	46	550262(52)
7	5040	27	108889(23)	47	258623(54)
8	40320	28	304888(24)	48	124139(56)
9	326880	29	884176(25)	49	608282(57)
10	326880(1)	30	265253(27)	50	304141(59)
11	399168(2)	31	822284(28)	51	155112(61)
12	479002(3)	32	263131(30)	52	806582(62)
13	622702(4)	33	868332(31)	53	427488(64)
14	871783(5)	34	295233(33)	54	230844(66)
15	130767(7)	35	103331(35)	55	126964(68)
16	209228(8)	36	371993(36)	56	710999(69)
17	355687(9)	37	137638(38)	57	405269(71)
18	640237(10)	38	523023(39)	58	235056(73)
19	121645(12)	39	203979(41)	59	138683(75)

Appendix 3

TABLE III

The Negative Exponential

(e^{-x} equals given fraction divided by ten to the power given in parentheses to the left. For numbers with asterisk, divide by ten to the power given in row immediately below.)

x		0.0	0.1	0.2	0.3	0.4	0.5	0.6	0.7	0.8	0.9
0		1.00000	.90484	.81873	.74082	.67032	.60653	.54881	.49659	.44933	.40657
1		.36788	.33287	.30119	.27253	.24660	.22313	.20190	.18268	.16530	.14957
2		.13534	.12246	.11080	.10026	*.90718	*.82085	*.74273	*.67206	*.60810	*.55023
3	(1)	.49787	.45049	.40762	.36883	.33373	.30197	.27324	.24724	.22371	.20242
4	(1)	.18316	.16573	.14996	.13569	.12277	.11109	.10052	*.90953	*.81297	*.74466
5	(2)	.67379	.60968	.55166	.49916	.45166	.40868	.36979	.33460	.30276	.27394
6	(2)	.24788	.22429	.20294	.18363	.16616	.15034	.13604	.12309	.11138	.10078
7	(3)	.91188	.82510	.74659	.67554	.61125	.55308	.50045	.45283	.40973	.37074
8	(3)	.33546	.30354	.27465	.24852	.22487	.20347	.18411	.16659	.15073	.13639
9	(3)	.12341	.11167	.10104	*.91424	*.82724	*.74852	*.67729	*.61284	*.55452	*.50175
10	(4)	.45400	.41080	.37170	.33633	.30432	.27536	.24916	.22545	.20400	.18458
11	(4)	.16702	.15112	.13674	.12373	.11195	.10130	*.91661	*.82939	*.75046	*.67904
12	(5)	.61442	.55595	.50304	.45516	.41186	.37266	.33720	.30512	.27608	.24981
13	(5)	.22603	.20452	.18506	.16745	.15151	.13710	.12405	.11225	.10156	*.91898
14	(6)	.83153	.75240	.68080	.61601	.55739	.50435	.45635	.41293	.37363	.33807
15	(6)	.30590	.27679	.25045	.22662	.20505	.18554	.16788	.15191	.13745	.12437
16	(6)	.11254	.10183	*.92136	*.83368	*.75435	*.68256	*.61760	*.55884	*.50565	*.45753
17	(7)	.41399	.37460	.33895	.30670	.27751	.25110	.22720	.20559	.18602	.16832
18	(7)	.15230	.13781	.12469	.11283	.10209	*.92374	*.83584	*.75631	*.68433	*.61921
19	(8)	.56028	.50696	.45872	.41507	.37557	.33983	.30749	.27823	.25175	.22779
20	(8)	.20612	.18650	.16875	.15269	.13816	.12501	.11312	.10235	*.92614	*.83800
21	(9)	.75816	.68610	.62081	.56173	.50827	.45991	.41614	.37654	.34071	.30818
22	(9)	.27895	.25240	.22838	.20665	.18698	.16919	.15309	.13852	.12534	.11341
23	(9)	.10262	*.92854	*.84017	*.76022	*.68787	*.62241	*.56318	*.50959	*.46110	*.41722
24	(10)	.37751	.34158	.30908	.27967	.25305	.22897	.20718	.18747	.16963	.15349
25	(10)	.13888	.12566	.11370	.10288	*.93094	*.84235	*.76218	*.68966	*.62403	*.56464
26	(11)	.51091	.46229	.41830	.37849	.34247	.30988	.28039	.25371	.22957	.20772
27	(11)	.18795	.17007	.15388	.13924	.12599	.11400	.10315	*.93336	*.84453	*.76416
28	(12)	.69144	.62564	.56610	.51223	.46349	.41938	.37947	.34336	.31068	.28112
29	(12)	.25437	.23016	.20826	.18844	.17051	.15428	.13960	.12632	.11429	.10342
30	(13)	.93576	.84671	.76614	.69323	.62726	.56757	.51356	.46469	.42047	.38045
31	(13)	.34425	.31149	.28185	.25503	.23076	.20880	.18893	.17095	.15468	.13996
32	(13)	.12664	.11459	.10369	*.93819	*.84890	*.76812	*.69502	*.62889	*.56904	*.51489
33	(14)	.46589	.42156	.38144	.34514	.31229	.28258	.25568	.23136	.20934	.18942
34	(14)	.17139	.15508	.14032	.12697	.11489	.10395	*.94061	*.85111	*.77011	*.69682
35	(15)	.63051	.57051	.51622	.46710	.42264	.38242	.34603	.31311	.28331	.25635
36	(15)	.23195	.20988	.18991	.17183	.15548	.14069	.12730	.11519	.10422	*.94305
37	(16)	.85330	.77210	.69863	.63214	.57199	.51755	.46830	.42374	.38342	.34693
38	(16)	.31391	.28404	.25701	.23255	.21042	.19040	.17228	.15589	.14105	.12763
39	(16)	.11548	.10449	*.94549	*.85552	*.77410	*.70043	*.63378	*.57347	*.51890	*.46952
40	(17)	.42484	.38441	.34783	.31473	.28478	.25768	.23315	.21097	.19089	.17273

TABLE IV

THE ERLANG DENSITY FUNCTION

Values of $ke_{k-1}(kx) = [k(kx)^{k-1} e^{-kx}/(k-1)!]$

x	$k=1$	2	3	4	6
0	1.0000	0.0000	0.0000	0.0000	0.0000
0.1	.9048	.3275	.1000	.0286	.0021
.2	.8187	.5363	.2964	.1534	.0375
.3	.7408	.6586	.4940	.3470	.1562
.4	.6703	.7189	.6506	.5513	.3612
.5	.6065	.7358	.7531	.7218	.6049
.6	.5488	.7229	.8034	.8361	.8261
.7	.4966	.6905	.8101	.8899	.9799
.8	.4493	.6461	.7838	.8905	1.0485
.9	.4066	.5951	.7349	.8499	1.0369
1.0	.3679	.5414	.6721	.7815	.9638
1.1	.3329	.4875	.6025	.6972	.8518
1.2	.3012	.4354	.5312	.6067	.7222
1.3	.2725	.3862	.4618	.5171	.5914
1.4	.2466	.3405	.3968	.4329	.4702
1.5	.2231	.2987	.3374	.3569	.3644
1.6	.2019	.2609	.2844	.2904	.2761
1.7	.1827	.2269	.2379	.2335	.2052
1.8	.1653	.1967	.1976	.1858	.1499
1.9	.1496	.1700	.1631	.1464	.1078
2.0	.1353	.1465	.1339	.1145	.0764

x	$k=8$	10	12	16	20
0.1	0.0001	0.0000	0.0000	0.0000	0.0000
.2	.0086	.0019	.0004	.0000	.0000
.3	.0660	.0270	.0108	.0017	.0002
.4	.2223	.1323	.0771	.0252	.0079
.5	.4763	.3627	.2704	.1444	.0746
.6	.7669	.6884	.6050	.4492	.3227
.7	1.0137	1.0140	.9932	.9158	.8170
.8	1.1600	1.2408	1.2995	1.3703	1.3980
.9	1.1886	1.3176	1.4299	1.6189	1.7734
1.0	1.1169	1.2511	1.3724	1.5875	1.7767
1.1	.9778	1.0853	1.1794	1.3388	1.4706
1.2	.8079	.8736	.9251	.9970	1.0396
1.3	.6357	.6605	.6720	.6687	.6438
1.4	.4798	.4734	.4574	.4103	.3562
1.5	.3495	.3241	.2943	.2332	.1788
1.6	.2467	.2131	.1803	.1240	.0825
1.7	.1694	.1353	.1058	.0621	.0353
1.8	.1136	.0833	.0597	.0296	.0142
1.9	.0745	.0498	.0326	.0134	.0054
2.0	.0480	.0291	.0173	.0059	.0019

TABLE V

Poisson Functions for Erlang Channels

ϵ_m, E_m, and D_m as functions of $\zeta = mx$

m		$x=0.1$	0.2	0.3	0.4	0.5	0.6	0.7	0.8	0.9	1.0
1	$\epsilon_1(mx)$	0.0905	0.1637	0.2222	0.2681	0.3033	0.3293	0.3476	0.3595	0.3659	0.3679
	$E_0(mx)$	.9048	.8187	.7408	.6703	.6065	.5488	.4966	.4493	.4066	.3679
	$E_1(mx)$	.9953	.9825	.9631	.9384	.9098	.8781	.8442	.8088	.7725	.7358
	$E_2(mx)$	.9998	.9988	.9964	.9920	.9856	.9769	.9659	.9526	.9372	.9197
	$D_0(mx)$	.9048	.8187	.7408	.6703	.6065	.5488	.4966	.4493	.4066	.3679
2	$\epsilon_2(mx)$	.0164	.0536	.0988	.1438	.1839	.2169	.2417	.2584	.2678	.2707
	$E_0(mx)$	.8187	.6703	.5488	.4493	.3679	.3012	.2466	.2019	.1653	.1353
	$E_1(mx)$	.9825	.9384	.8781	.8088	.7358	.6626	.5918	.5249	.4628	.4060
	$E_2(mx)$	.9989	.9920	.9769	.9526	.9197	.8795	.8335	.7833	.7306	.6767
	$E_3(mx)$	1.0000	.9992	.9966	.9909	.9810	.9662	.9463	.9212	.8913	.8571
	$D_1(mx)$	.9006	.8044	.7135	.6291	.5518	.4819	.4192	.3634	.3141	.2707
3	$\epsilon_3(mx)$	.0033	.0198	.0494	.0867	.1255	.1607	.1890	.2090	.2205	.2240
	$E_1(mx)$	.9631	.8781	.7725	.6626	.5578	.4628	.3796	.3084	.2487	.1991
	$E_2(mx)$	.9964	.9769	.9372	.8795	.8088	.7306	.6495	.5697	.4936	.4232
	$E_3(mx)$	.9997	.9966	.9866	.9662	.9343	.8913	.8386	.7787	.7141	.6472
	$E_4(mx)$	1.0000	.9996	.9978	.9923	.9814	.9636	.9379	.9041	.8629	.8153
	$D_2(mx)$	.9001	.8013	.7054	.6144	.5299	.4529	.3839	.3230	.2698	.2240
4	$\epsilon_4(mx)$	.0007	.0077	.0260	.0551	.0902	.1254	.1557	.1781	.1912	.1954
	$E_2(mx)$	.9920	.9526	.8795	.7833	.6767	.5697	.4695	.3799	.3028	.2381
	$E_3(mx)$	.9992	.9909	.9662	.9212	.8571	.7787	.6919	.6025	.5152	.4335
	$E_4(mx)$	.9999	.9986	.9923	.9763	.9473	.9041	.8477	.7806	.7064	.6289
	$E_5(mx)$	1.0000	.9999	.9985	.9941	.9834	.9643	.9349	.8946	.8441	.7852
	$D_3(mx)$	.9000	.8004	.7024	.6078	.5188	.4369	.3653	.2986	.2417	.1954
5	$\epsilon_5(mx)$	.0002	.0031	.0141	.0361	.0668	.1008	.1322	.1563	.1708	.1755
	$E_3(mx)$	.9983	.9810	.9343	.8571	.7576	.6472	.5366	.4335	.3423	.2650
	$E_4(mx)$	.9999	.9963	.9814	.9473	.8912	.8153	.7254	.6289	.5321	.4405
	$E_5(mx)$	1.0000	.9994	.9955	.9834	.9580	.9161	.8576	.7852	.7029	.6160
	$E_6(mx)$	1.0000	.9999	.9991	.9955	.9858	.9664	.9348	.8895	.8311	.7622
	$D_4(mx)$	.9000	.8001	.7011	.6045	.5114	.4269	.3498	.2811	.2240	.1755
6	$\epsilon_6(mx)$	.0000	.0012	.0078	.0241	.0504	.0826	.1143	.1398	.1556	.1606
	$E_4(mx)$	.9996	.9923	.9636	.9041	.8153	.7064	.5898	.4762	.3733	.2851
	$E_5(mx)$	1.0000	.9985	.9896	.9643	.9161	.8441	.7531	.6510	.5462	.4457
	$E_6(mx)$	1.0000	.9998	.9974	.9884	.9664	.9268	.8675	.7908	.7017	.6063
	$E_7(mx)$	1.0000	1.0000	.9994	.9966	.9881	.9692	.9360	.8867	.8216	.7440
	$D_5(mx)$	.9000	.8000	.7005	.6027	.5084	.4203	.3403	.2700	.2102	.1606

m	$x=$	1.1	1.2	1.3	1.4	1.5	1.6	1.7	1.8	1.9	2.0
1	$e_1(mx)$	0.3661	0.3614	0.3543	0.3452	0.3347	0.3231	0.3106	0.2975	0.2842	0.2707
	$E_0(mx)$	.3329	.3012	.2775	.2466	.2231	.2019	.1827	.1653	.1496	.1353
	$E_1(mx)$	.6991	.6616	.6268	.5918	.5578	.5249	.4933	.4628	.4338	.4060
	$E_2(mx)$	.9005	.8794	.8571	.8334	.8088	.7833	.7573	.7306	.7038	.6767
	$D_0(mx)$	.3329	.3012	.2775	.2466	.2231	.2019	.1827	.1653	.1496	.1353
2	$e_2(mx)$	.2681	.2613	.2510	.2384	.2240	.2087	.1949	.1771	.1615	.1465
	$E_0(mx)$	.1108	.0907	.0743	.0608	.0498	.0408	.0334	.0273	.0224	.0183
	$E_1(mx)$	.3546	.3084	.2674	.2311	.1991	.1711	.1468	.1257	.1074	.0916
	$E_2(mx)$	.6127	.5697	.5184	.4695	.4231	.3799	.3397	.3028	.2689	.2381
	$E_3(mx)$	.8193	.7787	.7359	.6920	.6471	.6025	.5583	.5153	.4735	.4334
	$D_1(mx)$	.2317	.1996	.1708	.1459	.1245	.1060	.0901	.0765	.0649	.0549
3	$e_3(mx)$	.2209	.2115	.2001	.1851	.1687	.1517	.1348	.1185	.1033	.0892
	$E_1(mx)$	.1386	.1157	.0992	.0779	.0611	.0477	.0372	.0290	.0224	.0174
	$E_2(mx)$	.3594	.3027	.2531	.2102	.1736	.1445	.1165	.0948	.0768	.0620
	$E_3(mx)$	.5803	.5151	.4531	.3954	.3443	.2942	.2513	.2133	.1801	.1512
	$E_4(mx)$	.7653	.7065	.6483	.5899	.5321	.4762	.4232	.3733	.3373	.2850
	$D_2(mx)$	.1850	.1519	.1242	.1011	.0819	.0662	.0533	.0427	.0344	.0273
4	$e_4(mx)$	.1917	.1820	.1681	.1515	.1339	.1162	.0992	.0836	.0696	.0573
	$E_2(mx)$	.1851	.1445	.1088	.0824	.0620	.0465	.0345	.0255	.0188	.0138
	$E_3(mx)$	.3594	.2941	.2381	.1906	.1512	.1189	.0928	.0719	.0554	.0424
	$E_4(mx)$	.5511	.4762	.4062	.3441	.2851	.2351	.1920	.1555	.1250	.0997
	$E_5(mx)$	.7198	.6509	.5810	.5118	.4458	.3838	.3269	.2759	.2308	.1911
	$D_3(mx)$	.1558	.1232	.0966	.0753	.0583	.0448	.0343	.0261	.0197	.0149
5	$e_5(mx)$	.1714	.1666	.1454	.1277	.1094	.0916	.0751	.0607	.0483	.0378
	$E_3(mx)$	.2017	.1512	.1119	.0818	.0592	.0424	.0302	.0213	.0149	.0104
	$E_4(mx)$	.3575	.2851	.2237	.1730	.1321	.0996	.0744	.0550	.0403	.0293
	$E_5(mx)$	.5289	.4457	.3691	.3007	.2415	.1912	.1496	.1157	.0886	.0671
	$E_6(mx)$	.6860	.6063	.5266	.4497	.3783	.3133	.2561	.2068	.1649	.1301
	$D_4(mx)$	.1356	.1036	.0783	.0585	.0433	.0318	.0232	.0168	.0120	.0086
6	$e_6(mx)$	.1562	.1445	.1281	.1097	.0911	.0736	.0581	.0450	.0341	.0255
	$E_4(mx)$	.2117	.1555	.1117	.0789	.0550	.0378	.0257	.0173	.0116	.0076
	$E_5(mx)$	.3547	.2759	.2103	.1573	.1157	.0838	.0599	.0423	.0295	.0203
	$E_6(mx)$	.5209	.4204	.3385	.2670	.2068	.1574	.1180	.0873	.0636	.0458
	$E_7(mx)$	.6582	.5690	.4812	.3986	.3239	.2583	.2027	.1567	.1191	.0895
	$D_5(mx)$	.1107	.0893	.0651	.0468	.0331	.0233	.0162	.0112	.0076	.0051

(continued)

TABLE V (*Continued*)

m	x=	0.1	0.2	0.3	0.4	0.5	0.6	0.7	0.8	0.9	1.0
8	$e_6(mx)$	.0000	.0001	.0025	.0111	.0298	.0575	.0887	.1160	.1337	.1396
	$E_6(mx)$	.9999	.9987	.9884	.9554	.8853	.7908	.6703	.5443	.4404	.3334
	$E_7(mx)$	1.0000	.9997	.9967	.9832	.9489	.8867	.7970	.6873	.5689	.4530
	$E_8(mx)$	1.0000	.9999	.9992	.9943	.9787	.9442	.8857	.8033	.7026	.5926
	$E_9(mx)$	1.0000	1.0000	.9999	.9982	.9919	.9749	.9409	.8858	.8096	.7167
	$D_7(mx)$	.9000	.8000	.7001	.6010	.5042	.4122	.3178	.2535	.1906	.1396
10	$e_8(mx)$	.0000	.0000	.0008	.0053	.0181	.0413	.0710	.0993	.1186	.1251
	$E_8(mx)$	1.0000	.9998	.9961	.9787	.9310	.8473	.7291	.5916	.4556	.3338
	$E_9(mx)$	1.0000	1.0000	.9989	.9919	.9681	.9161	.8305	.7166	.5874	.4579
	$E_{10}(mx)$	1.0000	1.0000	.9997	.9971	.9865	.9574	.9015	.8159	.7060	.5830
	$E_{11}(mx)$	1.0000	1.0000	.9999	.9991	.9945	.9799	.9467	.8881	.8030	.6967
	$D_9(mx)$	.9000	.8000	.7000	.6004	.5021	.4077	.3201	.2446	.1773	.1251
11	$e_{10}(mx)$	.0000	.0000	.0003	.0026	.0113	.0303	.0579	.0866	.1072	.1144
	$E_{10}(mx)$	1.0000	.9999	.9987	.9895	.9574	.8866	.7744	.6330	.4840	.3477
	$E_{11}(mx)$	1.0000	1.0000	.9996	.9960	.9799	.9371	.8571	.7411	.6031	.4616
	$E_{12}(mx)$	1.0000	1.0000	.9999	.9986	.9911	.9674	.9150	.8278	.7103	.5760
	$E_{13}(mx)$	1.0000	1.0000	1.0000	.9996	.9964	.9842	.9524	.8918	.7994	.6816
	$D_{11}(mx)$	.9000	.8000	.7000	.6001	.5012	.4051	.3151	.2349	.1676	.1144
14	$e_{12}(mx)$	.0000	.0000	.0001	.0013	.0071	.0225	.0479	.0757	.0983	.1060
	$E_{12}(mx)$	1.0000	.9996	.9996	.9948	.9730	.9150	.8102	.6665	.5077	.3584
	$E_{13}(mx)$	1.0000	.9999	.9999	.9980	.9871	.9514	.8786	.7624	.6169	.4644
	$E_{14}(mx)$	1.0000	1.0000	1.0000	.9993	.9943	.9749	.9265	.8391	.7152	.5704
	$E_{15}(mx)$	1.0000	1.0000	1.0000	.9998	.9976	.9875	.9578	.8964	.7978	.6693
	$D_{13}(mx)$	.9000	.8000	.7000	.6000	.5007	.4034	.3115	.2291	.1600	.1060
16	$e_{14}(mx)$	.0000	.0000	.0000	.0006	.0045	.0168	.0401	.0685	.0911	.0992
	$E_{14}(mx)$	1.0000	1.0000	.9999	.9975	.9828	.9358	.8391	.6954	.5281	.3675
	$E_{15}(mx)$	1.0000	1.0000	1.0000	.9990	.9918	.9638	.8963	.7810	.6393	.4667
	$E_{16}(mx)$	1.0000	1.0000	1.0000	.9996	.9963	.9806	.9364	.8495	.7204	.5659
	$E_{17}(mx)$	1.0000	1.0000	1.0000	.9998	.9984	.9901	.9628	.9011	.7976	.6593
	$D_{15}(mx)$	.9000	.8000	.7000	.6000	.5004	.4024	.3090	.2247	.1540	.0992
20	$e_{18}(mx)$	.0000	.0000	.0000	.0002	.0019	.0097	.0286	.0559	.0798	.0888
	$E_{18}(mx)$	1.0000	1.0000	1.0000	.9992	.9927	.9645	.8826	.7443	.5622	.3815
	$E_{19}(mx)$	1.0000	1.0000	1.0000	.9997	.9965	.9787	.9235	.8122	.6609	.4703
	$E_{20}(mx)$	1.0000	1.0000	1.0000	.9999	.9984	.9884	.9511	.8681	.7307	.5591
	$E_{21}(mx)$	1.0000	1.0000	1.0000	1.0000	.9993	.9939	.9711	.9107	.7991	.6437
	$D_{19}(mx)$	.9000	.8000	.7000	.6000	.5001	.4011	.3056	.2184	.1449	.0888

m	x=	1.1	1.2	1.3	1.4	1.5	1.6	1.7	1.8	1.9	2.0
8	$e_8(mx)$	.1344	.1112	.1033	.0840	.0655	.0493	.0360	.0256	.0177	.0120
	$E_6(mx)$	.2256	.1574	.1068	.0707	.0458	.0291	.0181	.0111	.0067	.0040
	$E_7(mx)$	.3478	.2584	.1865	.1307	.0895	.0599	.0393	.0253	.0160	.0100
	$E_8(mx)$	.4821	.3796	.2896	.2147	.1550	.1092	.0753	.0509	.0337	.0210
	$E_9(mx)$	.6136	.5089	.4090	.3192	.2433	.1793	.1297	.0919	.0636	.0433
	$D_7(mx)$	.0997	.0695	.0474	.0317	.0208	.0134	.0085	.0053	.0033	.0020
10	$e_{10}(mx)$	.1194	.1048	.0859	.0665	.0486	.0341	.0230	.0150	.0095	.0058
	$E_8(mx)$	.2310	.1550	.0997	.0620	.0375	.0210	.0126	.0071	.0039	.0021
	$E_9(mx)$	.3405	.2414	.1658	.1094	.0699	.0433	.0261	.0154	.0089	.0050
	$E_{10}(mx)$	.4599	.3477	.2517	.1757	.1185	.0774	.0491	.0304	.0184	.0108
	$E_{11}(mx)$	.5793	.4615	.3532	.2601	.1848	.1270	.0846	.0549	.0348	.0213
	$D_9(mx)$	.0853	.0564	.0361	.0215	.0137	.0081	.0047	.0027	.0015	.0008
12	$e_{12}(mx)$	.1081	.0925	.0728	.0534	.0368	.0240	.0150	.0090	.0051	.0029
	$E_{10}(mx)$	.2349	.1506	.0921	.0539	.0304	.0165	.0087	.0045	.0022	.0011
	$E_{11}(mx)$	.3332	.2277	.1481	.0920	.0549	.0315	.0175	.0094	.0049	.0025
	$E_{12}(mx)$	.4443	.3202	.2209	.1454	.0917	.0555	.0315	.0185	.0101	.0054
	$E_{13}(mx)$	.5511	.4227	.3083	.2144	.1427	.0911	.0560	.0333	.0192	.0108
	$D_{11}(mx)$	.0748	.0470	.0284	.0165	.0093	.0051	.0027	.0014	.0007	.0004
14	$e_{14}(mx)$	.0993	.0818	.0616	.0436	.0281	.0172	.0099	.0054	.0029	.0014
	$E_{12}(mx)$	.2357	.1454	.0845	.0467	.0246	.0140	.0060	.0028	.0013	.0006
	$E_{13}(mx)$	.3360	.2144	.1327	.0778	.0434	.0231	.0118	.0058	.0028	.0013
	$E_{14}(mx)$	.4453	.2977	.1953	.1214	.0716	.0403	.0217	.0111	.0057	.0027
	$E_{15}(mx)$	.5274	.3899	.2713	.1782	.1111	.0660	.0374	.0203	.0108	.0053
	$D_{13}(mx)$	.0667	.0399	.0218	.0114	.0065	.0033	.0016	.0008	.0004	.0002
16	$e_{16}(mx)$	.0920	.0748	.0543	.0359	.0219	.0124	.0066	.0033	.0016	.0007
	$E_{14}(mx)$	.2355	.1398	.0774	.0403	.0198	.0093	.0041	.0018	.0008	.0004
	$E_{15}(mx)$	.3191	.2021	.1192	.0659	.0344	.0170	.0080	.0036	.0016	.0007
	$E_{16}(mx)$	.4111	.2769	.1735	.1018	.0561	.0294	.0146	.0069	.0031	.0014
	$E_{17}(mx)$	.5065	.3614	.2399	.1491	.0872	.0481	.0252	.0125	.0061	.0027
	$D_{15}(mx)$	.0601	.0344	.0186	.0095	.0047	.0022	.0010	.0004	.0002	.0001
20	$e_{20}(mx)$	.0809	.0624	.0418	.0249	.0134	.0066	.0030	.0013	.0005	.0002
	$E_{18}(mx)$	.2325	.1283	.0646	.0300	.0130	.0051	.0019	.0007	.0002	.0001
	$E_{19}(mx)$	.3060	.1803	.0968	.0478	.0219	.0093	.0037	.0014	.0005	.0002
	$E_{20}(mx)$	.3869	.2427	.1386	.0727	.0353	.0159	.0067	.0027	.0010	.0004
	$E_{21}(mx)$	.4717	.3140	.1904	.1059	.0544	.0260	.0116	.0049	.0019	.0008
	$D_{19}(mx)$	.0503	.0265	.0118	.0058	.0025	.0010	.0004	.0001	.0000	.0000

TABLE VI

Distribution Functions for Hyper-Exponential Channels

Hyper-exponential distribution functions $V_0(t) = \frac{1}{2} e^{-2\sigma x} + \frac{1}{2} e^{-2(1-\sigma)x}$
$S_0 = -(dV_0/dx)$ and $(s/\mu) = -(dS_0/dx)$, where $x = \mu t$. (See Eqs. 5.16 and Appendix 2.)

x	j	1	2	4	10	20
x	σ	0.5000	0.2113	0.1127	0.0477	0.0244
0	(s/μ)	1.0000	1.3333	1.6000	1.8182	1.9048
0.2	(s/μ)	.8187	.9894	1.1284	1.2436	1.2897
	S_0	.8187	.7695	.7298	.6974	.6845
	V_0	.8187	.8242	.8286	.8322	.8336
0.4	(s/μ)	.6703	.7373	.7974	.8510	.8734
	S_0	.6703	.5981	.5393	.4904	.4709
	V_0	.6703	.6883	.7027	.7147	.7195
0.6	(s/μ)	.5488	.5521	.5651	.5827	.5915
	S_0	.5488	.4701	.4044	.3487	.3262
	V_0	.5488	.5821	.6092	.6316	.6406
0.8	(s/μ)	.4493	.4159	.4019	.3994	.4007
	S_0	.4493	.3740	.3087	.2517	.2282
	V_0	.4493	.4981	.5384	.5722	.5858
1.0	(s/μ)	.3679	.3154	.2873	.2742	.2716
	S_0	.3679	.3013	.2404	.1852	.1619
	V_0	.3679	.4309	.4839	.5289	.5473
1.2	(s/μ)	.3012	.2411	.2066	.1885	.1843
	S_0	.3012	.2460	.1915	.1394	.1169
	V_0	.3012	.3765	.4410	.4967	.5197
1.4	(s/μ)	.2466	.1861	.1498	.1300	.1250
	S_0	.2466	.2036	.1562	.1079	.0863
	V_0	.2466	.3317	.4064	.4722	.4996
1.6	(s/μ)	.2019	.1451	.1098	.0900	.0851
	S_0	.2019	.1706	.1305	.0862	.0656
	V_0	.2019	.2943	.3779	.4530	.4845
1.8	(s/μ)	.1653	.1145	.0815	.0627	.0578
	S_0	.1653	.1449	.1115	.0711	.0514
	V_0	.1653	.2629	.3538	.4373	.4729
2.0	(s/μ)	.1353	.0914	.0614	.0440	.0395
	S_0	.1353	.1244	.0973	.0606	.0418
	V_0	.1353	.2361	.3329	.4242	.4636

TABLE VII

Values of $Q_m(m\rho)$

$Q_m(mx)=[e_m(mx)/D_{m-1}(mx)]$.   (See Eqs. 8.2 and 8.4 and Appendix 2.)

x	$m=1$	2	3	4	6
0	0.0000	0.0000	0.0000	0.0000	0.0000
0.1	.1000	.0182	.0037	.0008	.0000
.2	.2000	.0666	.0247	.0096	.0015
.3	.3000	.1385	.0700	.0370	.0111
.4	.4000	.2286	.1411	.0907	.0400
.5	.5000	.3333	.2368	.1739	.0991
.6	.6000	.4501	.3548	.2870	.1965
.7	.7000	.5766	.4923	.4286	.3359
.8	.8000	.7111	.6472	.5964	.5178
.9	.9000	.8526	.8172	.7878	.7401
1.0	1.0000	1.0000	1.0000	1.0000	1.0000
1.1	1.1000	1.1524	1.1943	1.2307	1.2938
1.2	1.2000	1.3091	1.3985	1.4777	1.6181
1.3	1.3000	1.4696	1.6115	1.7390	1.9692
1.4	1.4000	1.6333	1.8321	2.0129	2.3441
1.5	1.5000	1.8000	2.0593	2.2979	2.7400
1.6	1.6000	1.9692	2.2926	2.5927	3.1543
1.7	1.7000	2.1408	2.5310	2.8961	3.5850
1.8	1.8000	2.3142	2.7742	3.2072	4.0301
1.9	1.9000	2.4897	3.0216	3.5254	4.4880
2.0	2.0000	2.6667	3.2727	3.8497	4.9572

x	$m=8$	10	12	16	20
0.1	0.0000	0.0000	0.0000	0.0000	0.0000
.2	.0002	.0000	.0000	.0000	.0000
.3	.0036	.0011	.0004	.0000	.0000
.4	.0185	.0088	.0043	.0010	.0003
.5	.0591	.0360	.0225	.0090	.0038
.6	.1395	.1013	.0748	.0419	.0242
.7	.2706	.2218	.1838	.1298	.0936
.8	.4576	.4093	.3687	.3049	.2560
.9	.7014	.6687	.6400	.5913	.5507
1.0	1.0000	1.0000	1.0000	1.0000	1.0000
1.1	1.3490	1.3991	1.4455	1.5307	1.6087
1.2	1.7438	1.8602	1.9700	2.1761	2.3695
1.3	2.1793	2.3769	2.5658	2.9255	3.2686
1.4	2.6510	2.9430	3.2246	3.7670	4.2907
1.5	3.1546	3.5524	3.9388	4.6893	5.4199
1.6	3.6861	4.1999	4.7018	5.6821	6.6420
1.7	4.2422	4.8808	5.5071	6.7358	7.9445
1.8	4.8199	5.5909	6.3494	7.8427	9.3163
1.9	5.4170	6.3268	7.2241	8.9959	10.7485
2.0	6.0309	7.0854	8.1276	10.1896	12.2333

BIBLIOGRAPHY

Fortunately there is no need to include here a complete bibliography for the subject of queues. Several adequate bibliographies exist in the following publications:

"Some Problems in the Theory of Queues," by D. G. Kendall, *J. Roy. Stat. Soc.*, **13,** 151 (1951).

Operations Research for Management, Vol. II, J. F. McCloskey and J. M. Coppinger (Eds.), Baltimore, 1956, The Johns Hopkins Press, page 541.

Introduction to Operations Research, C. W. Churchman, R. L. Ackoff, and E. L. Arnoff (Eds.), New York, 1957, John Wiley & Sons, page 415.

Most of the articles of importance in the field are referred to in one or another of the bibliographies given in these three publications. The list of references given below, therefore, includes only those that the author has found directly helpful in writing this book.

First, books that deal in part with one or more aspects of queuing theory:

Probability Theory and Its Applications, Vol. I, by William Feller, second edition, New York, 1957, John Wiley & Sons, pages 368 *et seq.*

Probability and Its Engineering Uses, by T. C. Fry, New York, 1928, D. Van Nostrand, pages 321 *et seq.*

The Life and Works of A. E. Erlang, by E. Brockmeyer, H. L. Halstrom, and A. Jenson, Copenhagen, 1948, published by the Copenhagen Telephone Co.

The following articles have suggested useful points of view with respect to queuing theory in general:

"Some Problems in the Theory of Queues," by D. G. Kendall, *J. Roy. Stat. Soc.*, **13,** 151 (1951).

"Stochastic Processes Occurring in the Theory of Queues," by D. G. Kendall, *Ann. Math. Stat.*, **24,** 338 (1953).

"Sur le Problème d'Attente," by A. Kolmogorov, *Math. Sbornik*, **38,** 101 (1931).

"Über das Warteproblem," by F. Pollaczek, *Math. Z.*, **38,** 492 (1934).

"The Problem of Waiting Time," by E. N. Bouchman, *Akad. Nauk SSSR Zhur. Prik. Matematiki i Mekh.*, **11,** 475 (1947).

"Stochastic Matrices Associated with Certain Queuing Problems," by F. G. Foster, *Ann. Math. Stat.*, **24,** 355 (1953).

Some articles discussing the analysis of special arrival or service distribution are:

"Delay Probability Formulae When Holding Times Are Constant," by C. D. Crommelin, *Post Office Elect. Eng. J.*, **25,** 41 (1932).

"State Probabilities in Congestion Problems Characterized by Constant Holding Times," by J. L. Everett, *Opns. Res.*, **1,** 259 (1953).

"The Influence of Servicing Times in Queuing Processes," by D. P. Gaver, *Opns. Res.*, **2,** 139 (1954).

"A Family of Queuing Problems," by P. M. Morse, H. N. Garber, and M. Ernst, *Opns. Res.*, **2,** 444 (1954).

"A Class of Queuing Problems," by H. N. Garber, Sc.D. thesis, Electrical Engineering Dept., M.I.T., 1955.

Articles on queue discipline and priorities are:

"Delay Curves for Calls Served at Random," by J. Riordan, *Bell Syst. Tech. J.*, **32,** 100 (1953).

"Priority Assignment in Waiting-Line Problems," by A. Cobham, *Opns. Res.*, **2,** 70 (1954) and **3,** 547 (1955).

"Waiting Lines Subject to Priorities," by J. L. Holley, *Opns. Res.*, **2,** 341 (1954).

Two articles on sequential arrays of service facilities are:

"Queuing Problems with Phase-Type Service," by R. R. P. Jackson, *Opns. Res. Quart.*, **5,** 109 (1954).

"Sequential Arrays of Waiting Lines," by G. C. Hunt, *Opns. Res.*, **4,** 674 (1956).

Articles on time-dependent solutions are:

"A Waiting-Line Process of Markov Type," by A. B. Clarke, *Ann. Math. Stat.*, **27,** 452 (1956).

"Stochastic Properties of Waiting Lines," by P. M. Morse, *Opns. Res.*, **3,** 255 (1955).

"Single-Channel Queuing Equations Characterized by a Time-Dependent Arrival Rate and a General Class of Holding Times," by G. Luchak, *Opns. Res.*, **4,** 711 (1956).

"A Continuous Time Treatment of a Simple Queue Using Generating Functions," by N. T. J. Bailey, *J. Roy. Stat. Soc.*, **16,** 288 (1950).

Articles which have been useful in describing various applications of queuing theory include the following:

"The Theory of Probabilities Applied to Telephone Traffic Problems," by E. C. Molina, *Bell Syst. Tech. J.*, **1,** 69 (1922) and **6,** 461 (1927).

"Analysis of the Erlang Traffic Formula for Busy-Signal Arrangements," by C. Palm, *Ericsson Technics*, **6,** 39 (1938).

"The Distribution of Repairmen in Servicing Automatic Machines," by C. Palm, *Industridningen Norden*, **75,** 75, 90, 119 (1947).

"Machine Utilization and Economical Assignment," by J. W. Field, *Factory Management and Maintenance*, **104,** 288 (1946).

"Delays in the Flow of Air Traffic," by E. G. Bowen and T. Pearcey, *J. Roy. Aero. Soc.*, **52,** 251 (1948).

"Productivity of Machines Requiring Attention at Random Intervals," by F. Benson and D. R. Cox, *J. Roy. Stat. Soc.*, **13,** 65 (1951).

"Marshalling and Queuing," a Report of a Conference on the Subject, *Opns. Res. Quart.*, **3,** 1 (1952).

"Traffic Delays at Toll Booths," by L. C. Edie, *Opns. Res.*, **2,** 107 (1954).

"Application of Waiting-Line Theory to Manufacturing Problems," by T. A. Mangelsdorf, Master's thesis, School of Industrial Management, M.I.T., 1955.

"On a Congestion Problem in an Aircraft Factory," by G. Brigham, *Opns. Res.*, **3,** 412 (1955).

For articles on other aspects, see the bibliographies in the three publications first mentioned.

INDEX

199